Annie Berlyn

Sunrise-Land

Rambles in Eastern England

Annie Berlyn

Sunrise-Land
Rambles in Eastern England

ISBN/EAN: 9783743383944

Manufactured in Europe, USA, Canada, Australia, Japa

Cover: Foto ©ninafisch / pixelio.de

Manufactured and distributed by brebook publishing software (www.brebook.com)

Annie Berlyn

Sunrise-Land

SUNRISE-LAND.

Rambles in Eastern England.

BY

MRS. ALFRED BERLYN,

("VERA")

Author of "Vera in Poppyland," etc., etc.

LONDON:
JARROLD & SONS, 10 & 11, WARWICK LANE, E.C.

[All Rights Reserved.]

1894.

PREFACE.

In the following pages I have made no attempt to guide, in the conventional sense, intending pilgrims through a part of the country that has only of late come to be duly appreciated.

In these days we are almost all conscious or unconscious impressionists, and I have merely sought to set before my readers a series of impressions of Eastern England which must necessarily be sometimes crude, and sometimes blurred, and in any case can have no pretension to be complete. How, for instance, could Norwich, or Cambridge, or Broadland be treated in detail within the scope of a little work like this?

But at the same time I am not without hope that these slightly sketched word-pictures may be sufficiently clear to give those who turn these pages a desire to visit the scenes thus described. They will everywhere find a wealth of interest which it would take many books to exhaust.

THE AUTHOR.

London, 1894.

CONTENTS.

CHAPTER		PAGE
I.	IN THE CITY OF CHURCHES	9
II.	ROUND CROMER	34
III.	AN INLAND DRIVE	48
IV.	ROUND THE "SHOULDER"	56
V.	A VILLAGE INDUSTRY	70
VI.	THE TOWN OF LYNN	80
VII.	A WALK TO SANDRINGHAM	93
VIII.	IN THE PRINCE'S PLEASAUNCE	107
IX.	BLOATERDOM	117
X.	ON PEACEFUL WATERS	134
XI.	ENTERPRISING IPSWICH	143
XII.	UP THE ORWELL	154
XIII.	HARWICH PORT	167
XIV.	FLOURISHING FELIXSTOWE	174
XV.	ALDEBURGH—ANCIENT AND MODERN	182
XVI.	A CITY OF THE DEAD AND SUNNY SOUTHWOLD	195
XVII.	FISH AND FASHION	209

CONTENTS.

CHAPTER		PAGE
XVIII.	The Saint's Sepulchre	223
XIX.	Cambridge	235
XX.	A Fane in the Fens	248
XXI.	In Fenland	259
XXII.	The Metropolis of the Turf	274
XXIII.	Whitechapel-super-mare	283
XXIV.	Chelmsford	293
XXV.	Boats and Bivalves	305
XXVI.	A Floral Shrine	313
XXVII.	'Twixt the Colne and the Naze	325
XXVIII.	The Camp on the Colne	334

LIST OF ILLUSTRATIONS.

	PAGE
Castle and Cattle Market	10
Bishop's Bridge	14
Tower Stairway (Castle)	15
St. Peter's Mancroft Church, etc.	16
St. John's Alley	18
St. Mary's Coslany	19
Bishop Hall's Palace	20
An Old Corner	21
Cathedral from S.E.	22
Pull's Ferry and Watergate	23
North-East Corner of Cloisters from Quadrangle	24
Interior of Cloisters of Cathedral	25
The Monks' Lavatory in the Western Walk of the Cloisters	26
Strangers' Hall (Exterior)	27
,, ,, (Interior)	28
The Guildhall	29
St. Andrew's Hall	30
Cow Tower	32
East Cliff, Cromer	35
West Cliff, ,,	36
Cromer Church	37
Overstrand Church	38
Poppies	40
Mundesley	42
Bacton	44
North Walsham Church	46
Sunflowers	48
Gateway at Baconsthorpe	51
Barningham Hall from Garden	52
Garden of "Crown Inn"	61
The Quay, Wells	62
In Holkham Park	64, 65, and 66

	PAGE
Stiffkey	71
A Village Industry	76
The Oldest House in Lynn	81
A Bit of Lynn	85
Mill Fleet, Lynn	86
St. Margaret's Church, Lynn	88
Lynn Ferry	90
From the Quay, Lynn	91
The Custom House and Purfleet, Lynn	92
Staircase, Castle Rising	96
At Rising Almshouses	98
In the Chapel, Rising Almshouses	100
Gateway at Sandringham	108
Sandringham House	111
A Corner of the Saloon at Sandringham	113
York Cottage, Sandringham	114
Sandringham Church	115
On Yarmouth Sands	118
The Quay, Yarmouth	122
St. Nicholas Church, Yarmouth	125
The Market Place, ,,	127
Fishermen's Hospital, ,,	129
Caister Castle	130
Burgh Castle	131
St. Benet's Abbey	136
Dyke near Coltishall	137
"Swan Inn," Horning	138
Horning Ferry	139
Yachts coming off Wroxham Broad into the Bure	140
On Rockland Broad	141
Wolsey's Gate, Ipswich	144

LIST OF ILLUSTRATIONS.

	PAGE
The Oldest House in Ipswich	148
A Sketch in the Dock, ,,	151
Chelmondiston, or Pin Mill, on the Orwell	156
A Ford near Chelmondiston	159
A Bit of the Bank opposite Pin Mill	162
Near Chelmondiston	165
The Orwell near Harwich	168
Parkeston Quay	168
In the Saloon of the 'Cambridge'	169
The 'Cambridge'	170
Great Eastern Hotel, Harwich Quay	171
Off Harwich	172
Landguard Fort, Felixstowe	177
Leiston Abbey from the Road	183
Leiston Abbey	184
The Moot Hall, Aldeburgh	187
A Sketch on the Sea-Front, Aldeburgh	190
A "Bit" at Southwold	196
Southwold Church	199
Southwold Church and Stocks	204
Walberswick Ferry	206
Fish Market, Lowestoft	210
Types in Fish Market, Lowestoft	211
A Lowestoft Smacksman	212
The Harbour Basin, Lowestoft	213
In Belle Vue Park, ,,	215
St. Margaret's Church, ,,	216
Pier and Reading Rooms, Lowestoft	218
Kirkley Cliffs, Lowestoft	220
The Norman Tower, Bury	227
The Abbot's Bridge, Bury, from the Gardens	229
In the Gardens, Bury	233
King's College	236
The Entrance, Trinity College	238
Clare College and Bridge	240
Part of St. John's College and Bridge of Sighs	242

	PAGE
Boys of King's Chapel Choir	244
On the Backs, Cambridge	246
Ely from the North-East	249
West Front of Ely Cathedral shewing the Galilee	252
A Part of the East End of Ely Cathedral	255
A Corner in Peterborough Cathedral	259
In the Fens	261
Ready for Shearing	263
Shorn	265
West Front of Peterborough Cathedral	271
Character Sketches at Newmarket	275 and 278
The "Rutland Arms," Newmarket	281
Southend Pier	285
Hadleigh Castle	287
At Southend	289
Southend at Low Tide	291
The Shirehall and High Street, Chelmsford	294
Tindal Square, Chelmsford	297
A Bit in Chelmsford	300
The River, Chelmsford	302
Brightlingsea Church	308
Phlox and Sweet Peas	314
Threshing Seeds at St. Osyth	316
Stripping Seed Pods at St. Osyth	318
Church of St. Osyth	319
Gateway to existing Priory	321
Interior of Quadrangle of existing Priory	322
Fragment of St. Etheldred's	323
Sea-Front, Clacton	327
Walton	331
Colchester Castle	336
Ruins of Priory, Colchester	339
St. John's Gateway	342
A Bit in Colchester	344

SUNRISE-LAND.

CHAPTER I.

IN THE CITY OF CHURCHES.

A CITY built, apparently, without a plan, the capital of Sunrise-Land is flung together in charmingly careless fashion, its labyrinthine streets winding in and out each other like a maze. One might wander backwards and forwards in them, coming again and again to the starting point, yet never reaching the two great centres of Norwich life—the one social, the other commercial—the Cathedral and its precincts, and the Market-place. It is on this account that Norwich holds sway as one of the most picturesque of English cities. Though one of the most progressive, it is full of old-world charm. About its quaint byways you may roam all day in an almost untainted atmosphere of antiquity; yet, if your tastes lie not in that direction, Norwich is fully equal to your needs, for it is very wide-awake, and the life here, especially on a Saturday market-day, will not a little astonish those who dream

Castle and Cattle Market.

of this ancient East Anglian city as drugged into somnolence by cathedral influence.

Its market is famous. One sees splendid Irish and Scotch cattle here on Saturdays as well as native beasts that do infinite credit to the county, and everything seems to be conducted with extraordinary neatness and order. Cobbett pronounced it the "best and most attractive" market in England; but could he have seen its modern improvements he would have been even more profuse with his praise.

Surely no Norwich citizen ever goes shopping in London; for all within a circle, so to say, in Gentleman's Walk and in London Street, everything that is newest and prettiest is obtainable. That there is plenty of money here no one could doubt who paused before the windows of the tempting emporiums and noted the number of fine jewellers' shops in these thoroughfares; but, then, everybody knows that Norwich is a rich city. Does it not abound with huge factories and foundries? Are not its charities well supported, its philanthropic and educational establishments all that could be desired? Messrs. Colman's starch and mustard works, covering many acres at Carrow, are famous throughout the world; and Harmer and Co.'s factories certainly deserve to be, for every care here is taken of the employés, and no other building of the kind in England can boast a finer system of ventilation. And there are monster boot and shoe and ready-made clothing factories, crape works, iron works, and mills, which are fast helping to make the city one of the greatest commercial centres of England, and have already made her wealthy. It is perhaps her commercial activity which makes the first impression upon strangers. Before one has been half an hour in the city it is apparent that progress is the watchword here. It is no ordinary town that can boast such excellent societies, such hospitals and charities, and its modern buildings are an earnest of what Norwich will be in the days to come.

The young blood of this great East Anglian city courses swiftly, and her sons have resolutely determined that she shall neither rest on her antiquarian nor on her manufacturing laurels alone. Norwich has always been a centre of activity and of progress, commercial and artistic; but, as in the rest of East Anglia, movement has hitherto been slow. Now the spirit of competition is aroused within her. The manufacturing element has strengthened her purpose, and Norwich is making haste to "catch up" with the larger cities of the Midlands and the North. It is hither that pilgrims through Eastern England will muster in force; it is round Norwich, so to say, that the whole life of East Anglia will revolve. There is still much to be done in the city, but schemes are already in hand that promise to bring it into greater prominence. River improvements, long contemplated, may yet be carried out, some of its ancient fame as a "city of gardens" may be restored, and visitors may ere long find that it is not behindhand in the matter of places of amusement.

Naturally the antiquarian interests of Norwich take precedence of all others, but it is beginning to dawn upon the younger folk of the city that even of these the most is not made. Hitherto even its own citizens, with a few exceptions, have not realised the wealth of interest existing in Norwich. It has been off the track, as it were, of tourists; it has never sought, like Chester and other cities, to constitute itself a "show" place; yet there is every reason why our American cousins, the intelligent foreigner, and the native holiday-maker, should include Norwich among the places to be "done." But as nothing succeeds like success, so does nothing bring fame like fame. Norwich until now has been too modest, too reticent, too uncertain of itself. It has gone forward commercially, but lagged behind in self-advertisement; it has not sought the prominence due to it as one of the most interesting cities of our kingdom.

The average tourist likes to be told at every step that the "light of other days" is full upon him. He reverences the old buildings, marvels at the commercial activity, appreciates the faded glories and the advances of civilization twice as much, if he is constantly reminded that he is expected to do so. And Norwich needs to bear this in mind. It must not suffer its splendid treasures and resources to be merely existent: they must be brought forward and interest reaped on them as in other cities with but half its advantages. With its churches and churchyards alone, what may not yet be done, if these latter are carefully laid out and due attention thereby drawn to the magnificent old buildings they surround? And will not hero-worshippers come in increased numbers from all points of the compass to the metropolis of Sunrise-Land, if only the shrines of the Norwich worthies, whose name is legion, are kept well before their eyes? Now one may pass and repass the famous houses with which the city abounds, stand on spots hallowed by memories of those whose names will ring through all ages, and know them not; whereas if a few tablets were judiciously sprinkled on the birthplaces and former dwellings of those who have brought honour to their native place, with what additional interest would one journey to this city of churches and of gardens to view her splendid old buildings and modern improvements!

From an artistic point of view, Norwich is "bad to beat." It is essentially a city of colour. Looking down upon it from the great Norman keep of the Castle, which once dominated the town, a fine panorama of tinted woods is unfolded. Mousehold, rich in colour, lies on the eastern side across the picturesque old Bishop's Bridge. It was here that Kett, of Wymondham, encamped with his followers, when the masses, maddened by oppression, rose against the classes and marched on to Norwich with the view of seizing the city. Kett swung in chains on Norwich Castle for his leadership of the rebellion, and his brother similiarly adorned the tower of their native village church at Wymondham. It is to this Castle of Norwich, closely resembling those of Castle Rising and Castle Acre, that the city owes its first importance. It has been painfully restored, and its interior, consisting of three stories, was, until recently, the county gaol;

but the Norwich citizens are now about to put it to more fitting use, and it is rapidly being converted, like Colchester Castle, into a museum; while its gardens are already laid out as a pleasant resort for those who have neither time nor inclination to go further a-field, and

Bishop's Bridge.

Tower Stairway (Castle).

who seek a change from the Chapel Field, wherein music is made an additional attraction on summer evenings.

But it is not necessary to seek this lofty position to see Norwich in its most artistic aspect. Strolling through its streets one finds pictures at every turn. There is no cathedral city in England possessed of so many fine churches, few richer in ancient buildings. The old grey towers, the grim flint structures, the brown and red gabled houses and the curiously-carved oaken doors and shutters to be seen upon them here and there, make up a series of scenes whose quaintness, colour, and picturesqueness at once endear the city to artistic visitors.

The worst of it is, one never knows when one has seen all there is to be seen. There is so much that can be missed down these twisting, twirling streets, so much hidden away in the most unlikely corners, that, even after a week's stay in the city, one may overlook some of its quaintest "bits." Its churches, like the cathedral, are happily not among

these, if Carrow Priory be excepted; for that, being without the walls and on the domain of Mr. Colman, who, at much trouble and expense, has had the foundations of this grand old Priory traced out, is often passed by.

St. Peter Mancroft, the great parish church of the city —a noble Perpendicular structure of black flint—has one of the finest peals of bells in England; so that, fortunately, is not long in making itself known. On Sunday morning the city runs Bruges very hard in the matter of bells. This famous peal of twelve in the tower of St. Peter Mancroft may be heard miles away, and crash and echo in every corner of the city. But, besides, there are some one hundred and forty others ringing in the steeples of the forty-nine churches that exist here exclusive of the Cathedral, and the combined effect would have taxed even the descriptive powers of Edgar Allan Poe. Perpendicular work is the leading characteristic of nearly all these Norwich churches, in which one finds so much to interest one that it is almost a wonder the rest of the city is ever seen. Tumbled among low-roofed Elizabethan dwellings, and the huge warehouses with which busy Norwich now abounds, these churches, which have made the city of so great worth in the eyes of antiquarians, and earned for it its title of the "City of Churches," are found in every form and condition, from mere ruined remains to the aforesaid St. Peter Mancroft, with its beautifully-toned old windows, its rich lofty tower overshadowing the Market-place, its finely-restored carved stone work. Close to St. Andrew's Hall, through a couple of the tortuous alleys of the city, a church dedicated to the same saint runs St. Peter's very close in the beauty of its architecture, and here, as at St. Michael's at Plea, the yard has already been tastefully laid out. This and the church of St. John Maddermarket are fine specimens of fifteenth century Perpendicular work, like the adjoining church of St. Gregory, under whose chancel, by the way, there is a public thoroughfare, St. John's likewise having a passage through the tower.

One might dwell at length on the architectural interests of SS. Lawrence and Giles, the splendid flint work and beautiful lady chapel of St. Michael Coslany; so too one would fain linger at the companion Coslany church of St. Mary, with its round tower, curiously-inscribed bells, and beautiful ceiling; but where is one to stop in Norwich when a tour of the churches is once commenced, unless it be at St. Julian's, which claims to be the oldest or one of the oldest in the city, or at Heigham St. Bartholomew, just without the walls? Picturesquely situated in one of the old narrow streets of Norwich, and opposite the house where Anne Boleyn's father lived, is St. Julian's, surrounded with sufficient interest to keep one busy for a week; for but a few yards further is the "Music House," once the dwelling

St. John's Alley.

of Moses and Isaac—a couple of Jews respectively famous
in the reigns of William Rufus and Cœur de Lion—and the
church of St. Etheldred, where sleeps Bishop Hall, who
spent his last years in the fine old Elizabethan house now
known as the "Dolphin Inn."

But, of course, the Cathedral first claims attention.
The process of getting there from any point in Norwich is
apt to be protracted, since in every alley, down every turning, there is either an old house, a ruin, a fascinating

St. Mary's Coslany.   Round Tower dating before the Conquest.

church overflowing with relics of the past, or a richly-
coloured "corner" to bring one to a standstill. It is
melancholy to have to confess that the Cathedral, grand as
it is, fails to impress as it should by reason of its low-
lying position. As the rambler through Sunrise-Land will
be continually haunted by the good Bishop Herbert de
Losinga, it is naturally with a special interest that one
comes upon his greatest work and last resting-place.

Bishop Hall's Palace. (The "Dolphin Inn.")

Once within its walls—even within its Close—one forgets everything in admiration of the beautiful Norman work of which it is chiefly composed; its picturesqueness, and the grandeur of the old gateways of Erpingham, facing the West front, with its noble arch, rich tracery, and statues; and St. Ethelbert's, less beautiful, though older by two hundred years, built with the monies of the penitent citizens, who had warred in 1272 with the monks, attacked the monastery, burnt convents, and brought an interdict on the city. It is the Bishop's Gateway, built some ten years later than that of Erpingham, whose date is about 1420, that is the principal entrance to the Cathedral, and is the more picturesque, leading as it does to the Palace which Herbert de Losinga built, and from the precincts to the quaint old water-gate (Pull's Ferry), whose black flint archway, with the cathedral spire towering above it, conjures up in the mind curious visions of the past, when sable-coated priors and richly-vested bishops landed here: of the busy days when Elizabeth visited her "dutiful" Norwich, and lodged in the Bishop's Palace hard by—a time, according to certain historians, when Norwich proved itself worthy of its once proved position as the

An old Corner.

third city of England by overwhelming the Queen with "rare bankets and shows and pageants and soletties." Elizabeth must have been specially interested in Norwich, as within the cathedral sleeps her mother's grandfather, Sir William Boleyn, whose arms and quarterings are on the

Cathedral from S.E.

four main arches; and in the city too, the Boleyns, whose home was at Blickling, where the hapless mother of Elizabeth was born, had a house. Colour runs riot through these gateways, where the rich red roofs of the houses, set back among the trees in the Close, blend with the greys of every shade to be seen in the gables and stone work of the Cathedral and its entrances. There, on the left, is the old Grammar School, once a chapel, built by Bishop Salmon in 1316, afterwards a charnel house, and finally secularised by Elizabeth, picturesque to look upon, and hallowed by memories of such scholars as Tenison, Archbishop of Canterbury; Cosins, of Durham; Caius, who gave to Cambridge the college which bears his name; and Lord Nelson, whose statue adorns the lawn of the Close. Within the precincts of the cathedral it is perhaps the cloisters, than which there are none more beautiful in England, which most fascinate. They not only form a quadrangle of unusual size, but the roof is so elaborately carved with incidents in the lives of the saints,

Pull's Ferry and Watergate.

North-East Corner of Cloisters from Quadrangle.

subjects from the Gospels and from the Revelation of St. John, that the eye is almost wearied in looking from end to end of these cloister walks. Though the grand Norman nave of Norwich Cathedral is with one exception the longest in England, it somehow fails to impress like that of Ely or Peterborough. But the triforium arches are magnificent, and the choir-stalls, of which there are sixty-two, are splendidly carved and of great beauty. As the centre of ecclesiastical work in Eastern England, Norwich has hitherto not held the honoured position that the See should claim as one of the very earliest bishoprics founded in England, and as one of the most important. Under the recently appointed Bishop Sheepshanks, there is good reason to hope that the diocese of Norwich will wake from its lethargy, and the Cathedral become, as it should, the core of spiritual life in East Anglia.

Already Dean Lefroy has taken in hand the much-needed restoration of the Cathedral, for which no less than £12,000 is required. The fabric has for some time been in a decaying condition, and within the apsidal Jesus Chapel, there is much restorative work to be done, the recent severe winters having played havoc with this building.

Interior of Cloisters of Cathedral.

Just without the gates of St. Ethelbert and Erpingham, through Tombland; may still be found a cluster of streets, pebbled and narrow, wherein are delightful old houses rich with colour, like the gabled fifteenth century dwellings hidden away in the yards of St. Peter Mancroft and St. Andrew's Broad Street. In and out of these cobbled lanes, now past huge warehouses that look almost too big for them, now through the yards of churches, black with age and crusted with historic interest, one comes, by the thoroughfare through the tower of St. John Maddermarket, to the Strangers' Hall, one of those many beautiful old treasures of the city that casual visitors may so easily overlook. It is now used as

The Monks' Lavatory in the Western Walk of the Cloisters.

a school, and is hidden away behind the little Roman Catholic chapel, which might well be dispensed with when the beautiful new cathedral, now in course of erection at the expense of the Duke of Norfolk, is finished. Not, perhaps, that it would be well to drag into greater publicity this old Strangers' Hall, which seems

Strangers' Hall (Exterior).

more fitly placed in retirement. One could wish, however, that Curat's House in the Market Place, one of the most beautiful of the old dwellings in the city, were more accessible. It is now used as a wine merchant's residence, and may be seen by the courtesy of the proprietor ; but few of those who come hither to ferret out antiquities know even of its existence. Just across the way the black-flinted Guildhall, grimly impressive as befits the "seat of civic honour, power, and glory," if not architecturally beautiful, is much more attractive within than without, provided always that one enters it "inofficially attended," for the council chamber remains almost as it was in 1547. From time to time, however, relics and pictures have been added, and besides "Old Crome" and Lord Chief Justice Coke and Archbishop Parker, who was, like Crome, a native of Norwich, and was Anne Boleyn's confessor, there is a goodly collection of the counterfeit presentments of civic worthies from the sixteenth century onwards. There are a few unconsidered trifles in the way of regalia and Corporation plate here, too, that might interest the enterprising burglar if he were sufficiently devoted to his

Strangers' Hall (Interior).

The Guildhall.

profession to "crack" so formidable a "crib" as the Guildhall. He might previously sample the wares at South Kensington Museum, where reproductions of the silver gilt laver and ewer, magnificent specimens of seventeenth century work, are to be seen.

It is, however, to none of these places that one first finds the way from Tombland. One of the best known of all the Norwich buildings gives one pause. It is the internally as well as externally beautiful St. Andrew's Hall, built early in the fifteenth century. This seems to have been one of the most useful structures ever possessed by the city, since it has served as a Dominican convent, a Royal residence, a civic banqueting hall, a Nonconformist place of worship, and now as the great public hall of the city, in which the Triennial

Norwich Musical Festival—always one of the best and most attractive in England—is held. Somehow, it is in this fine building, of which the citizens are so justly proud, that one realises how strong the artistic element is in this beautiful city of Sunrise-Land. One remembers here that it has given to the world both Harriet and James Martineau, William Taylor, and Dr. Caius, Cotman and Crome, Amelia Opie, Hansard of Parliamentary debates renown, the Wilkins, and Jane Austen. Here in St. Andrew's Hall the atmosphere seems specially charged with art, maybe because one is surrounded by excellent works of Gainsborough, Opie, Lawrence, and Hoppner, because there is music in the air, because it was here that Sir Thomas Browne, author of " Religio de Medici " received his knighthood from Charles II., who with his

St. Andrew's Hall.

Queen and Court lodged here when they visited "the city of gardens and churches," and were sumptuously entertained by "my Lord Howard" at his splendid palace in St. Andrew's Broad Street, which, says Macaulay, was the largest town-house in the kingdom out of London. His description of this pleasant residence, on the site of which is now built the Norwich Museum and Free Library, gives the best idea of its importance. "In this mansion," he says in his History of England, "to which were annexed a tennis-court, a bowling-green, and a wilderness stretching along the banks of the Wensum, the noble family of Howard frequently resided, and kept a state resembling that of petty sovereigns. Drink was served to guests in goblets of pure gold, the very tongs and shovels were of silver. Pictures by Italian masters adorned the walls. The cabinets were filled with a fine collection of gems purchased by that Earl of Arundel whose marbles are now among the ornaments of Oxford. Here all comers were annually welcomed from Christmas to Twelfth Night. Ale flowed in oceans for the populace. Three coaches, one of which had been built at a cost of £500, were sent every afternoon round the city to bring ladies to the festivities, and the dances were always followed by a luxurious banquet." When the Duke of Norfolk came to Norwich the bells of the cathedral and St. Peter Mancroft were rung, and the guns of the Castle were fired.

There is beautiful country round Norwich. To the other attractions of this grand old city may be added its suburbs. There is nothing in the whole of East Anglia that can compare with the stretch of country that lies between here and Cromer and round about that charming seaside nook. To tell of the drives and walks and scenic beauties that are without the walls of the growing capital

Cow Tower.   Quanting Wherry.

of Sunrise-Land would be to fill a whole volume. One lingers, on leaving the city, on its bridges, sorrowful that the Wensum has had its beauty spoiled by the mills and factories along its banks, and that Norwich has no longer a river worthy of her, though the inky waters soon bear one away past charming Thorpe—on the wooded hill slopes, one of the prettiest villages in England—and Whitlingham, Postwick, and Cantley, beloved of Waltonians, to Yarmouth; while they are crossed among others by the picturesque Bishop's Bridge, built in 1249, at whose foot, in the Lollards' Pit, burned Bilney and others for conscience' sake in Mary's reign.

On summer evenings Norwich folks have an embarrassment of riches in the matter of drives and walks, as the visitor has of interests in the city. Cossey, with its fine park, through which the Wensum flows, is naturally an attraction; and Catton and Sprowston, with their smart villas and pretty churches, have their charms. As a driving centre, Norwich, next to Stalham, is one of the most favourable pitches in Norfolk. The scenery is always good, the roads are excellent, and the County Council cannot be too highly commended for their care of the sign-posts. The Norfolk roads hereabouts are thick with them, and they are all delightfully legible. One may walk or drive through Keswick to Cringleford and Eaton back to the city without once enquiring the way. For small mercies such as these one cannot be too thankful. It is by way of Eaton and Keswick and Hethersett, where Kett and his followers took oath to sacrifice, as they did, "even life itself" in the cause of the people, that Wymondham, with its curious double-towered church, is reached. It was here that the Ketts of rebellion fame lived; it was on the tower of this same church that William Kett was hanged, a church which those who are interested in ecclesiology would as little like to miss, as those who revel in deeds of blood and historical associations would care to pass unheeded by the moated Tudor manor where Amy Robsart was born.

CHAPTER II.

ROUND CROMER.

FASCINATING as Cromer sands and Cromer cliffs may be, they are not by any means the sole resort of the Cromer visitor. There are always some excellent but indolent folk, of course, who deem it the greatest delight of the holiday-maker to burrow for hours in the deep sand, slowly browning in the sun, and "ever falling asleep in a half-dream," to the soothing murmur of the sea, and who, like the lotus-eaters, cry "we will no further roam."

At Cromer and the picturesque fishing hamlets that lie below it on the coast, there are miles of exquisitely firm, white sands, along which at times even the ubiquitous cyclist may spin, and of such wide extent that when the tide is out, the riders come gaily cantering, without even disturbing the children as they paddle and dig and play. But there is a still wider range of delights round Cromer, and though the sands are full and lively enough in the morning, in the afternoon they are practically deserted. It is then that the beauties of this most charming district are sought by those who, having once tasted its strong, sweet air, and joyed in its peace, come again and again to revel in its dreamful ease, its wealth of colour, the glories of its sunrises and sunsets and its opalescent sea.

East Cliff.

Cromer itself is a place of infinite possibilities. It is vain to hope that here all things will be as they have been. The time is close at hand when its borders, already fast increasing, will be greatly widened, when it will be even with other seaside resorts not more popular perhaps, but more populous and more pushing, when its narrow cobbled streets will be broadened into fashionable thoroughfares, and a pier and esplanade, and all the other "attractions" of a favourite watering-place will be "laid on."

Rumours are heard from time to time of a coming pier, but so far Lord Cromer is the only one the town has produced, and surely the only kind that is needed. With a long jetty, a band-stand at its end and troups of noisy excursionists making the glorious nights hideous with their noise, Cromer would indeed be given over into the hands of the spoiler. Even now, as the peace-loving frequenters of slumberous Poppyland stroll along the firm white sands or their beautiful cliffs to watch the sun die gloriously behind Cromer church, the quiet of the scene is sometimes sadly broken by the faint echo of the music from the primitive but inoffensive little wooden jetty, and the raucous strains of the nigger who happily never invades these beautiful little villages on the cliffs. It can, certainly, never have anything grander, or more interesting than its magnificent parish church, one of the finest in Norfolk. This church dominates not only the town but

West Cliff.

the whole district, for its tower, one hundred and fifty-nine feet high, may be seen for miles both at sea and on land. Tradition says that Cromwell, who certainly did play havoc in East Anglia with all ecclesiastical structures, is responsible for the destruction of this grand building, which has only lately been restored to its former shape, the chancel and north porch having both undergone extensive repair. Its "Galilee" porch is in fairly good condition,

Cromer Church.

and keeps local as well as stray artists in perpetual work. Probably the church has been painted almost as many times as the "Garden of Sleep" has been sung in Cromer, for it makes a most effective picture from any point of view. Pictures of Cromer from the hills, Cromer from the north, east, south, or west, Cromer town, or Cromer from afar, principally consist of this huge Perpendicular church. If a sketch is made from a distance, the tower alone stands out conspicuously; if the town itself makes up the picture is not this huge, many-windowed and lofty-towered building, round which dead and gone mariners and humble Cromerites take their rest, the most prominent object?

Despite the terraces of handsome houses it already possesses, its imposing hotels, the smart villas that are overflowing into the roads that lead to neighbouring villages, Cromer is less able, as each season comes round, to provide for the thousands of holiday-makers who pour in from its two railway stations. Fine shops are springing up perpetually, and still there is a cry for more; and as yet, though it would perhaps be surprising, if they were counted, to learn how many vehicles of different kinds there are in the town, there are but half as many horses and traps as are needed for the bright August days, when everybody is panting for the lanes and woods and interesting sights without Cromer town.

There are those who grumble that Cromer built up and extended will be Cromer spoiled. Others there are who

Overstrand Church.

delight, as they come year after year, to find it hurrying along towards the inevitable end. It must come now. Such charms could not for ever be kept secret; their fame is spreading rapidly, and Cromer must provide for those who seek them. But without, in the villages near at hand, and yet untouched by the rush and bustle of life, there will always be peace, there will always be the same calm delights, and hither the Cromer visitors wander in the long summer afternoons. It is here, after all, where those joys are really found that make Cromer to be so highly esteemed. Where along the coast is there anything more charming than Overstrand with its ruined church, that happy little village between the sea and the hills, the now famous "Poppyland," the Othestranda of the Doomsday Book? In the yellow cornfields that stretch away to sleepy Sidestrand, glow the poppies that ruddle the cliffsides and incarnadine hedges that overflow, too, with dog roses and honey-suckle, hare-bells, and ox-eyed daisies. You may follow the same scarlet track along the roadways where quaint rambling farmhouses, set back among clumps of silver birches and elms and old oaks, are sheltered from the fierce winds that blow across the wide waters from the North Pole itself, by massive stone walls, overgrown with ivy and moss.

Overstrand, by the way, threatened awhile since to become "a place." But the extension of Lord Battersea's cliffside domain has fortunately nipped its young ambition in the bud. Two or three harmless rows of picturesque red cottages have sprung up; its pristine simplicity has been marred by a shop or two; but there is, happily, no more building-land to be had for love or money—and there an end.

Across Toll's Hill, where in former days the smugglers, who flourished hereabouts, hid their goods, lies Northrepps,

Poppies.

a village of flowers; and Northrepps Wood, always charming, is most beautiful in June, when, in the deep valley opening to the sea, the rhododendrons are in bloom, and the picturesque Hermitage is almost hidden by the dazzling masses of these beautiful flowering trees. Like children in a wood gay with wild flowers, one is thus tempted further and further along the coast. The influence of the poppy may be strong, and it is sweet to lie on these purpling hills overlooking the green and blue and pink sea; but there are always allurements beyond. Climb to the hill-top, and look down on the scene,

"Deep-meadowed, happy, fair, with orchard lawns,"

and wide stretches of orange sands, and the tiny village of red houses clustering on the cliff's edge, and so surely will you be tempted to go further along up the ever-ascending cliffs to the dreamy little fishing hamlets that lie yonder.

So exquisitely clear is the atmosphere that every spot of colour stands out vivid and distinct. The impression is never blurred. And what great rolling waves of colour there are in this land! Under the pink slopes of the purple heathery hills the corn gleams like copper and gold, from which the eye finds rest in the cool sage-green of the great patches of mangolds. The red admirals flitting by, the green and grey and sapphire waves, fringed with white, the great brown bees buzzing over the red and white clover, all add to the mass of dazzling tints that catch the eye. Under the shady hollow of the hills, a group of roan horses form a picturesque knot. It is almost a relief to turn into a lane where there are only masses of blue-grey "smoke-Jack" and cool feathery grasses.

On the lonely Beacon at Trimingham, three hundred feet above the sea, not a sound save the drowsy plash of the sea and the song of the lark can be heard. It is hard to believe that at one time the still, lifeless little village drew many pilgrims to its church, once possessed, says tradition, of one of the many heads of St. John the Baptist, formerly venerated by the faithful. Trimingham no longer has this attraction to offer, but it has perhaps the finest air of any coast place between Southend and Scarborough. It is a grand place to rest in, as Mr. Walter Besant and other tired brain-workers will doubtless readily admit. Its lanes are positively blue with delicate hare-bells, its crumbling grey and yellow and red cliffs, down which part of a wood has slipped, are the highest land in Norfolk, and, walk as one will, weariness is unknown. The glorious air is like some potent elixir. It fills one with strength and energy, feeds the body, and sets the brain dancing like sparkling wine.

What wonder that at Cromer they are never tired of golfing, that the girls all about the district scamper like fawns through the fields and lanes, that even the older folk walk briskly up the hilly roads and are not the least appalled at the prospect of an extra mile or two! What does anyone think of walking from Cromer to Trimingham, taking in Northrepps Cottage and village by the way! And once at Trimingham, it is nothing to jog on another two or three miles to Mundesley. The air is keen, the lanes are so full of flowers that one halts every few minutes to pick them and admire; and after all, eight miles in such an invigorating atmosphere but compare with a stroll elsewhere. This is not "dreamful ease," did anyone say? Let him only saunter along these irregular cliffs, fringed with yellow "luck" and red and white campion, through these flower-embowered lanes and over these heathery hills; ask then where are peace and rest found, and he will surely answer—it is here.

Mundesley.

Mundesley is not an ideal village. It is best described by that depressing adjective "rising." The speculative builder is busy here. The village is laid out in plots, and glaring new red-brick villas are springing up on all hands. Very shortly there will be a railway station. At present the village is delightfully distant—five miles distant in fact—from whistles and signals and express trains; but already it is losing its old-world air. There are excellent hotels here, in one of which—the most comfortable Royal—one may occupy the tiny room in which Nelson slept as a school-boy; for it was here, whilst he was a scholar at North Walsham Grammar School, that he spent his holidays. But withal there is a tumble-down, untidy, unkempt appearance about the village that is unpleasing, though the sea is magnificent. On the sands everyone seems busy. Shrimping operations are in full swing, men are raking the great masses of seaweed into heaps, that will presently be collected, carted up the winding path, and flung on the land as manure. Through the ravine that divides the cliffs a streamlet somewhat sadly trickles its way to the sea, and there is a distinctly depressing air about the church, now in ruins, with the exception of a portion of the nave, which is used for service, and is, as regards the interior, cheerfully and reverently adorned and decorated. Altogether a melancholy interest clings about Mundesley. Phœnix-like it is rising from its ashes, and will doubtless be a brisk resort some day. At present, despite its many signs of future prosperity, it retains mournful suggestions of decay and sadness. It was here, on these same firm white sands, that poor Cowper, the poet, whose mother's relations were all Norfolk "dumplings," spent many an hour tramping to and fro when his mind became clouded, finding something, as he said, "inexpressibly soothing in the monotonous sound of the breakers."

Bacton.

It is a relief to press on to Bacton and Paston, trim, bright, and unpretentious hamlets, teeming with interest, where undoubtedly the Romans were formerly established, and where, so to say, one meets the Pastons on their own ground. It was from Paston Hall that many of the famous "Letters" were written. In the Pastons everyone learns to take an interest who explores much round Cromer. They appear in almost every village, and one is goaded at last into tracing their history and following their careers. Here at Paston they naturally have it all their own way. Bromholm, once one of the most famous priories in England, now a mere heap of ruins in a farmyard, was founded in 1113 by William de Glanville, Lord of Bacton, and at once fell under the patronage of the Paston family. Threshing machines and wagons now stand within the walls where, it is said by Matthew Paris, the holy rood was once enshrined and miracles were performed by its virtue; and where friars chanted and the "holy cross of Bromeholme" rested, where pilgrims came and kings made vows, turkey gobblers and pigs now hold sway; where altars once were raised, farm sheds now stand; and where John Paston sleeps, heavy-footed labourers and lowing cattle tramp their way day after day. Withal it is picturesque. The old Norman gateway is ivy clad, wild flowers spring up among the ruins of the dormitory and chapter house; the village, a collection of fishermen's cottages with droll little porches made of old boats, together with Edingthorpe, Bacton, and Knapton churches help, to make an effective foreground. There were grand doings here when they brought this same Sir John Paston from London in 1466 to rest by the "Roode of Bromholm," to which both Piers Ploughman and Chaucer make reference. Pigs and calves and various other beasts were slain right and left to furnish forth the funeral baked meats; beer and wine flowed freely, and "a barber was occupied five days in smartening up the monks for the ceremony," which apparently was unusually elaborate, as "the smoke of the torches at the dirge" necessitated the removal of several windows in order that the mourners and officiating clergy might breathe. Later on Master Oliver Cromwell took out a few more windows from a convenient situation on the hill, whence he played havoc with this fine old building. Very curiously, Paston itself is a replica of Baconsthorpe on the other side of Cromer. At both places the Pastons are greatly to the fore, in both villages an Elizabethan building erected by a Paston is now one of the Hall barns.

Rattling into North Walsham, past the fine old Grammar School founded by Sir William Paston in 1606, which has numbered among its pupils Nelson and Archbishop Tenison, one seems to have suddenly come to a centre of gaiety. After the stillness of the lanes, the weird solitude of the cliffs, the sleepy coast villages, this spick-and-span little market-town is undoubtedly gay. On the whole, North Walsham rather prides itself on its "life." It is close to the Broads, for Potter Heigham and Hickling, Horsey, Somerton, and Heigham are all within reach, and at holiday-time there is always a great discharge of passengers from the London trains at this station. Moreover it has a public library and recreation ground and assembly rooms, and it revels in

North Walsham Church.

places of worship of almost every denomination. Here then, to start with, are a few of the elements of life. Viewed seriously, however, the little town is not without its merits. It is certainly not so dreary as many an East

Anglian market-town. To Saxmundham, for instance, it can give points, and it leaves Halesworth and Holt a long way behind. Then it is pleasantly disposed. The market-place with its restored cross, built in the reign of Edward VI., on which, of course, one looks for and duly finds the Paston arms, and the church, make at once the town picturesque. The church, built in the very early lanceo-lated style, is handsome without and within, and in the market-place the shops and cottages seem to be mingled in sweet confusion with the churchyard. However little one may be interested in matters of this kind, it is impossible to pass without notice the wonderfully-trimmed flint work of the Norfolk churches, and especially of this one of North Walsham, which is strikingly fine. John of Gaunt, who seems to have had a country residence at Gimingham, has his memory perpetuated on the porch of this church. In the spandrils of the arch his arms are engraved, but there is no trace of his having done anything special for the town. Sir William Paston, however, whose tomb and effigy are within, gave the Grammar School. Just opposite to his monument, erected in 1607, is a memorial tablet to the father of Sir John Lubbock, who was a native of these parts. The font cover profusely carved with saints and angels is alone worth the journey to North Walsham; and if there were less Puritanical simplicity about the chancel and the services, it would be a church to which visitors from neighbouring places would gladly flock in the season, in which case, perhaps, there might be a chance of rebuilding the massive tower which fell in 1835, and has never been restored for lack of funds.

CHAPTER III.

AN INLAND DRIVE.

Sunflowers.

AMID a tangle of flowers, where the wild thistles grow as tall as an average man, and a veritable thicket of meadow-sweet fills the air with its delicate perfume, one may trace out with difficulty the remains of Gresham Castle.

From Cromer to Gresham, and thence onward through the cluster of beautiful villages adjoining it, to Blickling Hall and Gunton Park, and so homewards, when the shadows are fast lengthening and the woods are dark, is one of the most beautiful drives imaginable. Not half a mile of the road is unattractive, for the way lies by Sherringham, and thence through cool pine groves and exquisite lanes heavy with the odour of wild flowers, past some of the finest old Elizabethan halls in this part of the country.

Gresham Castle is rather a snare and a delusion, though, to the ordinary excursionist who paints in his imagination a grey old fortress with picturesque turrets, through whose open windows he can shout facetious remarks, and on whose crumbling walls he can inscribe his name and leave his plebeian mark. It is in vain that he searches for this stronghold when he comes at last to the quiet little village where Chaucer's son once held the living. Apparently there is nothing here, even when one finds the way to the "Chequers Inn," supposed to be within the grounds of the Stutevilles' domain. "The castle is yonder," they tell you here before you make enquiries, for they conceive that for no other reason would one journey hither. But "yonder" is only a shady meadow, where the cows are peacefully browsing.

At the further end the trees form a circle, and coming closer one finds that the little mount on which they grow is surrounded by water dark with reeds, and that the moss and ivy are thick upon the tree-trunks. As yet, though, there is no castle in sight, and it is not until one pushes a way through the tangled ferns and reeds, and the masses of ivy and meadow-sweet, that the first indications of what must once have been a fine stronghold are discovered. The trees shut it in completely, the mosses and hart's-tongues and grasses, the spiky loosestrife and the ivy cover over the fragments that remain of the four huge towers originally standing in the great square of the castle. It is a wilderness of flowers, a handful of stones, nothing more. Only by tearing away the brambles, and trampling down the delicate maidenhairs and feathery grasses, are these bits of walls seen at all; and, truth to tell, there is little in them even when they are disclosed to suggest their origin. It is imagination that is needed most at Gresham, and having that, one may spend a delightful hour here under the trees, with only gauzy-winged dragon-flies and golden-belted bees and twittering birds for company; filling once more in fancy yonder meadow with the band of yelling, fierce-visaged insurgents under Lord Molynes, who are intent upon taking the castle by force from the Pastons. The wind rustling through the trees helps the illusion. It is, one fancies, the roaring of the rioters, in sallettes and glaives and cuirasses, rushing hither and thither, trying this gateway and scaling that wall, battering at the portcullis with the trunks of the trees they have felled in yonder forest, and tearing down by savage strength the solid walls with their long crooms. There are a thousand of them all told, pitiless, determined, plundering ruffians, and presently even this stout masonry gives way before them.

Up in one of the turrets a pale-faced woman, Margaret Paston, watches them with strained eyes and the calm of despair. She has held out with her women till the last. She has defended the castle with but a few frightened attendants against this marauding host. But the end has come.

Presently, with a shout that brings the trembling women to their knees, Lord Molynes and his followers gain the courtyard. Margaret Paston's brave fight is over and surrender has to be made. Then the waving trees shut out the picture again, and one looks round wonderingly at the desolate scene, the wraith of the old stronghold, the mass of weeds, the moat choked with rushes and brambles, and silently and thoughtfully, with many a backward glance into the stagnant moat and dark recesses of the gloomy grove of trees, one moves away. *Tout passe, tout casse, tout lasse.*

But the Pastons are not left behind, for along the sunny lanes one reaches Baconsthorpe, and half hidden away behind the stacks and sheds of Mr. Mott's farm, is

Gateway at Baconsthorpe.

Heydon Hall, where, in the reign of Edward VI., John Heydon, a legal luminary of the times, held a small court. It is easy enough to picture as one passes through the grand old gateway, now leading to a charming kitchen garden, where scarlet runners and tall languid lilies and peaches and marrow-fats run riot, how extensive and beautiful this old

Tudor house must have been. It is picturesque even now though the cows are littered down in it, and far more interesting than Bromholm, since there is more of it to be seen. The barn across the yard, with its mullioned windows, is still architecturally beautiful, and may possibly have once served as a chapel.

This John Heydon was an inveterate enemy of the Pastons, and there was continuous warfare raging between him and his neighbours. His legal mind revolted against their system of oppression and extortion, and the tedium of country life seems to have been considerably relieved by the constant skirmishes between these lawless Pastons and the justice-seeking Heydon.

Baconsthorpe Church, one of the most beautifully kept churches in this neighbourhood, contains a fine monument of the Heydons, upon which the colours are still bright, though it is nearly four hundred years old.

Near at hand, a while later, the irrepressible Pastons

Barningham Hall from the Garden.

built unto themselves a lordly house in Barningham Hall, which is unquestionably worth coming a long way to see. Ruin has not touched this fine old mansion. Mellowed with age and situated in the midst of the most charming scenery, it appeals strongly to the artistic eye, not only as one of the best specimens of seventeenth century domestic architecture in Eastern England, but by reason of its almost ideal position.

Below it in the valley there is a ruined church, in which some extremely good brasses are to be seen; and taking all things into consideration, Barningham is, maybe, the most fascinating of this trio of interesting villages, peopled with Paston ghosts.

They are not vastly interesting, it is true, to those who love not quiet beauty and cannot hark back to the days that are no more, who cannot dissociate the farm buildings from the crumbling gateways and hide their eyes to ploughshares and reapers in old courtyards. But there is a rich feast of delight for such as appreciate the beautiful landscape unfolded in a drive hereabouts, and can potter cheerfully among the grey remains of decayed halls.

This finely-toned old Tudor hall of Barningham is framed in woods—woods that look deeply purple as one glances back at them, and against which the poplars and pines that border the lanes are sharply silhouetted.

Hence to Wolterton, the home of the Walpoles, of which Horace was pleased to approve, the way is charming. Imperceptibly hilly so far as the ascent and descent are concerned, the roads at every bend open up a prospect of fresh beauty. Now one looks back on long leagues of moorland dyed crimson with heather, now on patches of emerald green fields as bright and fresh in summer as if spring had come again. Then a great glistening ocean of corn rolls over the land, and the hedges on either side the roadway gleam with bright fragile hare-bells and golden rod, cool-looking eyebright, and flaming poppies.

Suddenly there is gloom as more woods are reached, and thus one comes to Blickling, a house partially Jacobean, and partially in the atrociously ugly style prevailing towards the close of the eighteenth century, when part of it was rebuilt.

Blickling, now in the possession of the Marchioness of Lothian, once belonged to Shakespeare's "old Sir Thomas Erpingham," who gave Norwich Cathedral the beautiful gateway which bears his name, and who has found in the Cathedral "a good soft pillow for that good white head." He was a brave old moustache, this Thomas Erpingham, knightly, pious, an honourable member of an honoured family, but his connection with Blickling was brief. It soon passed from his hands, and eventually came into the possession of the Boleyns, and as Blickling was in those days it is now.

In these avenues of yew and chestnut and oak, beside the famous wood-encircled lake that is one of the glories of this part of England, pretty Anne Boleyn must many a time have walked, musing, maybe, of possible lovers, but still happily unconscious of her coming honours and her coming doom.

There is in the church a brass to a baby Anne Boleyn, who died in 1479, a little aunt of the poor queen; and one cannot help thinking how much better it would have been for the mother of Elizabeth if she, too, had found an early resting-place in Blickling Church. Hither it is said the king came to privately wed Anne, and from one of the oriel windows in the gables she may have watched her royal lover ride up the road across the stone bridge over the moat.

There would seem to have been some fatal disposition

on the part of the Boleyn family to lose their heads, for Blickling possesses a decapitated Boleyn ghost, Sir Thomas, the father of Anne herself, who, maybe, out of sympathy for his daughter, is said to annually drive round his former house in a coach driven by four headless horses, carrying his own head comfortably tucked beneath his arm. It is to be hoped he did not have the bad taste to make his little tour during the visit of Charles II., who came here to stay in 1676 on his way to Oxnead, where he was the guest of Robert Paston, afterwards Earl of Yarmouth. References to headlessness in the presence of the merry monarch might not have been altogether appreciated.

After Blickling Hall and its magnificent park, which is said to comprise a thousand acres, Lord Suffield's place at Gunton Park pales its ineffectual fires. But it is a far cry to Blickling, while Gunton is within easy reach of Cromer and its adjacent villages, and Lord Suffield generously places his lovely gardens at the disposal of the public on certain days of the week. So on the principle that it is ungrateful to look a gift-horse in the mouth, one shuts one's eyes as much as possible to the uninteresting Hall, and, forgetful of Blickling, one has only admiration for the splendid avenues, the fine trees, and the abundance of game at Gunton. The brown pheasants and hares are thick on the ground. They start from the roads as one drives beneath the shady canopy of the trees, and almost dart between the slender legs of the deer in the park. And a visit to Gunton means a drive home in one of those magnificent sunsets for which this corner of Norfolk is famous; sunsets to which neither word-painter nor artist could ever do full justice.

CHAPTER IV.

ROUND THE "SHOULDER."

WERE it not for the beauty of the drive thither from Cromer through the most picturesque portion of the county and the extreme interest of the surrounding neighbourhood, Wells would certainly not be a town that anyone need pine to visit. But it serves the useful purpose of making a destination for such as care to explore by road the delightful country lying between the two towns.

Cromer, with its evidences of modernity, is very soon left behind when once the start is made, and almost before the great tower of the church disappears from view, rustic Runton with its famous mill is at hand, and Beeston looms in sight. There is no doubt about the peace here. The trees, maybe, are beginning to look a trifle tired of the sun's fierce embraces; and at oppressively red-brick Sherringham, with its background of hazy blue woods, attempts at seaside gaiety are in progress; but at Beeston Priory absolute stillness prevails. The grey ruin down in the valley and within sound of the sea was an Augustinian Priory, founded about the time the Magna Charta was signed. Like most other ruins hereabouts, it is now encircled by farm buildings, and among the fast crumbling remnants of the Priory the fowls cluck contentedly and the cattle calmly graze. Except for the steady crunch of the cows down by the pool overshadowed by ash and elm and sycamore, and the occasional observation of a pensive hen, not a sound is heard. The sea is calm as a lake, the villagers as silent and as invisible as Isabel de Cressy, the foundress, and the black-garbed priors, who once had such comfortable quarters here.

It is not easy to "move on." The horse, infected by the dreaminess and the lotus-like influence of the picturesque old church, browses among the graves of the monks whilst his driver dozes, and the faint rustle of pigeons in the ivied belfry, soon to go the way of the rest of the building, lulls one into inertia. But without the least disturbing the peace of fast decaying Beeston—for the way out lies over soft, springy turf—the dark lanes are reached again, almost overshadowed by tall thistles and ferns, and masses of hawthorn in the hedges. Here and there, as a gateway is passed, or where the hedgerows have been thinned, a glimpse of sea is caught, or a patch of heather brightly gleams through the sombre pines. It is like passing through a natural picture-gallery of Constable-like landscapes, though Constable found most inspiration for his brush lower down the Saxon shores, Dedham's beautiful vale and the quaint and picturesque villages about Hadleigh and Southend supplying him with endless material.

East Anglia, once scoffed at and maligned as the least interesting and least picturesque part of England, has nevertheless produced and attracted some of our most delightful landscape painters. Collins, at Cromer; Gainsborough, at Ipswich; Crome and Cotman, round about Norwich; and Constable further south and east, at least testify to its artistic worth. And here by beautiful Beeston, in the bowery lanes of Sherringham and Weybourne, with woods and hills and sea and wild heathland at command, who shall venture to say that Norfolk is not scenically deserving the attention of the best modern painters?

Was there ever such a place for trees? Pines, blue in the full light of day, and glowing like pillars of fire under the setting sun; fringed and ragged larches and firs—glorious firs—are in the greatest profusion; and presently, when Aylmerton's round church tower is lost to view as a plunge is made into the deep recesses of Felbrigg Wood, the sunlight drips and trickles through great masses of chestnuts, sycamores, heavy with "Adams and Eves," elms and oaks, ashes and golden beeches.

Then again Sherringham comes in sight, lying red against a purple sea. On the light wind that softly stirs the trees is borne the sweet pungent scent of bracken and pine, and the distant murmur of the sea. Beyond lies the heathery Roman encampment, whence one looks down on Beeston vale, the sea, Cromer, and the winding, shady road leading to Sherringham Bower, than which few more beautiful and romantically-situated houses are to be found in England.

Sloping seawards, the huge clumps of fern and heather, the trees of many tints, through which, from the sea and the little fishing village, are gleaming brighter spots of colour, make a foreground to which the eyes turn for rest from the dazzling gold of the undulating corn-fields, the glories of wood and vale beyond. At such a moment one does not feel kindly-disposed towards one's fellow-creatures who have come hither in donkey-chaises with spirit kettles and picnic-materials to vulgarise the finest scene in Norfolk, to bestrew the wild moorland with paper-bags, and disturb the weird silence with discussions as to the best position for the table-cloth and the advisability of letting the children sit on the grass. The average Cromer holiday-maker cares for none of these quiet beauties. His children tramp ruthlessly and noisily knee-deep in ferns and heather through the peaceful glades. He himself sleeps within sound of the sea as the afternoon sun gathers heat, only regretful that "no smoking is allowed here;" while the donkey boys and flymen fraternize, and the young men and maidens alone appreciate the romance of their surroundings. But there is balm in Gilead. Peace and repose are found again within a couple of hundred yards down the winding road, and in the shady lanes bright with wild mignonette and poppies, lady's smock and scabious.

Felbrigg and Sherringham Park cause bitter regret that Wells has yet to be reached. It is pleasant idling here under Squire Upcher's mammoth trees, watching the rabbits among the heather on the wild tracts of moorland, and Felbrigg—Elizabethan as to its Hall and unrivalled as to its woods—is a sore temptation.

"Mad Windham" and Sir Simon de Felbrigg would be a strangely-contrasted pair to unearth from its church vaults, if it were not impossible to do so for the excellent reason that neither of these interesting persons sleep here. But their brasses—which, with the others here, are said to be among the finest in the country—set forth something of their histories, enough at all events to spur that lazy jade, memory, into action, and set one dreaming of Richard II.'s standard-bearer, now at rest in St. Andrew's Hall, Norwich, and those fine old English gentlemen, the Windhams, from whose family the estate has now entirely passed.

The quiet respectability of neat little Holt is as water unto wine after Felbrigg and its surroundings. But it is meritorious in that it has a decent inn, that it lies amidst charming scenery, was the birthplace of that worthy knight, Sir Thomas Gresham, founder of the Royal Exchange, and Gresham College in Basinghall Street, and that on either side of it are places of extreme interest. For, but seven miles distant is Melton Constable, dear to the sporting mind, and welling over with artistic treasures and antiquities; while six miles northwards is the beautiful old church of Cley; the weird, wild stony shore of Weybourne; and the mud flats of Blakeney, a paradise for sportsmen and ornithologists. But the smugness and stiffness of Holt and its air of dull country-town propriety, creates a longing to be on the road again; and in strange contrast to it presently come the moorlands of Saxlingham—whereon the more or less merry Zingari and the Romany lads are encamped, doubtless with an eye to the plump fowls and any other unconsidered trifles that Field Dalling may produce—and the picturesque calm of Binham Abbey, in hopeless ruins, but rich in archæological interest. Wells is at last in sight, and again the wonderful variety of the trees becomes a striking feature of the landscape, that by degrees grows not beautifully less, but decidedly less beautiful. It is with something like dismay that the dreary marshy shore and depressing quay are viewed for the first time, but once within the comfortable, hospitable, and picturesque old "Crown Inn," hopes revive, and wonder diminishes that visitors ever come hither for a summer holiday.

To be doomed to stay in Wells, and elsewhere than at the "Crown," would be a punishment for which one can conceive no adequate crime. But with Holkham and Burnham Thorpe and Stiffkey to explore and study, and with the "Crown" as headquarters, Wells becomes endurable. Here, in a real old garden, a veritable wilderness of sunflowers and hollyhocks and stocks and sweet peas, one speedily becomes reconciled to the decayed and uninteresting port. The shady old bowling-green is now a tennis-lawn, and visitors between the sets gather their

Garden of "Crown Inn."

own dessert from among the tangle of raspberry canes, old-fashioned blossoms, strawberry layings, and currant bushes surrounding it. The church, much more attractive without than within, for it is a sad specimen of the bare, open-one-day-a-week order, peeps through the trees, and makes a picture at once of the "Crown" garden, wherein, says its hospitable and cheery hostess, have walked many worthies, whose names would seem to belong more rightly to the visitors' list of a fashionable resort than to this slumberous little town.

It is not easy to realise without the undeniable evidences

of a playbill produced by the intelligent Mrs. Glazebrook that Wells once revelled in a theatre of its own, and that the "legitimate" was played here. The fact is undisputable, however, in face of that long, heavily-leaded bill, dated 1826, and by degrees Wells appears in the

The Quay, Wells.

light of a gay theatrical centre; for presently, from among the treasures of the house, other relics of the good old days of the Drama are produced, and Phelps and Macready, Mr. and Mrs. Keeley, Mrs. Nisbet, Miss Helen Faucit, Madame Vestris, and J. C. Lambert become in a measure associated with the quaint old posting-house overlooking the village green. For here the last-named actor, a relative of mine host, fretted his last hour upon life's stage, and his theatrical possessions, his agreements with Macready, and the criticisms of his performances when he was a member of companies to which these other artists belonged, are still carefully preserved.

Wells Quay, lined with malt-houses and tumble-down beer-shops, suggesting by such signs as the Dogger, the Lord Nelson, the Ship, and the Anchor, the marine character of their patrons, and the long dreary walk along the marshy level to Holkham village combine to engender in a pedestrian with a disordered liver a frame of mind calculated to render him dangerous alike to himself and his fellows. No London fog could ever produce such profound melancholia and blood-curdling thoughts as the promenade of Wells-next-the-Sea. If Mr. G. R. Sims were to walk this way in a drizzling rain one shudders to think what "Mustard and Cress" would become; but any melodramatic playwright who could not produce a ghastly murder scene after a stroll from Wells to Holkham along this dismal shore, would be unworthy of the name.

When the pretty red-brick model village of Holkham comes in view life once more seems worth living. The Earl of Leicester is evidently determined to do his best to render the existence of his tenants less depressing. The charming little model cottages, with their verandahs, their garden patches, and modern improvements, let to the labourers of Lord Leicester's estate at half-a-crown a week, put to the blush many Queen Anne villas in suburban London, at a rental of £40 per annum. Hodge, moreover, is not only decently housed and his artistic tastes cultivated, but he is also provided with means for mental improvement. In the centre of the village is a pleasant and picturesque reading-room, one of many that the kindly descendant of "Coke of Norfolk" has erected on his vast estate. It is hard to realise, looking around at these

In Holkham Park.

charming cottages and the tracts of fertile land that encircle gloomy Holkham Park like a golden band, that "the first farmer in England" and the first Earl of Leicester, on succeeding to the estate in 1776, found it all a barren waste—so many dreary, profitless acres—farmed by agriculturists of the old and bad school, and tilled by labourers who, could they rise and see the dwellings and hear the views and aspirations of their descendants, would probably expect the sea to promptly overflow the land and swamp them for their "presumption." Holkham is, of course, agriculturally, one of the most notable places in Norfolk, the very Mecca of all good farmers; but unless one is prepared to enter scientifically into turnip culture, and the nature of the soil which the popular and judicious "Coke of Norfolk" so completely changed, it is not particularly interesting without the hideous great hall, which like Devonshire House, Piccadilly, is one of Kent's most ghastly erections. The Park is very vast, it is true, but it is also woefully depressing with its miles and miles of funereal evergreen oaks and grass-grown roadways. It is unconventional, though, in a way; for browsing with the deer in what we may call the front garden, are flocks of beautiful black-faced sheep, and the fine shorthorns for which the estate is famed. Every inch of ground is used to the best advantage, and the excellent pasturage round the house is not wasted on merely ornamental deer, which,

In Holkham Park.

after all, are hardly more effective in the picture than these finely-shaped, rich-coloured bullocks and fleecy sheep.

With a triumphal arch on the Fakenham road facing the house, and an eighty-feet Obelisk, setting forth the virtues and enterprises of the Coke of whom Norfolk men are so proud, in the rear, the Hall can hardly be said to be picturesquely situated; and, indeed, the bewildered stranger is apt to rub his eyes and wonder whether he is not dreaming that a kind of combined British Museum and National Gallery, the Monument and old Temple Bar have not got somehow mixed up in the midst of Richmond Park. But this

In Holkham Park.

strange edifice, which, says Ferguson, is an "ingenious architectural puzzle," is a storehouse of artistic treasures, reserved, unfortunately, only for privileged eyes. There are marvellous marbles, fine Claudes, and old MSS., which are the envy and admiration of every bibliophile in England. Within the Holkham Library are stored priceless missals and old treatises, including one written by Leonardo da Vinci *sui ipsius manu*, and a sketch-book of Maratti's, of whose works there are some delightful examples in the state bed-chambers. It is terrible to turn from these artistic glories, from the Lorraines and Canalettis, the Poussins and Rubens, the ancient marbles and the fascinating old books and manuscripts, to the vista before the drawing-room windows, with its trumpery stone arch and Kew Gardens suggestiveness.

A long walk under the gloomy oaks across the Park brings one to Burnham Thorpe, the quiet little village where Horatio Nelson first saw the light, and for which he never lost his affection. It was to the old Rectory House, with its surrounding beeches and elms, to his mother's grave in the chancel of his father's church, and to the peaceful God's acre where, with his last breath, he expressed a wish to be laid, that his thoughts turned as he lay bleeding to death in the cockpit of the "Victory." "Don't throw me overboard," he said to Hardy. "I wish to be buried by the side of my father and mother, unless it should please the King to order otherwise." Who shall say what visions of the dear old Norfolk home may have passed before his glazing eyes? Maybe, afar off in Trafalgar's Bay he saw again the brawling brook where he and the boy Fish struggled, the leafy lane leading to the church, the pump in Downham market-place, whence he made streams of water flow that he might float his paper boats. There is a wealth of pathos as one traces the history of the great Admiral's life from his early days in this Norfolk hamlet to that fatal October 21st, 1805. A puny baby; a little motherless lad, with a gentle, affectionate, tender disposition, sent to rough it at sea; a young husband bird's-nesting in Burnham Woods with his lighthearted bride, the pride of the village and the naval hero of his country, he is always a sympathetic figure in the pictures framed by sylvan Burnham.

Happily the reproach that so long rested on the great hero's native village of neglecting to fitly honour his memory, is at last being rolled away. It should be the nation's care as well as that of the Burnhamites to keep the church under whose shadow he was born, and in which he was baptised, as a memorial of England's greatest naval commander. At the suggestion of the Prince of Wales steps are being taken to restore it; but the patriotism and gratitude of his fellow-countrymen have so far not been greatly stimulated, and the burden of perpetuating his memory in his "dear, dear Burnham," has chiefly fallen upon the Royal Family, the rector, and a few who honour the naval hero's valour and services to the country. The church is still undergoing repairs and restoration; it was until a year or two ago in the most deplorable condition, and still is a disgrace to the county upon which Nelson brought so much honour. Six years ago the lectern alone existed to remind one of his life and death. It is inscribed,

To the glory of God
and the memory of
HORATIO NELSON,
This Lectern
made from the wood of
H.M. Ship VICTORY
on the deck of which
He fell,
Thanking God
That he had done his duty,
is dedicated,
A.D. 1886.

THE WOOD AND THE TWO PLATES
FROM PART OF THE VICTORY,
THE FLAGSHIP OF LORD NELSON
AT THE BATTLE OF TRAFALGAR,
 21 OCT., 1805;
THEY WERE GIVEN BY THE LORDS OF THE
 ADMIRALTY TO BURNHAM THORPE,
 HIS NATIVE PARISH, A.D. 1881.

But in the summer of 1892 the Dean of Norwich opened the Nelson Memorial Village Hall, erected with money advanced by the rector and his family; and maybe as the inglorious Hampdens of his native village meet together here, and read of his immortal deeds and of his undying love for the village "the thought of which," he wrote, "brings all my mother into my heart, which shews itself in my eyes," even they, too, may be stirred to keep his memory green among them for all generations, by striving to maintain the resting-place of his father and mother as he would have wished to see it. "England expects every man to do his duty," was his last command; but he being dead surely will not in vain appeal to his countrymen and his country, whose obvious duty is, at least, to preserve to his memory the church in which he first learned that great lesson of Duty, which guided his whole life.

CHAPTER V.

A VILLAGE INDUSTRY.

THERE is evidently something strange about it. The trim waiting-maid looks askance when asked if she knows it. Boots smiles and thoughtfully scratches his head when enquiries are made as to the nearest way.

"Stiffkey," he repeats. "'Stewkey' is what it's called round these parts. It ain't so far away as a walk goes, though the roads is awful; and it ain't what you care to do after dark, and they're none of us," he adds, suddenly dropping into the plural and a whisper, "they're queer folk."

Curiosity is thus whetted afresh about this mysterious village with the quaint name. Is it then some fearsome swamp, reached only through dangerous morasses? Or can it be that it is inhabited by wild men of the East, a savage tribe, who invade surrounding villages and raid on dismal Wells? It would hardly be surprising to find it so; for with these dreary shores and lonely mud-flats, these wastes of sand and swamp, whence strange birds start up with hoarse cries, it is impossible to associate the plodding, peaceful Norfolk field-hand, or the simple, honest fisher. Instinctively one listens for slow music. Behind these "Meols," or desolate coarse grass-tufted sand-hills, must surely lurk some gnome-like wild-eyed creatures, who execute fantastic dances on the moonlit shore as the sea laps, laps, laps against the pebbles. Are these the "queer folk" we shall find at "Stewkey," the village which the women seem to speak of with bated breath, and the men regard with evident distrust?

Stiffkey.

The road thither truly is "awful." Deep-rutted, grass-grown, lonely, bare. It seems, too, to be the original long lane without a turning. On and on it stretches, always dreary and ill-kept, treeless, hedgeless, with never a bend in it to break its terrible monotony. What will be the end? Suspense becomes painful. If only there were a wayside cottage to give some life to the scene, a signpost, a stile, anything to bring rest from this long, straight, stony road. At last! The road slopes upwards, the summit is reached, and one catches one's breath in speechless admiration.

"Stewkey" lies below in no dank, dark swamp, but in a sequestered vale of perfect beauty. Around rise the hills, bare of trees, it is true; but at their base are dark, sombre woods, rich in deep shades of brown and green, and meadows of finest verdure, their vivid verdancy contrasting sharply with the gloomy darkness of the thick clumps of trees surrounding the village. Slowly babbling down the hillside through these pleasant pasture lands, a silver rivulet winds to the sea, and adds the final touch to a scene which Arthur Young, the Suffolk agriculturist, whose tours were as wide as his views were broad, temperately describes as "a most complete and pleasing picture." The tree-tops and the vale are touched with a soft tinge of grey, over-mastered by the brownness of the hills and the red roofs of the cottages huddled together in the hilly village street high above the wooded valley. The roadway is narrow, the houses turned this way and that as their builders' fancies have dictated; this one's front windows overlooking that one's back door. But the picture has its dark side. The valley may be very sweet and very pleasant, but squalor reigns in the village. Its picturesqueness is obviously its only charm. Stay, there is the old farm down yonder in the hollow, not "behind the little wood," but behind the desolate-looking church, whose vicar must have a sorry time. Its carved doors are sadly out of repair, and many of its mullioned windows are boarded up. The fowls and pigs scrape and wallow before its handsome doorway, yet it is well "within the picture," and still a delight to the eye.

This is Stiffkey Hall, now a humble farm-house, but once intended to have been a seat of Sir Nicholas Bacon, Lord Privy Seal to Elizabeth, and Premier Baronet of England. As a recreation from his State duties, this astute son of a Bury St. Edmund's sheep-shearer seems to have indulged in house-building. Close to Bury, at Culford, he reared himself the mansion now occupied by the Earl of Cadogan, which probably was the one frequently visited by Elizabeth, who on one occasion remarked to him, "My Lord, what a little house you have gotten," whereupon he artfully replied, "Madam, my house is well, but it is you who have made me too great for my house." Stiffkey Hall he, for some reason, never finished. Maybe his means would not permit him to carry out his scheme; for, unlike most other statesmen of his time, he seems to have been wholly guiltless of peculation and corruption. Possibly if he had completed this "delightfully situated residence," Stiffkey might now have been an ideal village. For, with the Hall fitly occupied, its people would have been somewhat cared for, and have become conventional and respectable Hodges instead of the pitifully interesting studies of humanity who now lure the curious to "Stewkey." Where, by the way, are they all? The village is strangely quiet, and only an occasional unkempt urchin darts out from a cottage to peep at the strangers in the street. What are they all doing? Presently a group of stolid-looking men, who glance sullenly at the passers-by, are espied at a corner. It is morning, yet they seem to have no occupation, and apparently they belong to one family, for without exception they have all a tangled crop of fiery-red hair. So, too, it is presently discovered, have all the tousled, unwashed little imps rolling like kittens in the grime of the neglected gardens.

Gradually it is borne in upon one that these Stewkeyites are a race of Rufuses. Men, women, lads, and maidens, even the fluffy-pated infants are crowned with Judas locks of every tint, from the dull red that Titian loved to the fiercest scarlet, and from the dingy "ginger" to the gold just tinged with a rosy glow. Can it be that these dwellers by the Northern Sea are descended from Norse invaders of the coast, and have all inherited the complexion of their ancestors? Alas! there is a more prosaic explanation forthcoming, when the manners and customs of "Stewkey" are revealed, an explanation that serves, too, to account for the puny frames, the stunted forms, the dull wits, and worse, of at least half the population. Inter-marriage is the secret of it all. Without this peaceful valley no ruddy-haired youth ever seeks a bride, nor do the "foreigners" ever take hence the "emancipated" maidens, who have freed themselves from the shackles of conventional domesticity and relegated man to "a back-seat." It would be a brave-hearted wooer who should come hither in search of a bride. The girls are not uncomely, it is true; but what would the "foreign" mother-in-law, the sisters, the cousins, and the aunts of the valiant wooer say to a wife who docked her skirts above the knees and sent her husband to potter round while she did the hard work; who "farmed" out her babies and never cleaned her house, or did needlework, or cared about a best bonnet? And what gipsy-faced, dark-eyed girl would ever care to share the fortunes of—or in other words, work for—a "Stewkey" lover in such circumstances as these? So they continue to mate among themselves, forming one vast family, alike in feature, in complexion, in habits. They suffer physically and mentally, of course, and there are sad sights within those picturesque dwellings in the pretty Stiffkey Valley.

"Queer folk" indeed! who stand sorely in need of sanitary inspection, of civilisation, of moral suasion, of everything that lifts a human being out of the rut of ignorance in all its forms to the level of thinking man.

There are no mills and factories on the banks of this gentle rivulet, meandering through meadows and woods, to make the women independent and motherhood unwelcome, yet in this seemingly simple Norfolk village we have a replica of all the evils of a manufacturing town. The children are uncared for, the women supply the domestic treasury, home life is not sacred, "service" is regarded as degradation. By degrees the gloom gathers round the picture. As one learns more of Stiffkey and its people, the scene which looked so charming from the hill-summit seems to lose its brightness. Is there not something, after all, weird and gloomy and lifeless about the still vale, and that dark stream trickling its way slowly under the trees to the dreary shore?

One feels somehow that it is not Peace but Death that reigns in this valley. It is hard to repress a shudder even though the sun gleams on the picture and the children's voices break the silence. Withal there is a grim fascination, too, about these queer folk, who live and move and have their being in Stiffkey Vale, undisturbed by any considerations without their village, spurred by no ambition save to get a half-penny or a penny a dozen more for the cockles they gather on "the main;" but content to grub on among themselves, a race apart from the people of other villages, heedless of their appearance, for the women are rarely seen even in the gay stuff gowns which it is every cottager's pride to don on high-days and holidays. One looks in vain for the wives and maidens of the village.

Early in the morning, before the sun was up, and while as yet the men slept, the women and girls were plodding

heavily down the rutted road on their way to the " main."
In the dawning light one of their number had been the
round to rouse them for action, and then, banded together
in gangs similar to those one sees in Fen-land, they took
their way shorewards, their sacks bound about their backs,
their legs bare to the knees, and their long rakes serving as

A Village Industry.

staves to help them along the heavy lanes. What an
admirable picture it would make! An artist of the new
French school would rejoice in its strength and unconven-
tionality. It is almost possible to see reproduced on
canvas the long grey road in the grey morning light,
the bent figures, quaintly garbed, of the women armed with
the cockle-rakes, hard-featured, brawny-limbed, weather-

beaten creatures, whose ruddy hair is the brightest note of colour in the picture. Away on the lonely shore they will work till the tide comes in, and then, bent almost double beneath the weight of their loaded sacks, which they strap upon each other's backs, cold and saturated with spray, they will tramp back again to the cheerless homes, where neither warmth nor food awaits them. For, excepting the witch-like doubled-up old crones, who can no longer pursue the industry, and the little maids upon whom the School Board happily keeps a vigilant eye, every female in the place goes away to the "main," and things at home must take their chance till the "cockle-ers" return.

Peep through the door of the squalid cottage yonder, and see what becomes of the babies while the mothers and the sisters are away. Within sits one of the least helpless of the superannuated old "cockle-ers," surrounded by wicker cradles and infantile paraphernalia. The tiniest of her little red-haired charges are screaming in every key. The older ones tumble over each other on the floor, and cry and re-cry themselves to sleep in the intervals of feeding. Across the road another poor old creature is "minding" another batch of youngsters at a more advanced stage of existence, and apparently heeding their falls and baby troubles as little as if they were a litter of puppies or young pigs. In due course these wee girls will grow up and go to work on the shore and marry these ruddy-polled little men, who, like their fathers, will not do more than they can help. It is not an ideal life from any point of view. The babies and the toddling children certainly know little of the joy of life under the care of the village grand-dames. The women look upon hard work as their heritage, the men reap the advantages of their wives' "emancipation." Mention "service" to the girls of "Stewkey" and they recoil in horror. Nor do their mothers urge them to it. It is more than probable that they would not be in great demand as domestics even if they were willing to seek such employment. A childhood on the shore and such training as they receive at home scarcely predisposes them to become neat-handed Phyllises. A parlour-maid who preferred bifurcated and abbreviated skirts, and scorned hosiery and shoe leather, would not be likely to keep her situation for any lengthened period; and cleanliness, judging from the appearance of the village as a whole, would certainly not be a strong point of any "Stewkey" maiden.

It is to Lynn and Wisbech that the "bluestones," gathered by these women on the "main," ultimately find their way. The dealers come out almost daily and bargain for their spoils; but it is rare that the price exceeds fourpence a peck, and as a bushel would be as much of a load as each woman could bring back with her from the desolate, bleak shore, "cockle-ing" is not the most lucrative profession in the world. When the east wind blows in from the sea it cuts like a flail on the naked legs of the women, stooping hour after hour to pick the slimy, glistening molluscs from the pools, and rheumatism, say the old "minders," is the inevitable lot of them all; for however bleak and cold it may be, and whatever may be their constitutions, they will plunge into the water knee-deep again and again, day after day, to rake from the incoming waves an extra peck to swell their sacks. Sometimes it is in the waning light, according to the tides, that the women come down for their spoils, but always in gangs, for the sea is treacherous; and once, they say, it carried away one of their number, who, working alone in the gloaming with her back to the waves, learnt only of her danger when it was too late. Moreover, they need each other's help. As they gather the cockles they place them in rough aprons held up by the corners, and as these fill they are emptied into the sacks in which the cockles are carried home. But to lift these on the bearers' backs when full would be impossible without help, so each one assists to raise her burden on the other's shoulders, the last one having hers literally pushed upwards by the united efforts of her heavily-laden sisters. "As strong as any man," the men and women of neighbouring villages pronounce these thick-set, auburn-headed toilers by the sea, and one can hardly doubt it seeing them tramp homewards after their rough labours with their heavy loads. As strong as the men they may be, but how infinitely braver and more industrious than the pale-face louts who dawdle round the fields and hang about, while their womankind work like slaves and their children and homes are neglected. Strong they may be as mere beasts of burden, but their stunted, pallid offspring do no credit to their "strength" as the mothers of the coming generation, nor the squalor of the village to the power which it is Woman's privilege to wield.

As the mist creeps up from the valley the blue smoke begins to curl from the cottagers' chimneys. The babies are being collected by their weary mothers, the men are coming home to be fed, and one turns sadly and sorrowfully from this unlovely picture of village life. It is in the shadows that it is most fitly left.

CHAPTER VI.

THE TOWN OF LYNN.

MOST people, before they visit it, are impressed with the idea that Lynn is a very charming place, above all things a place to be seen. Possibly its name has something to do with this superstition. There is a pleasant ring about Lynn. The name is quaint, suggestive of Devonshire, with a fine old Saxon flavour about it. To those who know it not nor its neighbourhood, Lynn possibly suggests, too, shady old quays, quaint alley-ways, fine river scenery, and much activity of a marine and picturesque kind. They dreamily associate it with bells :

> "O'er the shining sands, the wandering cattle homeward
> Follow each other at your call, O Bells of Lynn,"

and with Eugene Aram and his arrest; and having, too, a hazy notion of its antiquity and ancient history, it must necessarily, they think, be a delightful place. Illusions, alas, are so difficult to retain, that it is best for all who think thus pleasantly of Lynn to keep as far from it as possible. With a nice turn for antiquarianism, one might perhaps find time hang less heavily on one's hands in this Norfolk town, for there are a couple of fine churches and a Guildhall of extreme interest. But more than this is somehow expected in Lynn, and the expectations are unrealised. Picturesqueness is most assuredly not one of its charms, and for this there is no excuse.

An important seaport, with such a church as St.

The Oldest House in Lynn.

Margaret's, and quartered, so to say, by the four "fleets" that run through the town from the river, it ought to be a tolerably presentable place. But it is not. It is snug and clean and respectable, and drearily modern as a whole. Its narrow streets are

cobbled, it is true—painfully cobbled, for the flints pierce the toughest boot soles, and absolutely wreck the "uppers"—but they are not picturesque. Smart shops line them on either side, and the houses with a few exceptions are of the terrace order, eminently respectable but architecturally dismal. Here and there one comes on a quaint old building, jammed between a couple of hideous modern brick houses, such as the residence of the Sandringham Hall chimney-sweep, who proudly but inaccurately boasts that his is the oldest house in Lynn. Upstairs on the plaster walls are some curious old paintings, and from an artistic point of view the sweep "by appointment to H.R.H. the Prince of Wales" has a more interesting dwelling-place than many an important Lynn burgess. But in Nelson Street—Nelson recurs like a decimal in all these East Anglian ports—the sweep's antiquity card is unmistakably trumped by the dwellers in the two quaint old houses with quadrangles. Doorways, too, and curiously-carved and obviously antique archways, are constantly appearing in unexpected places in Lynn, which has a way of preparing little surprises for its visitors. Carmelite Terrace, for instance, has an alluring sound, suggestive of old priories and walled-in gardens and ruins, but it consists in reality of a row of modern ugly cottages; while "the hill" to which one is constantly being directed, is none other than the Tuesday Market-place, a quadrangular space as guiltless of the slightest elevation as the Strand or Cheapside.

> "Pleasantly shone the setting sun
> Over the town of Lynn,"

says Hood, describing the "evening calm and cool" when that melancholy usher, Eugene Aram, froze the young blood of the little Grammar School boy with his ghastly confession. And from this evidence it is to be concluded that the rain, which apparently raineth every day here, sometimes ceases to wash the streets of King's Lynn. And what rain it is! It comes down in torrents, swishing along the gutters, bubbling over the cobbled roadways, and enveloping the Grey Friars' steeple and the churches in mist. Hood evidently knew the place well, for he leaves us with no pleasant picture of a sunlit port, when he describes how

> "Two stern-faced men set out from Lynne
> Through the cold and heavy mist."

That "evening calm and cool" was evidently an exceptional one, of which the four-and-twenty happy boys very wisely availed themselves.

Unhappy Aram! that his conscience could not sleep in Lynn was small wonder. The Grammar School, now a modern building, was always overshadowed, so to say, by the grim and gloomy steeple of the old Franciscan convent across the way, now its only remaining fragment. If it always rained, and he had to look out upon this frowning tower, standing stark and lonely against the grey sky, while its bells chimed the weary hours, and were answered by others across the "fleet," it is not surprising that "a burning thought was in his heart, and his bosom ill at ease." The only wonder is that, with his propensity for dispatching his fellow-creatures, he did not fall upon other victims in Lynn to their destruction, by way of relieving the monotony of existence and providing the townsfolk with a little excitement. One can fancy him moodily tramping the winding avenue of elms that leads to the dismal and romantically-situated Chapel of the Red Mount, the lodgment of Edward IV. after his defeat by Warwick, when he made his way to Lynn "en route for the Continent." He would be alone here, shut in by the trees, and it is such a walk as one would imagine a mind-tortured man seeking, when affrighted by every sound.

The best impressions of Lynn are taken in the early morning and in the twilight. It is in the morning, when fine, that this mall, so like to the beautiful college groves of Cambridge, is best seen, and especially if it is Spring-time, when as yet the leaves are in the full glory of vivid greenness. The nakedness of the land is hidden by this leafy screen. One cannot then see the flat marshlands, the smoky chimneys, the mercantile aspect of the town. The walk runs parallel with the fragmentary remains of the old town walls, which in 1643 were sufficiently strong to keep out the Parliamentarians for three weeks. On the meadow land the sheep and cattle graze, the birds twitter among the branches, and the mellowed Old Red Tower on the hillock, encrusted, so to say, with legend, lends the needful touch of romance to this ideal lover's walk.

Seven miles from the sea, in a fertile valley in the direction of Wells, there is one of the quaintest little towns in Norfolk, Walsingham, where once a shrine, set up

A Bit of Lynn.

to Our Lady, was as celebrated for its miraculous properties as that of St. Thomas à Becket at Canterbury. Pilgrims from all parts of the world landed at Lynn and thronged to Walsingham to this famous Augustinian Priory, the remains of which are still to be seen, and it is supposed that this beautiful little Chapel of the Red Mount at Lynn, once evidently most elaborately decorated within, was built as a station for the pilgrims bound for the shrine at Walsingham.

The building, three stories high, and in the form of a cross, contained an inner and outer staircase; the one intended for pilgrims to ascend to the relic in the upper storey, whilst the outer one enabled them to pass down without disorder. The internal ornamentation of this upper room must have been singularly elaborate. Even now the tracery and panelling are beautiful, though both places have been sadly ravaged by time and soldiers and other depredators; for, while in the Great Rebellion the chapel was used as a powder magazine, it served also a pest-house at the time of the plague in 1665. It has, therefore, in its time played many parts, and Robert Curraunce, its founder, was certainly well advised to build it. Its date, 1484, is determined by records in possession of the Corporation, and taking into consideration its age and history, this unique—so far as England is concerned—chapel is in a fair state of preservation. There is a legend to the effect that a subterranean passage exists between the Red Mount and

Mill Fleet, Lynn.

Castle Rising, and that some years ago a fiddler undertook to traverse it, playing his violin on his way that there might be "no deception" about the fulfilment of his wager. For awhile the strains of the instrument were plainly heard, then they suddenly ceased, and of that fiddler and the subterranean passage the rest is silence.

Returning from an early stroll in the mall, past the slimy, suicidal-looking, and not ineffective if scarcely picturesque Mill Fleet, with Grey Friars' Steeple and the fine towers of St. Margaret's rising above it, the town is found to be waking into life. The country wagons rattle over the cobbles, and creep in one by one to the Marketplace; gipsy vans and carriers' carts gradually make their appearance; agricultural implements, cattle troughs, and stalls of produce spring up as from the ground before the windows of the comfortable old "Globe," where the farmers will by-and-bye have their market dinner; the whistles of the seed and oil-cake factories and of the vessels going out of the harbour strike shrilly on the ear, and all the romance of the Red Mount and of the melancholy usher Aram fades rapidly before the commonplaces of a dull provincial mercantile life.

No, not quite all the romance of Lynn, if St. Nicholas— carefully shut up, of course, like the majority of Norfolk churches,—is skirted by way of Black Goose Street, and the Gothic Guildhall, with its quaint black and white chessboard front of flint, is sought out. There is a grimness that is absolutely grand about this old Elizabethan Townhall, the mere sight of which, as it is now used as a police court and "lock-up," should act as a deterrent to would-be breakers of the peace in Lynn. Horace Walpole, who like his father, Sir Robert, represented Lynn in Parliament, declared his constituents to be "sensible, and reasonable, and civilised," so maybe this peculiarly drear-looking building does over-awe the inhabitants. Within there is much to see, besides the portraits of William and Mary, and Sir Robert Walpole, afterwards Earl of Orford. Lynn is rich in charters, the earliest of which was given to the town in 1216 by John, who was then on his way to meet Louis of France, whom his despairing Barons had called to their rescue. Probably he afterwards repented of his grant, for but a day or two later, like many a modern householder, he lost all his clothes in the Wash, and not only his

St. Margaret's, Lynn.

clothes, but his money, jewels, and all the records of the kingdom. His loss was followed by a fever, possibly induced by agitation, and possibly by the malarious air of the marshes round these parts. At some time before or after this event, he presented Lynn with a cup and a sword, and although these have disappeared, their place has been taken by a very beautiful and curious goblet and an engraved sword, which respectively belong in all probability to the fourteenth and sixteenth centuries. These are both preserved, with John's charter and others, in the Guildhall, together with the famous "Red Book of Lynn," said to be the oldest paper-book in existence, and at all events an extremely interesting work, containing as it does the entries of wills from the year 1309. Here then, at all events, modernity has not laid a withering hand. One may potter round the Guildhall and St. Margaret's Church opposite, and almost be persuaded that Lynn is, after all, an interesting town.

That familiar East Anglian figure, Herbert de Losinga, reappears on the scene here; for it is to him that the town owes this splendid church, which is somewhat similar to his St. Nicholas at Yarmouth. Within and without it is worthy of its founder, for it is a magnificent, cathedral-like building; a patchwork of architectural styles, it is true —Norman, Early Decorated, and Perpendicular—but all admirable specimens of their kind. The finely-carved fourteenth century stalls and Misereres, the famous "Peacock brass" and vintage brass, bearing the date 1349, of Adam de Walsoken, whose name is singularly appropriate to the decoration of his memorial, and the carved Elizabethan pulpit, amply reward the patient seeker after the key that has to be fetched from a remote verger before the church can be entered. It is a misfortune that the counties of the East, which are so specially rich in beautiful old churches, should be so spiritually behind the times as to adhere to the miserable old open-only-on-Sunday principle. It is rare indeed that an open church is found; rare, too, that their interiors are worthily appointed, and here in Lynn, St. Margaret's and St.

Lynn Ferry (Wet Evening).

Nicholas' typify the unfortunate condition of the majority. One wonders, in connection with St. Margaret's, what manner of service was conducted here when Dr. Burney, father of Madame D'Arblay, the authoress of "Evelina" and "Cecilia," was organist of the church. During the time he lived in Lynn, his daughter Fanny, his son Charles, and his son James, afterwards Admiral Burney, were born, so that the town has added to the long list of literary and naval celebrities produced by the Eastern Counties. Lynn, by the way, has always had somewhat of a reputation for producing members of both these professions. In 1330, one Nicholas, a brother either of the Franciscan or

Carmelite order established in the town, set sail from Lynn to "the most Northern Islands in the World," preceding by some five hundred years Dr. Nansen, who is on the very same quest that Friar Nicholas undertook without tinned provisions and the scientific appliances that are now indispensable to Arctic explorers. The first printed English and Latin dictionary was compiled by a distinguished Lynn scholar, Galfridus, and another, Alan, was an indefatigable literary worker in the intervals of performing his clerical duties, for he too, was a Carmelite.

When the shadows begin to fall over the grey streets, and the "cold and heavy mist" prominently asserts itself, the most effective, if not the pleasantest impression of Lynn Harbour and Lynn Ferry is received. The effects are such as delight Mr. Whistler and other distinguished etchers. In the fading light the black barges move stealthily up the darkening stream; a steamer, flying the yellow quarantine flag, hoots its way past the vessels in the harbour and wakes the echoes of the curious old riverside buildings, which doubtless the opulent Lynn merchants and burghers built for private residences in the days when they kept their businesses always under their eye. Old Lynn

From the Quay, Lynn.

church, half hidden in trees, becomes shadowy in outline, the figures of the men leaning over the crazy little balustrade of the landing stage awaiting the ferry boat grow less and less distinct, and the sailors, shouting from the quaint old balcony of the "Ship" to their comrades on the river, appear in the misty gloaming to have come from Davy's locker to hold revel once more by the river-side. Against the slimy steps the water sullenly plashes. The dogs across the river bark hoarsely, and are answered by invisible and seemingly distant canine friends, and the silvery pall of twilight falls lightly over the great stretches of mud, and the curious cupola-crowned Custom House, erected, as an old Lynn historian has said "at the proper Cost and Charge of Sir Jno. Turner, Knight, Three times Mayor here, and for many years one of the Members of Parliament, for an Exchange for Merchants, Anno Domini 1683."

The Custom House and Purfleet, Lynn.

CHAPTER VII.

A WALK TO SANDRINGHAM.

LYNN resolves itself into a stack of chimneys and a couple of towers as a backward glance is taken of the town from the pretty lane leading village-wards from Wootton station. The air blows fresh and keen, and the scene is full of brightness, though when once the small railway station is out of sight there is nothing ahead but a long, narrow road, bounded on either side by hedges, just now brilliant with vivid hips-and-haws and trails of bryony berries. However, the sun streams down on the sandy path, the pine trees glow like copper in the light, and so clear is the atmosphere that the smoke, curling upwards from a few wayside cottages just skirting the village, presently to be entered, is as blue as a summer sea.

There is a momentary indication of life as Wootton itself, a peaceful and miniature hamlet of cottages, is passed; but a hundred yards beyond all is still and lonely again, save when a lordly cock pheasant in full plumage runs across the roadway, or a hare scutters over the wild heath-like tract that lies between Wootton and Castle Rising. If one wanted to show a foreigner a typical English village, none better could be selected than Castle

Rising. It has been liberally provided with all that goes to the making of a picturesque and tranquil scene; for what more could be needed than a ruined castle, a fine church, a village green, a sheltered position, a group of the most charmingly quaint almshouses to be found in the country?

The tourist, who comes here in his might from Hunstanton and Lynn, has not been able to rob it of its peace and beauty. True, the Castle enclosure is not always guiltless of paper bags, and the bicyclists' warning "hooters" too often break the stillness of the leafy lanes about the village, but withal it is delightfully quiet and literally overflowing with studies of rural life. There is no need to hunt about for "bits," no occasion to go further indeed than the threshold of the ideally planned and perfectly situated village. One has no desire to remember that

> "Rising was a seaport town
> When Lynn was but a marsh."

If the local rhyme is not without reason, Rising is the more to be congratulated on the changes which have come about; but it is more than probable that, like the majority of traditions, this one is wholly without foundation, and that the Wash, now more than two miles distant, was never much nearer.

Round the village green, with its central cross, a restored one it is true, but none the less picturesque in this case on that account, the pretty little cottages, with their glowing gardens of roses and sunflowers and marigolds and pansies, seem to have been set down designedly for the benefit of artists and word-painters. They are all so marvellously spick and span and ivy-mantled. They all have the regulation trails of roses clambering over their fronts, their gardens are full of the dear old sweet-scented blossoms that country-folk love and cherish. On their white gates swing flaxen-haired, rosy-cheeked little lads and lassies, who might have just stepped out of an illustrated toy-book; and even the cats, who lie sunning themselves in the open doorways, are just the sleek, clean, well-behaved pussies one associates with the ideal country cottage.

The whole village looks cosy and comfortable. Hodge evidently knows how to live hereabouts, and not a few pallid London clerks and pent-up shopmen would envy him his lot, could they but see these clean and quaint little homes set amidst a wilderness of flowers, and overshadowed by the beautiful ash trees and sycamores that encircle Castle Rising.

Folks make straight for the Castle itself as a rule without pausing to enjoy the first picture of this old-world village. The ruin is, of course, a magnificent example of Norman architecture, and stands unequalled in the county as a specimen of a mediaeval stronghold; but it is by no means the only "lion" of the place, especially from a picturesque point of view. Indeed the Castle is rather disappointing at the first glance to those who come in search of a pretty picture only. It is square and bare, and destitute of all the romantic attributes beloved of picnic parties and amateur lady artists. But when the "season" is over and the custodian of the Castle is no longer called upon to supply hot water to thirsty tea-making tourists, there are few more really picturesque and interesting ruins in Norfolk than this grim Norman fortress, hedged in with immense earthworks. Round the massive grey keep, with its fine staircase, the white pigeons whirl and whirr and coo, and without the myriads of birds in the shrubbery and trees that completely fill the fosse alone break the stillness. One may wander in

Staircase, Castle Rising.

and out the galleries and chambers then and find endless archaeological treasures, and see pictures enough through the open doorways and richly-moulded windows to fill a gallery. From the summit of the keep one may look across the salt marshes to the shining sea, over Babingley, the first Christian church built in England by Felix the Burgundian, who converted Sigeberht, king of East Anglia, to the faith; over the sandy heaths and plantations of fir and heather to the golden and purple hills that lie between Wolferton and Sandringham.

Yonder is all that remains of Flitcham Abbey, Lynn lies behind, and in the distance the outline of the low Lincolnshire coast is traced in the sunlight. Within this dreary keep Isabella, "the she-wolf of France," spent the greater portion of her time after the death of Edward II., in 1330. It could scarcely have been a lively place of residence, especially if, as some assert, she was kept here as a prisoner; but it was, in all probability, not more lonely for her in this "goodly castle" than for her wretched husband, Edward, in the keep of Berkeley, especially as the views from the windows were extensive, and there must always have been much coming and going between Lynn and Flitcham and Rising Hall. Throughout there are indications of her tenure of the castle. The arms of Edward II., and of his successor, Edward III., are to be traced in many of the rooms, which, judging from the remains of their decorations, must have been exceedingly handsome if not always snug apartments.

Rising Church, just peeping from a veritable thicket of sycamores and elms, and the wonderful ash trees that are such a special feature of the district, is not a whit less interesting than the Castle. It possesses all the attractions of the fortress, for it is a splendid example of Norman work, one of the most remarkable ecclesiastical specimens of this style of architecture in England; and those who are not merely content to be told that the mouldings are fine, the archways curiously carved, and that the font is of such and such a date, but who, in the true artistic spirit, and with a right reverence for such beautiful specimens of ecclesiastical architecture and decoration as are to be found here, will not easily be lured from the beautiful interior of this grand old Norman

At Rising Almshouses.

church. It is an ideal church for the village. Standing in a grove of magnificent trees, it is altogether charming. The little God's acre is most lovingly tended, the appointments of the church as rich and handsome and reverent as it is possible to secure for such a parish, and the interior of no Continental church could, in the matter of effect and colouring, outvie the picturesqueness of St. Michael's,

Castle Rising, on a bright Sunday morning. In the dark chancel, curiously separated from the nave by the tower, the altar stands out conspicuously against the grey Norman walls, with its rich hangings, its lights and flowers. The shadows cling about the interlacing arches, and deepen into cimmerian darkness in the tower chamber; and as the sun streams through the row of little round windows on the south, the scarlet cloaks of the "sisters" from the almshouse just without the churchyard supply the needful touch of colour. What a charming picture these old ladies would make, too, as they file out of the porch down the shady path into their little Jacobean houses, built round the grassy quadrangle opposite. How full of brightness it would be! How delightfully quaint! For, as they pass along under the trees, with the grey church in the background, and the old almshouses, built early in the reign of James the First, just seen through the gateway, there is nothing in the scene to indicate that the first of the Stuarts is not still on the throne; that nearly three hundred years have elapsed since the first recipients of Henry Howard, Earl of Northampton's bounty, went along this same path to piously pray for the founder of the charity. To this day they wear the curious Jacobean peasant garb. Their gowns are bright blue, their capes a fine rich red, and for headgear they have the high black steeple-crowned beaver hats, lined with a white frill, in which the wicked old women in the children's story books are invariably represented. Within the quadrangle the scene as they enter is even more charming. Here surely must Peace abide. The enclosure is gay with flowers. The door of the common hall stands open, and the "sisters" clatter over the red-bricked floor into the cool, exquisitely neat "hall" where their garments are kept in oaken presses, and where they are banqueted once

a year, according to the terms of the founder's bequest. Finely carved oaken chests, benches and settles, black with age and shining like ebony, and a long narrow table of the same wood, furnish the room; without, in the entrance hall, there is an eight-day clock to match, and in the little chapel, where daily prayers are offered by the inmates for the founder, the oaken seats with their carved corners are almost as black as the beaver hats of the "sisters." It was well, maybe, that the eccentric Earl of Northampton thus provided for his soul's health. He died in 1614, suspected of almost as many crimes as he had years; but though he had his faults like many other gentlemen of his period, he also had brains and turned them to good account, so far as he himself was concerned, for in the space of eight years he contrived to get himself created a Privy Councillor, Warden of the Cinque Ports, Lord Privy Seal, Knight of the Garter, and Earl of Northampton. He could

In the Chapel, Rising Almshouses.

evidently well afford, therefore, to perpetuate his memory, and provide for all time for twelve "sisters" of Castle Rising. It was to his family that the Castle had passed in Henry the Eighth's reign; and, until recently, the Hall, now occupied by the Duke of Fife, had been in possession of the Howards.

To this most complete and typical English village the Prince of Wales' family are greatly attached. It is but a pleasant walk past half-ruined Babingley church, on the bank of a willow-bordered stream, over the wild, undulating tract of heath and fir-scented plantation, to Sandringham, a walk that astonishes and charms the stranger who may picture this quarter of Norfolk as a sandy, dreary, treeless waste. It is a way of flowers. The air is heavy with the pungent odour of heather and pine and fir, with the fragrance of lilies of the valley, of which there are vast tracts hereabouts; and the bright broom and gorse and pale pink heath, foxgloves and wild crab cheer the eye, until the famous Norwich gates, presented by the county to the Prince on his marriage, are reached, and the greater glories of the Park absorb attention.

Of Sandringham there is literally nothing save the house, the church, and the park. The village no longer exists.

The Prince of Wales has, during his tenure here, built his tenants and labourers charming little rustic houses in West Newton, and that is now to all intents and purposes the "village," unless the Hall, York Cottage, the Rectory, and Sir Francis Knollys' house may be considered to constitute a hamlet.

Sandringham Hall is not beautiful as an architectural work, but is finely situated, and the estate is so charmingly varied that it is not in the least surprising that the Prince and his family should take the greatest delight in their Norfolk home. For thirty years the Prince has been ceaselessly making improvements, and probably there is now no more diversified estate in England. There are woods and hills, heathlands, meadowlands, cornfields, and marshes, where wild-fowl abound; there is the sea, whence the strong northern air blows keenly; beautiful lakes have been made in the grounds, whole plantations and shrubberies laid out; and so plentiful are the hares and partridges and pheasants that they cluster in the roadways and scarcely move as the very occasional pedestrian passes by. Birds and beasts abound everywhere. The meadows are full of beautiful cattle—fine, sleek, carefully-bred creatures—whose ancestors have been well known as they, too, are at London and county agricultural shows; and in the glades of the Park, under the enormous oaks and beeches, the grazing deer give life and colour to the scene.

Secluded, remote and wooded as it is with sombre firs and pines, Sandringham is never dull. The barking of the dogs that occupy the long series of kennels, close to the West Newton side of the gardens, may be heard in the neighbouring villages; and above the stables, in the shrubbery walks, and on the lawn, where they gather to be fed by their Royal mistress when she is here, hundreds of rocks and ring-tails, Jacobins, fan-tails, and other pigeons, cluster and coo and strut.

Across the garden, through an avenue of Scotch firs, the Prince and his family reach the tiny but beautifully decorated little church of St. Mary Magdalene, full of memorials of those "loved long since and lost awhile." Newspaper readers know this little church well by reputation. They have grown accustomed to read that the "Prince and Princess of Wales attended divine service in the church of St. Mary Magdalene." Few of them know, however, how miniature is this church. To enter it the Royal party have always to pass by the little green mound where, among the "village Hampdens," lies the infant Prince, who died after a day's experience of this world's life in 1871. Within, among many other windows presented by the Prince of Wales, is one to the memory of this day-old baby, while the west window, presented by the officers of 10th Hussars, will for ever hereafter be a memorial of his gentle brother, the Duke of Clarence, who passed from life, as he would most have wished could he have chosen his last scene, in the Norfolk home he loved so well. Opposite the pew in the chancel in which they sit, the Prince and Princess of Wales have placed a tablet to the memory of their beloved son. The simple pathos of the inscription catches the reader by the throat.

ALBERT EDWARD CHRISTIAN VICTOR
DUKE OF CLARENCE AND AVONDALE, K.G.
LOVING AND BELOVED

We, thy sorrowing parents, Albert Edward and Alexandra, by this simple token, record our lasting grief for the loss of thee, our first born.

"Man looketh on the countenance, but God
on the heart."

To his sister, the Princess Alice of Hesse, to his beloved brother-in-law, the late Emperor Frederick, and to his brother, Prince Leopold, the Prince of Wales has also erected marble memorials in bas-relief within the chancel of this beautiful little church, to which the Queen has also given a stained window as a thank-offering for her eldest son's recovery from illness, and the Princess of Wales has presented the brass lectern inscribed—

> To the glory of God. A thank-offering for His mercy 14th Dec., 1871. "When I was in trouble I called upon the Lord, and He heard me."
>
> ALEXANDRA.

It is but a short drive through Dersingham and Snettisham, whose fine church tower is a well-known sea-mark, and where, so to say, the influence of the L'Estranges is first manifested, to Hunstanton, or, as it is locally called, "Hunston," a "tripper"-infested resort, with few redeeming features.

Compared with Cromer or Southwold, or even Felixstowe, Hunstanton is but a poor place. The L'Estranges, who have been lords of the manor here since the Conquest, have done their utmost to make the town attractive. Under their supervision the pretty little villas and pleasant streets have been built and laid out. There are excellent hotels, a pier, an attractive church, good shops, and various other seaside attractions, and in particular the tennis and pleasure grounds on the cliffs; but, withal, Hunstanton is neither a centre of marine gaiety, nor the peaceful but picturesque and accessible village by the sea, which people are always seeking and so seldom find.

When Mr. Toole used to deliver comic lectures, he was wont to open one on "China" by remarking that "China is divided into two parts, China proper and China improper," adding in his inimitable manner, "of course with the latter we have nothing whatever to do." It is in this fashion one is tempted to describe Hunstanton. Hunstanton "proper" is the old village, which, since the Conquest, the L'Estranges have made their home. The old Hall, a fine, moated, "Family Herald" kind of ancestral manor, built in the fifteenth century, is almost intact. A wing of the original house was burnt down some years ago, but the greater part remains as Sir Roger Le Strange built it; and both without and within, especially in the chapel, hung with crimson velvet, and opening to a fine staircase and gallery, it suggests a "set" at the Haymarket or St. James's. Here was born the famous Roger Le Strange, who fought so pluckily for Charles I. at Lynn. He was altogether "too previous" in his appearance on life's stage. Had he only flourished two hundred and fifty years later he would probably have been running a smart evening paper as an organ of the Tory party, and have secured a peerage for his family. For, after the Restoration, having, unlike his Royal master, saved his head, which he very nearly lost at the hands of the Parliamentarians, he took to journalism, established no less than three papers, "The Public Intelligencer," and "The London Gazette," and the "Observator," became Licenser of the Press, and translated Erasmus, Æsop, and Seneca more or less successfully.

Looking up the street towards the Hall, one may view the whole of Hunstanton proper, or old "Hunston," at a glance. A mere handful of quaint old cottages, rich in colour, and doubtless as comfortless as they are picturesque: an Inn, whose front bears the sign and arms of the lord of the manor; the Hall, and the beautiful church, so tastefully restored by the family, whose ancestors occupy a considerable portion of the interior, make up the village. It is altogether a pretty, quiet, sleepy old place, but wholly without the fascination of the beautiful cliff villages clustering at the north-east corner of Norfolk. Nor have the cliffs the beauty of those of Cromer, nor the sea the same charm and colour and grandeur here as there.

The Hunstantonians boast of their sunsets, which are fine in their way, but they are "as moonlight unto sunlight," compared with the glorious sky and sea effects further along the coast. On the cliffs, past the lighthouse, when the tide is out, and the huge white and red boulders, half-covered with slimy brown and green seaweed, are sharply outlined in the clear light, the scene is often extremely effective. To get along the sands over these great masses of solidified marl, leaping-poles are used, and as the sun sinks into the sea and incarnardines the pools between these massive grey and green and white and red-brown fragments, and the figures of "grown-ups" and little folks in every variety of costume and in all sorts of grotesque attitudes are silhouetted against the darkening sky, the picture is very striking. But though the colouring is still good, all fades into the light of common day as St. Edmund's, or Hunstanton "improper," is neared. The pier is crowded with troups of excursionists, who overflow the green before the picturesque "Golden Lion" and the steps of the village cross in its midst. All is noise and confusion and vulgarity. It is Yarmouth on a small and ineffective scale, robbed of its interest and its amusing features. Old Hunstanton is Paradise compared with this, and in re-seeking its peace and picturesqueness one no longer wonders why the L'Estranges have done their best to popularise St. Edmund's, since there, with its pier and promenade and niggers and cheap delights to draw them, the "trippers" congregate, and thus Hunstanton proper is left in silence to those who love repose.

CHAPTER VIII.

IN THE PRINCE'S PLEASAUNCE.

EXQUISITE in design, and wonderfully wrought by the skilful iron-workers of Norwich, the gates which form the principal entrance to Sandringham Park give pause to all who find their way for the first time to the secluded, picturesque corner of the beautiful county which the Prince and Princess of Wales and their family affectionately call their "home." Presented to the Prince after the close of the 1862 Exhibition, they are fully worthy of this great and prosperous county of Norfolk; but though their beauty is subdued, and their value unostentatiously apparent, no one could possibly pass them by unnoticed and unadmired.

The occasional stranger without the gates is disappointed to find, on reaching the principal entrance to the Prince of Wales' country seat, that the house is still concealed from view. It is only when the gates have closed behind one, and the beautiful avenue of limes upon which they open has been traversed, that the house comes in sight, and even then, the front is, so to say, round the corner. The north entrance is cold and cheerless; in winter it is never used at all, and for many reasons the eastern entrance, looking over the lawn and through the park towards the cottage which is now the country house of the Duke of York, is much the pleasanter way into the house.

Gateway at Sandringham Presented by the City of Norwich.

Simplicity is the keynote of life at Sandringham. It is the impression at once received so soon as one is within the precincts of the Royal home. The park, admirably kept, is, of course, much like all other parks; the gardens are pleasantly and picturesquely laid out; and the shrubbery walks are delightful in spring, when the lilacs and laburnums are in bloom, and the air is heavy with the scent of spring flowers, with which the garden-beds are filled. But all is very homely; there are many such country houses and estates in England, but none more thoroughly comfortable, and few so carefully managed and laid out to such good advantage as Sandringham Hall and Park. Whichever way one turns outside the house it is plainly to be seen that the Prince and Princess of Wales are not merely content to have their house and estate set in order for them. There are everywhere evidences of the

Royal master's own guiding hand, of the Royal mistress's loving care and thought.

Of the farm the Prince of Wales has every reason to be proud. It is not an agricultural plaything, but a good working concern. The land is admirably farmed, the beasts are of the best strains, and not even Mr. Clare Sewell Read could take more interest in its practical working than the Prince, to whom the splendid shooting is not more dear than the crops and the stock of his six-hundred-acre model farm. And hardly less of a joy both to the Prince and Princess is the kitchen garden across the road without the park. Here, and in the dairy-house, where they often make butter and brew tea for themselves and visitors in a delightfully cosy little tea-room, the Princess and her daughters spend many an hour when they are at Sandringham. Fruits and vines and vegetables are most carefully cultivated in the most attractive fashion. In blossom time the apple trees, quaintly trained so that the branches fall round the trunks on all sides and form complete balls of pink blooms, and the curiously-trained plum and pear trees, are a wonderful sight; and in due season, when all has come to ripeness, and the branches of the trees, the vines, and the glazed walls on which the peaches and nectarines grow are laden with the rich fruits, these kitchen gardens are as beautiful as anything to be seen around the house. At all times and in all seasons they are interesting, and so indeed are all the external arrangements of the Prince of Wales' country home. Everything is admirably ordered, yet formality is wholly absent.

The stables and the kennels are as fascinating as the gardens and the dairy. Upon both the Princess of Wales and the young Princesses bestow their personal care. Each horse, each dog knows and is known by its Royal mistress. Some are, of course, especial favourites, and to them their owners are deeply attached. Just under the dining-room windows there is a little tablet inscribed, "Dear old Rover, for sixteen years the constant companion of the Princess of Wales. Died Xmas Day, 1886," and in one of the rooms of the stables there are several mounted hoofs of dead-and-gone horses and ponies that were favourites in the Prince's family. In this same room, by-the-way, lined with autographed portraits of sporting celebrities, the late Fred Archer's saddle holds an honoured place; and an interesting and curious present, offered to the Prince and Princess on the occasion of their silver wedding by Mr. John Porter, the well-known trainer, is to be seen. It is a large silver horse-shoe, round which the names of the Derby winners from 1863 to 1888 are inscribed, and small plaits of their manes are let in. Viva, Toynbee, and Nigel, the favourite steeds of the Princess and her daughters, have an adjoining stable of their own, which they share with a hunter belonging to Miss Knollys; and opposite, four dainty little stables, lined with green-and-white tiles and ornamented with silver, are devoted to the especial use of Bena, Huffy, Beau, and Belle—knowing little creatures—who are driven by the Princess in a small phaeton through the neighbouring villages. Sometimes, too, she takes out Puffy, another wee animal, harnessed to a tiny T-cart. But besides these equine pets, there are some forty other horses. There are four famous Hungarians—Balos, Bator, Csillag, and Fulesa, who go like the wind—station horses, brougham horses, and hunters; and almost as many vehicles of different kinds, from a coach to a donkey-chaise, as there are dogs in the kennels yonder, whose more or less honest bark fortunately grows fainter as the house is entered.

Recently, since the fire which played sad havoc with some of the rooms and personal knicknacks of the Royal ladies, the Prince of Wales has greatly improved the interior of the comfortable, pleasantly-irregular red-brick house which he built in 1870 on the site of the old and ugly manor. A storey has been added over the bowling-alley, and the billiard-room and the house thoroughly re-decorated. Since the death, too, of the lamented Duke of Clarence, a turret has been added to the new wing, in which is placed the four-faced clock presented by the local tradespeople as a memorial of the young Prince, to whom everyone round Sandringham was sincerely devoted. They

Sandringham House.

had all known him from babyhood, and though it is pleasant to find a singular absence of garrulity on the part of the villagers and officials hereabouts respecting the habits, sayings, and doings of the Royal residents, they become eloquent to a man directly Prince "Eddy" is mentioned.

Within doors it is those rooms most occupied by the Royal family that specially interest. Sandringham Hall is not particularly large, but it is well planned and arranged, with a strict view to comfort. The ball-room, built about a decade ago, is, however, of magnificent proportions, and not only is it of great size, but it is most tastefully and elaborately decorated. Many of the Prince of Wales' Indian trophies are here displayed. The decorations being white and gold, and the walls painted in the most delicate shades, this fine room appears even vaster than it is, though even when the beautifully-kept floor is full of dancers there is still an enormous amount of space. Next in importance come the drawing-rooms, looking on the terrace and lake, a suite of pleasant and home-like apartments, opening into the conservatory at one end and a corridor at the other, hung with stags' heads shot by the Prince, engravings, and paintings. This leads to the billiard-room, bowling-alley, and the charming dining-room, all of which face, too, the beautiful broad terrace, from which one may almost see—and most certainly smell—the sea across the salt marshes. In some respects the dining-room is the finest room in the house, for it is entirely hung from floor to ceiling with the beautiful tapestry presented by the late King of Spain. When the family are in residence and the room is lighted, and the plate, most of which has been presented to the Prince on various occasions, such as his marriage and silver wedding celebrations, is displayed, the room produces a more striking effect upon the visitor than any other in the house. An annex to this room, too, contains a fine collection of most interesting trophies of the chase at home and abroad. Sandringham, for that matter, is overflowing with souvenirs of the Prince's foreign travels and gifts from other distinguished travellers. Most of those possessions which have a personal interest for their Royal owner have found their way hither, where he and his family best like to spend such time as need not be devoted to social duties in the metropolis. On all sides this is apparent. Here, maybe, is a little statuette of the two young princes as "middies;" here a little bust by the late Prince Victor of Hohenlohe or the Marchioness of Lorne; and there are everywhere pictures and photographs of the children and old and dear friends and departed pets.

There is, too, one room entirely fitted up with the furniture of the Prince's saloons on the "Serapis," a snuggery of which he is particularly fond, his own business room being an exceedingly plain and unpretentious apartment. Visitors, as a rule, exhibit a marked liking for the saloon, into which they immediately pass through the eastern entrance. It is a charming, informal apartment, really a vast hall, where the pet parrot incessantly chatters, the young Princesses make music on the grand piano, everybody lounges about during the daytime in shooting or riding dress, and the dogs lie at length on the beautiful Eastern rugs. Over the fireplace there is a fine copy of a

A Corner of the Saloon at Sandringham.

York Cottage, Sandringham.

portrait group by Angeli of the Prince and Princess of Wales, the latter holding Princess Maud, then a wee maiden with laughing eyes, upon her lap, while at her side, in Highland costume, stands the eldest born, who was so dear to his devoted mother.

Into this saloon and the adjoining tea-room it would be perfectly possible to put the whole of the pretty little cottage across the park which has been given to the Duke and Duchess of York as a Norfolk residence. A new lake, spanned by a rustic bridge, and charmingly bordered with shrubs and plants, was lately made to face the windows of the dining and drawing-rooms of this little "nest," and from all windows a beautiful view across the park is obtained. Everything in the Cottage, as it is called, is marvellously simple and very light; but it is an ideal little home for a young couple, and though but a stone's throw from the "house," has its own private road to Wolferton Station, with which it has telephonic communication as well as with the "house," the stables, the Rectory, and the adjacent residences.

In the "house," by-the-way, there is a telegraph, postal, and telephone office; so that everything seems to be done by magic, taking into consideration the absolute

Sandringham Church.

seclusion of the Royal residence, and the distance it is from the station and villages, any of which are swiftly enough reached, however, when the horses from Sandringham stables are speeding one along. The drive to Wolferton, indeed, is all too short in these circumstances, for the private road thither is beautiful in the extreme. Pheasants and rabbits scarce move from beneath the horses' feet ; the air is full of the odour of firs and the sea, just visible before the road dips into the valley ; the rhododendrons in early summer, the heather and gorse in autumn, flood the scene with colour ; and as the pretty little station is reached, a glimpse of the beautiful church of St. Peter, Wolferton, standing boldly out against the trees, leaves one full of regret that this charming neighbourhood, with its group of fascinating churches, has to be left behind.

CHAPTER IX.

BLOATERDOM.

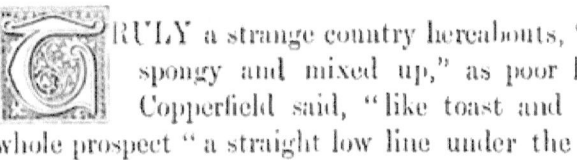RULY a strange country hereabouts, "soppy and spongy and mixed up," as poor little David Copperfield said, "like toast and water," the whole prospect "a straight low line under the sky," with masts and sails unexpectedly coming in sight where only fields and meadows apparently exist.

Yarmouth, the paradise of excursionists, who are poured in here by the thousands in the glorious summer weather, is, too, as strange as its surroundings. One scarcely knows how to take it, so to say, whether to look upon it as the haunt pure and simple of the cheap "tripper," or to regard it as a charming, quaint old seaport, picturesque in the highest degree, interesting from end to end; a place wherein to study the old "salt" in his native lair, or to take "impressions" of the East-end holiday-maker in his most festive mood. A single impression of Yarmouth would be little better than a blur; a wild confused jumble of shipping, crowds, sands, barrel-organs, eating-saloons, and public-houses; noise, vulgarity, perpetual movement, and vivid colouring. Whereas Yarmouth to be thoroughly appreciated must be seen in detail. Thousands of those who come here annually know nothing of this fine old town, save that it has a magnificent extent of beach—the

On Yarmouth Sands.

scene of wild orgies on the part of excited excursionists—that refreshments and ships, greasy paper-bags, "niggers," and lodgings are abundant, and all the advantages of the Old Kent Road are pleasantly combined with those of a seaside resort of peculiar excellence. They come to "enjoy" themselves, and for that purpose they hie them to the shining sands, wherein they dig holes and deposit their many babies, duly provided with feeding-bottles; while they themselves, fortified at the frequent and conveniently-adjacent saloons, dance to the strains of piano-organs, cornets, and various other musical instruments. Of its "sights" they know nothing, when the Aquarium, the Nelson column, the Market-place, the pier, and, maybe, the race-course have been excepted. These they can scarcely help seeing, for the pier in the holiday season is certainly not a sight to be overlooked, and the Nelson monument is visible to the naked eye for miles around. Moreover, the unfortunate, long-suffering donkeys, and poor, broken-kneed ponies that afford the excursionist such exquisite enjoyment, can be sometimes induced to go so far as this fine memorial of the great naval victor along the beautiful Marine Parade and Drive, the West-end of Yarmouth.

One is so accustomed to associate the "home of the bloater" with cheap day-trips and vulgarity, that it comes upon one as a distinct surprise to find a seaport almost equalling, so far as its width and fine residences are concerned, the more fashionable south-coast resorts. At one end, as one comes to the front down St. Nicholas Street, there is quite an outbreak of smart red-brick mansions, gorgeously curtained and brass-knockered, suggestive of Hove as it was in the earlier stages of existence; and further along, past the Assembly Rooms, and opposite the prettily laid-out little "Garden by the Sea," wherein Yarmouth's more select visitors take refuge with their babies and their dogs to watch the magnificent panorama of vessels passing the "Roads," there are some really fine residences, which must certainly find other inhabitants than those one is apt to loosely associate with this town. Shadingfield Lodge, for instance, has been occupied more than once by the Prince of Wales during his stay here, and there are other houses betwixt the Aquarium and the Naval Hospital that might equally well serve the purposes of a temporary Royal residence.

When, therefore, the "tripper" has ceased from tripping, and the excursionists do not quite overflow the beach into the roadway and dance in dozens round the barrel-organs that seem to be imported in large quantities from Saffron Hill, Yarmouth is not a place to be passed over as an "impossible" holiday-haunt. For a time, even in the heyday of the excursionists' visits, it has its fascinations, for there is a vast amount of amusement to be extracted from the contemplation of the sands when one is comfortably disposed within doors. Nowhere else does one see

"''Arry" and "'Arriet" in such profusion, and rejoicing in such freedom. On the magnificent stretch of sand they refresh themselves incessantly at oyster stalls, and revel in the delights of what is practically a gigantic marine fair. And what multitudes of children! They are literally turned out in thousands, and swarm like ants on the hillocks and in the holes they build and dig for themselves on these glorious sands. Mr. Clement Scott has called Yarmouth "a playground by the sea," and it could not be more fitly described. It is truly a playground for the myriads of children who are brought here—not to be dressed up and shown off as they are on Lowestoft pier and on the King's Road at Brighton—but to paddle and dig and burrow and grow brown, to shout and roll about. And not less a playground for the city folks, who come here by the trainsful for the sole purpose of enjoying the sea and making merry in pure air. They love these long wide Yarmouth sands better than the finest scenery that England could offer. To loll about them all the day, while the niggers and the peripatetic vocalists, gipsies, gymnasts, and conjurers provide ceaseless entertainments, is to them unspeakable bliss; and when it is too late to sit and watch the waves and the children, there is a wealth of amusement elsewhere for them in this centre of east coast gaiety.

There are entertainments for everybody, but the "high-class" music which, as Mr. Corney Grain says, "though a trifle melancholy is always so refined," is comparatively infrequent. Genuine Yarmouth visitors prefer the works of Mr. Chevalier and Mr. Coborn to musical classics, and those who have come to see Bloaterdom as it is, want to have the picture complete. There is no attempt at "selectness" in this breezy old resort. People do as they like, and represent as it were *en masse* the music-hall public. Nor are they relegated to different quarters of the town and the seaport, according to their lodgings and their tastes, as in other seaside places. Even in "merry Margate" there is, as it were, a great gulf fixed between that portion of the town and sands adjacent to the "Hall by the Sea," and Cliftonville with its monster hotels and handsome villas; and a kind of intermediate state is furthermore provided by the neighbourhood of the Fort. But not so in Yarmouth. The oyster and whelk stalls are just as numerous opposite the best part of the Marine Parade as anywhere else in the town; the "trippers" are as welcome and as prevalent at one end of the beach as at the other. As a matter of fact, the "upper suckles" do not come here to monopolise the best and widest roads and cleanest sands. Yarmouth is truly the "people's playground," and so they take their pleasure in it as they like and where they like.

But stay behind in the quaint, Dutch-like old town after the excursionists' reign is over, and the songs have ceased for the season in the Aquarium, and the sands are only covered by the great rolling North Sea. Forget it as a town of summer visitors and bathers, all noise and bustle and merriment, and seek for another "impression" of Yarmouth, the Yarmouth of Peggotty, smelling of "fish and pitch and oakum and tar," with its curious old "rows" and wonderful Quay, thronged with shipping, and overshadowed by the lime trees that have lost their glory ere the holiday-maker sees them. It is in the spring, when the sea runs high, and the mackerel boats are going out and coming in with their huge iridescent loads, that this avenue of limes is at its very best, and the beautiful old houses along the Quay, one or two of which are far more elaborate and interesting within than without, contrast finely with the vivid colouring of the trees.

There is no season, though, when the Quay does not present a fine sight; no time when it is not full of "pictures" and the scene unsurpassed by any of the kind in England. One seems to have been suddenly transported, so soon as this part of the town is reached, straight to Rotterdam or Antwerp. The whole country round about, with its dykes and ditches, its everlasting mills and soppy

The Quay, Yarmouth.

flat wastes, is irresistibly suggestive of Holland, but here on the leafy Quay the illusion is complete. The towering masts, the bulging old fishing, salt, and grain boats with their strangely-painted masts, the perpetual movement, the solid, respectable old houses and public marine buildings and offices, make as colourable an imitation of the Boompjes as could be well conceived. From end to end there is life and movement, from the comfortable "Star Hotel," an old Elizabethan mansion with a fine broad oaken staircase, and a richly-panelled and decorated room, known as the "Nelson" room, opposite to which they appear to be for ever loading up grain or timber, to the Fish Wharf, where the "luggers" and the "cobbles" discharge their cargoes.

Standing on the "Star" balcony, and looking down on the scene below, one may almost fancy that a gigantic piece of mechanism has been set working, so much has been crowded into the picture. There is, of course, the eternal mill ceaselessly turning in the background, and a perpetual vessel in the foreground, into which sacks of grain are always being carried. At intervals the huge clock in the tower of the strikingly-handsome new municipal buildings musically chimes the time. Cabs and carriages and Yarmouth "trolls" rattle along continually, and if it be summer, when the steamers of the General Steam Navigation Company disgorge their passengers, crowds suddenly appear and disappear, as if by clockwork, on the scene, which is, however, not half so characteristic of the port as that enacted down by the Fish Wharf.

Everybody is literally on the *qui vive* here. Not in tens, but in hundreds, are the smacks crowded into the Haven at this point, their pennons of every shade and device almost mingling with each other, and making with the brown and red and black and white sails, and the many-coloured masts, a gay enough sight. Here we find the Peggottys and Gummidges in their habit as they live. The men, great sturdy fellows, are of such metal as composed brave Ham Peggotty; and the "reivers," in their short oilskin petticoats, look hardly less hardy and capable of battling with the elements. It is, as a matter of fact, with the herrings that they are chiefly concerned. So soon as the fish is landed it is counted into "marins," thence tumbled into the "swills" and trundled away on the strange little carts that traverse the rows to the herring-houses with which Yarmouth abounds. Here they are salted, the "reivers" then run them through the gills on sticks, and assist the men in suspending them for the necessary "blow" which converts them, according to time, into "bloaters" or "Billingsgate pheasants." The former are only exposed once to the fires of oaken billets, over which all the herrings are suspended in the curing-houses, while the latter hang for two or three days and undergo several firings.

One meets with strange names about the Wharf, regular Dickens names like Tuttle and Huke, and Williment and Fiddyer; and curious-looking old salts, with huge gold rings in their ears and long ringlets, carefully oiled and curled, hanging on either side of their sou'-westers. These are they, who with their families, live down the "rows" which Dickens himself called the "ribs of Yarmouth." They are curious little narrow passages, at the most but five or six feet wide, running between the Quay and King Street, the principal thoroughfare of Yarmouth. Like those in the Lowestoft "scores," the houses on either side almost touch each other; but, though quaint, these "rows" lack somehow the picturesqueness of the "scores." They are dingier, possibly because they do not open on the sea, and almost too closely packed together, at all events from a sanitary point of view. Up and down them ceaselessly rattle the funny little two-wheeled barrows, drawn by horses, like children's penny carts, which they exactly resemble in shape. They take up the whole width of the "row" as they pass up and down, and make as much noise on the cobbled roadways as if they were huge vans. These "trolls" or trollies are no modern invention. Mr. Harrod, Norfolk's distinguished antiquarian, has discovered that

they were known in the town in the reign of Henry VII.
as "Harry carries," and that their drivers and owners were
described as "Harry carmen." They could never have been
more primitive in shape than they are now, so that as far as
they are concerned Yarmouth still preserves a characteristic
that was hers four hundred years ago.

One of these lanes, which bears the uninviting designation of Gaol Row, leads to one of Yarmouth's quaint
old sights, the Tollhouse, and the ancient Gaol, now used
as the Free Library; and down another, George and Dragon
Row, one comes upon a most curious specimen of domestic
architecture, which possibly not one in a hundred of
Yarmouth's visitors ever sees. Not that this is surprising,
for "sweetness and light" are not to be found down these
"rows" and in the older parts of Yarmouth. One may
trace out the town walls if one is duly equipped and

St. Nicholas Church, Yarmouth.

indifferent to a series of odours rivalling those for which Cologne is foully famous; and there are a couple of picturesque and interesting old fragments, the Blackfriars and the First Towers, built into the walls, that are seldom seen except by the most persevering lovers of antiquities.

But there is, however, little need to go poking into malodorous corners of the old port for relics of the past, when so fine a treasure-house as the grand old church of St. Nicholas, the finest parish church in England, can be seen. Alas! that so beautiful a building should be in danger of suffering from the excess of clerical vandalism with which the town has of late been unfortunately seized. No appointments and no services could be too elaborate or dignified for so noble a church as this, which, with Norwich Cathedral, and the magnificent church of St. Margaret's at Lynn, was founded by Herbert de Losinga, who removed the See of East Anglia from Thetford—it having been previously removed from Dunwich—to Norwich, he himself becoming first Bishop of the latter town. Bishop de Losinga was evidently an architect of exceptional merit, and a most energetic churchman. His work pervades all this district of East Anglia, and wherever he laid one stone upon another, the result, as we see at Norwich, at Elmham, at Lynn, and at Yarmouth, was as enduring as it is beautiful. To undertake the foundation of two such ecclesiastical structures as the cathedral at Norwich and what is almost a cathedral at Yarmouth could have been no small task, yet there is only five years' difference in the dates of these two buildings. St. Nicholas has been three times enlarged since Bishop de Losinga's death, and has many times suffered spoliation, the Puritans making disgraceful havoc here with the statues, brasses, windows, and chapels, of which there were at one time no less than eighteen. Happily this beautiful church has been most carefully restored, and it is to be hoped that every effort will be made to keep the interior fitly appointed. Its carved pulpit is said to be unrivalled in this country, and its organ is a particularly good one. At present there is no difficulty in getting in to see the church and its many interesting contents, which include a remarkable collection of valuable books; but as all the other places of worship in the town are now hermetically

The Market Place, Yarmouth.

sealed from Sunday to Sunday, one fears lest difficulties may be placed in the way of those anxious to see within the church dedicated to the patron saint of seamen.

One cannot help being vastly impressed with "unconventional, breezy" old Yarmouth on coming out from her grand parish church into the old-fashioned and enormous market-place. It seems as if everything were done on such an extensive scale. Yarmouth evidently proceeds on the principle that whatever is worth doing at all is worth doing well. Its quay, its fishing-fleet, its sands, its market-place, its parish church, and its catches of fish are all much bigger than anywhere else in the kingdom; and one might add that, for its size, its charitable and public buildings are unusually numerous. It has been laughingly said that Yarmouth is decidedly unromantic in the matter of its buildings, which run in the direction of charity schools, hospitals, asylums, and cemeteries; and it is true enough, for in the neighbourhood of the market-place alone there is quite a cluster of what may be called distinctly useful institutions, while one finds similar buildings in whichever direction one may turn. Even the sea front, usually guarded most jealously for hotels, private dwellings, and places of amusement, is here occupied by the Royal Naval Hospital and the Sailors' Home. It has its theatre, its Aquarium, and its Assembly Rooms it is true; but Yarmouth's sons are much prouder of their Smack Boys' Home, their institutes and hospital for fishermen, their reading and mission rooms and schools dotted profusely about the leafy old town.

This leafiness is another of its pleasant features. The Quay has already been mentioned as a delightfully shady promenade, but in the very centre of the town five acres of well-timbered ground have been converted into a public park, and round the parish church—everywhere in fact—there are well-grown, sturdy, branching trees to rest the eye dazzled with the brightness of the sands and the fierce light of these eastern shores.

Over this quaint, marine-flavoured old town they want presently to flash the electric light, which now only illumines the Quay opposite the municipal buildings. Imagine Peggotty's hut with an electric lamp outside its

The Fishermen's Hospital, Yarmouth.

low door! Picture the scene of Steerforth's death in the glare of electric light from the seafront! There is, unfortunately, no chance of seeing the former even in these circumstances, but the terrors of shipwreck will be always too plentifully illustrated on these dangerous shifting sands. Peggotty's hut no longer exists; it has been swept away to make room for a modern villa. Behind the Quay, still "past gas-works, rope-works, boat-builders' yards, ship-wrights' yards, ship-breakers' yards, caulkers' yards, riggers' lofts, smiths' forges," and close to St. James' church, the faithful may find in an old tool-house all that is left of

Little Em'ly's home; but the imagination needs not to be unduly stretched hereabouts to conjure up visions of the scenes and the "Yarmouth bloaters" made familiar to us by Dickens' glowing pen.

The inducements to leave Yarmouth, its fish and its yellow sands, are not great. Once comfortably ensconced in the town the visitor can do nothing better than stay there, unless the Broads lure him to their bosoms. Gorleston and Caister are, however, places that one must see as a matter of course, and no one ever regrets the visit. Gorleston pursues one round Yarmouth, as it were, and insists upon being seen. Views of it in water-colour, photographic views, ghastly oil paintings of its pier and

Caister Castle.

its harbour are in every other shop window. It breaks
out in sixpenny panoramic form, on children's mugs and
the tops of buttered toast dishes; it stares one in the face
on the Quay, until at last in desperation a rush is made
over the bridge for the tramway that bears one through
Southtown, Yarmouth's smart and salubrious suburb,
to this wonderful village with the wonderful pier. One
never returns disappointed. The houses rising one above the other, the magnificent view over Yarmouth

Burgh Castle.

Denes, the great roaring seas that lash against the cliffs
and fill the picture with colour, never fail to excite the
wildest enthusiasm. It has a charm of its own that is
undeniable. Nowhere else in England, maybe, is the
craft of fishing presented in such a picturesque light, and
unless one is either very unromantic, very strong-minded,
or a peculiarly keen critic and judge, one of these views
of Gorleston photographed or re-produced in water-colour

or oils is certain to be ultimately included among one's possessions. And there are those, presumably, who in souvenir of this altogether fascinating fishing village purchase the mugs and the tea-pot stands adorned with more or less blurred impressions of its charms, "made in Germany."

At Caister one meets again with those old East Anglian friends, the Pastons, into whose hands the castle—one of the first brick buildings ever erected in this country—ultimately fell, after the death of its famous builder, Sir John Fastolfe, one of the bravest and busiest soldiers of his time. This grand old commander did not live long to enjoy his castle when he had built it; but during the few years he occupied it, he lived *en prince*, and brought his military tactics to bear very severely upon his retainers, at whom he swore freely. He had fought all his battles by this time, for it was not until 1450 that he completed Caister, and only nine years later he died an octogenarian. It was certainly an eligible residence, as its remains show; it is said, too, to have been sumptuously furnished for the period, and on Sir John's death there was a pretty family squabble over it. The Pastons, his kinsmen, claimed the property, but the other claimant, the Duke of Norfolk, wasted no time arguing the matter. He simply besieged it with three thousand faithful retainers and walked in. Eventually the Pastons got possession of "this fair jewel," which, wrote Sir John Fastolfe's secretary, "my master would rather he had never builded than it should be in the governance of any sovereign that will oppress the country." From Caister were written many of the famous Paston letters, but despite their anxiety to enter in and dwell here, the family entertained no sentimental affection for their distinguished kinsman's castle; for when a *nouveau riche* of the period came along, one Crow—the London

Maple of the period—they sold their castle and ancestors without compunction to the wealthy trader, and themselves moved on to Oxnead Hall, built by Sir Clement Paston, in Elizabeth's reign. Of this old castle of Caister only the tower and three walls of one of its quadrangles remain, but what there is of it is charmingly picturesque. It is interesting, in "excurting" from Yarmouth to Caister, to trace a connection between the Star Hotel of the town and this ruined fifteenth century stronghold of a fine old English gentleman and his noble kinsmen. The former was built as the residence of a well-to-do-Yarmouth merchant, who in these days would probably have been mayor of the town. Even at that period he was somewhat of a municipal "big-wig," and his son, who was born in this house, started business as an upholsterer in the then fashionable neighbourhood of Smithfield. He not only furnished smart houses but helped their owners—at so much per cent. of course—out of little financial difficulties, and it was probably while redecorating and upholstering Caister that he negotiated a little bill or two for Sir William Paston. At all events he supplied Sir William with something more than oaken presses and bedsteads, and was apparently well satisfied to take over Caister in payment of his little account and play the country gentleman for the rest of his life.

CHAPTER X.

ON PEACEFUL WATERS.

YARMOUTH is the gate, so to say, of Broadland. Looking at it from a purely practical point of view, it is essentially the best starting point for a tour of these East Anglian lakes, as from this town the largest and more important are within immediate reach; but, even assuming that artistic considerations outweigh all others, Yarmouth still remains the royal road to the Broads, since it affords so striking a contrast to the district to be explored. It is doubly delightful to pass from the noise and rush and bustle and life of Yarmouth to the perfect peace, the solitude, and the quiet beauty of the Broads; to leave Yarmouth behind with its miles of shipping and its ubiquitous herring, and sail straightway to these silent scenes, where one has only the whirring wild-fowl for company.

There is a fascination about these wild and lovely lakes that draws one again and again to seek rest on their silvery bosoms and to lure from the same, by-the-bye, the mammoth eels and lordly perch that lurk therein. In the golden summer days, when the young man's fancy lightly turns to thoughts of wherries and fishing tackle, and the maidens bethink them of the glorious opportunities of displaying pretty boating costumes and of more or less dreaming away the sunny hours in quiet back-waters under the shadows of the woods, the lovers of the Broads go down by thousands and waken into life the solemn stillness of these lonely meres, startling from their sedgy coverts the sharp-billed snipes and water-fowl that abound. But, withal, there is always to be found, by those that seek, the silence and the solitude, the wild and lonely scenes dear to lovers of peace and the picturesque.

It is not by taking boat at Norwich and puffing noisily over the beaten track of Broadland that lies between the cathedral city and Yarmouth that the spell of their fascination is woven, nor after many days are the charms of the lovely string of lakes, beginning with Breydon Water, exhausted. "Many an hour of summer suns" may be spent upon these glancing waters, and fresh beauties will perpetually unfold themselves as they wind in and out among the low-lying meadows, past many-tinted woods and sleepy little villages, now running like narrow streamlets between grassy banks, and almost overgrown with white and yellow lilies as at Walsham, now widening into great lonely wastes of water like Hickling Staithe. Among these "haunts of coot and hern," literally overhung by the huge bulrushes and osmunda fern, the bright irises and sedges of every shade, whole days may be passed almost in solitude, the silence only disturbed, maybe, by the fluttering wild-fowl, the lowing of cattle in the misty meadows, or the plashing of falling water as the wheel of a gabled mill on the bankside goes round. A ceaseless panorama is unfolded of sunny waters, of woods and meadowlands, of villages with their ivied churches peeping from behind the masses of tall poplars, firs, elms, and alders, of flowery banks and of deep, dark reedy pools. Monotony is a word not understood by those who know the Broads thoroughly and love these peaceful haunts. It is no weariness to eye or mind to float silently along these flower-fringed lakes, under the drooping trees, whose branches often dip to the water's edge, sometimes wandering inland while one's boat lies moored in some woodland pool among masses of white and golden water-lilies, rose-coloured plantains and clumps of spiky, purple loosestrife, and the beady-eyed, snowy-crested coots that croak as tamely about the wherries as farmyard ducks.

St. Benet's Abbey.

There are quaint old churches and ruins like St. Benet's, founded by Cnut, to be visited on shore in picturesque little villages, there are delightful walks to be taken through the woods that skirt the waterways, and in the gleaming cornfields encircling the red-roofed farms. Even on the lakes one may make miniature excursions from the wherries into those dreamy recesses which cannot be entered by larger craft than punts. In these shady solitudes there are wondrous sights to be seen, undreamt of in the philosophy of the ordinary Broadland excursionist.

There you shall see the fish darting in shoals under the clear waters, and find the graceful herons and stately grebes feeding their young; the air is full of the pungent odour of rushes and the sweet fragrance of wild flowers. Sometimes a sloping garden, gay with blossoms, over which the bright blue butterflies of the district hover in myriads, unexpectedly opens on the view; sometimes sudden darkness seems to descend, as a bend in the sinuous stream brings one to some unfrequented pool shut in by trees, which would appear to have brought the wanderings to an end. But, steering shorewards, a narrow track is found through the rushes and water weeds, and from the gloom of the woods one emerges once more into sunlight to find fresh pathways, new caves of beauty, wherein the only sound is the droning of the snipe's wings, or the sharp, shrill scream of a black-headed gull, startled by the intruding punter.

What a charm there is about the red-sailed wherries

Dyke near Coltishall.

"Swan Inn," Horning.

with their broad, bulging sides and great gaunt masts! They have none of the smart spick-and-spanness of the fashionable yachts, they do not dart and dash over these lazy waters. Dipping low into the water, and of proportions akin to the typical Mynheer van Dunk, they push surely and steadily along, their mammoth sails, some of gleaming white, some of a rich, red brown, swelling out in the breeze. No toy-boat has gear more simple, and the mind of man could scarcely have desired a more useful and at the same time picturesque craft for these East Anglian lakes, which appear to increase in beauty as one sails from one to the other. In each the perfection of quiet beauty seems to have been found, whether one goes Burewards, Yarewards, or Antwards. Each of these rivers, as well as the Thurne, has its group of broads, each with distinctive characteristics only learned and recognised by those who lovingly explore their waters, and linger on them. Picturesque Filby, for instance, is alive with teal and mallard.

Heigham Sound is a weird, wild waste of rustling, swaying reeds, than which apparently nothing more lonely and desolate can be imagined. Yet life is abundant enough here. In the darkling waters there is an incessant plashing and dashing of fish and fowl; here and there among the glistening leaves of the lilies one spies the coot, "swimming in the reedy pond;" and when the clouds lower and the water runs swiftly under the lash of wind and rain, from the muddy recesses among the weeds, the elusive eel may be captured to furnish forth a dainty dish

Horning Ferry.

for the wherry dining table. But, by and bye, when the great expanse of Hickling is reached, with its islets of rustling reeds, over which the water rushes under the wild cloudy sky, the weirdness of Heigham is well-nigh forgotten, and here it seems is the very perfection of forlornness. Of all the Broads none most certainly can equal in impressiveness this great sheet of shining water, which, if one would enjoy its full beauty, must be seen under heavy clouds that darken the lake and deepen into blackness the great masses of plantain and bright green weed beneath. On the wind is borne the refreshing odour of the sea that lies but a little beyond, and is so forcibly suggested by the foam-flecked ripples—one might almost say wavelets—of the Staithe itself. The wherry sails—they are not seen in profusion—are sharply outlined against the sky, and the lines of posts, throwing deep shadows, stand like ghostly sentinels along the wide, wild stretch of open water. Hereabouts one might potter for weeks with ever-increasing delight. Here is wee but charmingly picturesque Horsey—beloved of anglers—with Palling beyond, where the ruins of Eccles church, half buried in the sand, are visible, and back again by shallow Martham, over-shadowed by its fine old Perpendicular church tower, and Ludham Bridge, to beautiful shining Ormesby, with its surrounding woods, its interesting bank-side churches, and fertile meadowlands. But fain as one would be to linger among a particular group of these silvery meres, one is tempted on and on in fresh directions by the glories of others. There is great

Yachts coming off Wroxham Broad into the Bure.

On Rockland Broad.

broad-bosomed Barton, full of sweet little islets, with a background of trees of every shade of green, sloping upwards from the blue, pellucid waters, fringed by mammoth *osmunda regalis* and the sweet *myrica*. Over this placid lake echo and re-echo the bells of Barton and Irstead and Stalham churches, whose towers are reflected in its glassy waters.

Sunset in Barton is one of the glories of Broadland. On the huge sheet of water, glowing like a crimson lake, are thrown the inky shadows of trees and spires, which themselves loom darklier still against the purple and gold, the crimson and orange, and tender greens of the dazzling sky. Further on, too, is Ranworth, covered with its cool mantle of reeds and its myriads of lilies. Between the trees, which almost meet across and kiss its flowery face, rises the great square tower of Ranworth church set on a hill.

There is Irstead, too, haunted by the wild ducks and the lordly kingfishers, and full of charming, deep, shadowy pools, where the water-lilies abound, and the pretty, bright-eyed coots sail in and out among the scanty reeds of metallic hue. Through leafy channels and sunny South Walsham, quiet little Horning, with its picturesque ferry, its quaint irregular "street," the adjacent St. Benet's, and homely, artist-haunted "Swan Inn," is reached, a village of marsh and flowering rushes, of mist and of rustic beggars, who pursue one along the banks of the river like the gnats at Barton. And as yet but half the journey through Broadland is made. For there is Woodbastwick, half hidden by trees, and Wroxham, encircled by woods and park-like meadows, with its myriads of flower-gemmed islands, its emerald waters, and fleet of white-sailed wherries from Coltishall—the birthplace of these crafts—a busy aqueous little village with Hautbois or Hobbies on the one side and Belaugh Church on the other. There are few of the Broads more charming than those which lead one to picturesque Norwich. Surlingham, with its famous ferry; wild Rockland, with its wealth of flowers; Salhouse's deep waters; Whitlingham, close to which is Thorpe, one of the prettiest little villages in Norfolk; and Wroxham itself—the scene of the annual "water-frolic," which Crome, the great artistic light of Norwich, had set himself to paint the very day that he was seized with his fatal illness—are all within an hour's journey of the famous old city, from under the shadow of whose huge factories on either side of the inky Wensum, the yachts and wherries go sailing away all day long to the peaceful and lonely waters stretching for miles through the country beyond.

CHAPTER XI.

ENTERPRISING IPSWICH.

TO see the county town of Suffolk in its most picturesque aspect, it is well to withstand for a time the fascinations of its old houses and interesting buildings, and to proceed to the Upper and Lower Arboretums, from whose gentle slopes Ipswich may be viewed at a glance. Until you have found your way into these leafy glades, and admired Mr. Fonnereau's magnificent beeches and chestnuts, until Christchurch Park with its old Tudor mansion has charmed the eyes, and suburban Ipswich has been seen taking its pleasure in the trim gardens of the Lower Arboretum, the residents of this strikingly enterprising and most ancient town do not consider that the glories of the Suffolk capital have been properly unfolded. Maybe they are right. Ipswich is full of interest from every point of view; but it is not, like many another quaint old town, seen to the best advantage by wandering in and out its streets.

The march of civilisation and progress is rapidly modernising its narrow picturesque thoroughfares, and even the Butter Market, which withstood the innovator longer than most of the streets, has now little left to mark the fact that it is, perhaps, the oldest of them all. The stranger is very apt to find that, as all roads lead to Rome, so all the streets here seem to lead to the Butter Market. Up this one, down that, backwards and forwards as you may seem to go, in the end you are pretty nearly sure to find yourself back again in the vicinity of "Sparrow's House," still, as it must always have been, the most conspicuous building in this unavoidable Butter Market. But there is much to be seen in many of these narrow, winding streets whithersoever they may lead

you, though the energetic manufacturers, whose tall chimneys rear themselves in all directions, have evidently determined that their town shall be more useful than

Wolsey's Gate, Ipswich.

ornamental. Once a walled-in city with a castle built by the Normans, it is now denuded even of the traces of its fortifications, while of the stronghold not a trace remains. Here and there, though, an ancient gateway soothes the antiquarian soul, such as the Archdeacon's Gate, a gabled Tudor structure, and the gateway to Wolsey's College, a delightful picturesque corner hidden away behind St. Peter's Tower, and sadly ravaged by the stress and storm of many ages.

The dazzling shops of Tavern Street—most fascinating to the feminine eye—those handsome modern buildings, the Town Hall, the Corn Exchange, the Public Hall, and the Museum, are apt to lure the stranger from the backways, wherein are to be found the curious old carved posts and brackets, "pargetted" house fronts, and quaint gables which still entitle Ipswich to be included in the list of picturesque English towns. It is curious to think that some of these neglected byways were once the busiest and the "smartest" in all Ipswich, and that nothing now remains of all their former glory. "Broc" Street existed in the reign of Henry III., and was in those days the Berkeley Square of the town; and it is difficult, as one wanders along now sleepy "Brook" Street, to fancy the gay and handsome Charles Brandon, Duke of Suffolk, bringing home his bride here from the French Court. Yet it was in this same quiet back street, on the site of the present "Coach and Horses" Inn, that the brilliant young nobleman's house stood, and one may well imagine that the lovesick Mary Tudor, freed from her marriage with the elderly Louis XII., found its seclusion charming after the rush and intrigue of the French court. One may conjure up endless pictures of the sixteen-year-old bride and her handsome young lord riding down the cobbled street; of the great Cardinal Wolsey, who lived close by, coming backwards and forwards to the young couple, in whom he seems to have taken a fatherly interest; for it was he who made peace for them with the mighty Henry VIII., whom the lovers had probably thought so busy with his own matrimonial affairs that they had not troubled him for his sanction to their union.

At a later period, Gainsborough lived in Brook Street, and through the quiet lovely lanes, without the town and on the picturesque banks of the Orwell, he found material for some of his happiest work. In this part of the street the old character has been better preserved, but in Tacket Street, which bisects it, one is again reminded of the glories for evermore faded by the gloomy old Theatre Royal, which, together with the "Tankard Tavern," occupies the site of another famous mansion, whose owner, Sir Anthony Wingfield, must have been almost a next-door neighbour to the gallant Duke of Suffolk.

Here, by the way, Garrick made his first appearance, a fact of which Ipswich folk are intensely proud; but not more so than that their prime favourite, the genial "Johnny" Toole, and the veteran Mrs. Keeley—a native of the town—likewise first trod the dusty boards of this same playhouse. Round about here one may wander for hours, recalling the good old days, when the rich and portly merchants built unto themselves, in the Fore Hamlet, comfortable and richly-decorated dwellings. Rows of poverty-stricken, dreary modern cottages now make up the Fore Hamlet, for mercantile Ipswich has betaken itself further out of the town, round about the Arboretum aforementioned; but for those that seek there is, nevertheless a mine of interest in the neighbourhood.

Up the narrow courts you will find clusters of carved houses, like the "Neptune Inn," the old shops opposite the "Sorrel," and the wine-merchant's a little higher up, whose dates of erection, still to be seen upon many of them, carries one back into the early part of the seventeenth century, when doubtless these streets were lively and gay, and gay enough with the beruffled and satin-doubletted gallants who rode to and fro. Some of the dingiest and narrowest of the "yards" round here are associated with persons whose names have been historically handed down through the generations, as, indeed, are most of the Ipswich streets; for harking back through Tacket Street to the neighbourhood of Silent Street, we find ourselves again among a ghostly company of Ipswich celebrities: "my Lord Curzon" having entertained Henry VIII., here when he visited the town, in 1552. Here, too, was the great Cardinal Wolsey born. A portion of the original premises occupied by his father is still standing. Round here the thoroughfares are all associated with him; for there are Wolsey, Cardinal, and College Streets: the latter so called from the college built here by Wolsey, and destroyed by Henry VIII. on the Cardinal's fall. The gateway still stands, and is at once one of the most picturesque and interesting objects of the town.

For a town of its antiquity and importance, Ipswich is singularly uninteresting so far as its churches are concerned. There are plenty of them, but none are specially remarkable. St. Mary-le-Tower takes precedence, although it has been so completely restored as to be practically a new building, though it actually dates back to the time of the Confessor. It is an exceedingly well-appointed church, and its beautiful oak screen is, presumably, as fine a piece of carving as there is in the county. Its peal of bells are, certainly, unequalled in Suffolk. But of the other churches, St. Margaret's,— with its fine tower and roof, internally despoiled by the wretched Dowsing—St. Mary-at-Key, St. Lawrence's—in

The Oldest House in Ipswich.

which Milton's brother is buried—and St. Nicholas, both of which date back to Saxon times, are alone interesting, though there is little now in any of them to detain a visitor to the town, however conscientious he may be about "doing" all the antiquities.

It is Sparrow's House that invariably attracts the larger number of sight-seers, and it is, certainly, one of the most remarkable specimens of domestic architecture in this part of the country. It bears the date 1567, and its front and sides, gables and interior, are all most richly carved, and "pargetted" with floral and other designs. The house derives its title from the Sparrow family, who occupied it for many generations, and who believe firmly in the apocryphal legend of Charles II.'s concealment within its walls after his flight from Worcester Field. But, like many other pretty historical romances, it has been made to fit the surroundings, which in this case are admirably suited to the picture.

Those of less antiquarian taste find most agreeable and diverting pastime in searching out the scenes immortalised in the "Pickwick Papers," and "interviewing," as it were, Sam Weller, the "lady in the yellow curl-papers," and Job Trotter. The little "green gate," upon which Mr. Weller's eye was fixed, is not so easy to find, but the ancient and historical "White Horse Tavern" still flourishes and gives its name to one of the busiest streets of the town.

Besides Mr. Pickwick, whose adventure in the wrong bedroom occurred in this very hostelry, its comfortable roof has sheltered many a famous and infamous historical character. Mr. Pickwick's room—No. 16.—is always asked for by admirers of Dickens who visit this ancient house, and they will tell you here that the adventure was no fictitious one, but actually did happen to Dickens himself in this identical bed-chamber. Lord Nelson, probably *en route* for Yarmouth, or possibly on his way to re-visit the beloved home of his childhood at Burnham Thorpe, where he had been staying for the whole previous year, brought the beautiful Emma Hart, Lady Hamilton, here in 1800, and previously George II. had engaged rooms here for a night or two. This Tavern Street is a fine and busy thoroughfare, and impresses one with a sense of the "liveliness" of Ipswich. That is, however, very speedily made apparent.

One cannot be long in the Suffolk capital without being struck by its progressiveness and enterprise. The natives will tell you, and with truth too, that they send forth the most enterprising journalists to the metropolis. Rightly, too, they boast of their Grammar School—the oldest in the kingdom—and High Schools, and the other educational advantages which place Ipswich so high as a centre of light and leading. But the immediate impression one receives, after a few hours' stay in the busy, thriving little town, is that it has "progress" written over it from end to end.

Look at the crowds passing up and down Tavern Street. Keen-faced mechanics, laughing, noisy factory girls, jovial farmers, prosperous manufacturers, and smartly-dressed women pass in an incessant stream, representing the interests of the town. Everybody seems busy, and there is always plenty to do. They have everything they need, provided by an excellent municipality.

East Anglians are certainly not "slow going" in Ipswich, which has a magnificent Free Library, an Art Gallery, voluntary schools, smart newspapers, a racecourse, Mechanics' Institute, recreation grounds, schools of science, and, as a well-meaning person, who was descanting on the advantages of the town, remarked, "a cemetery which is laid out as tastily as a gentleman's park." Its great aim, apparently, is to be like London. Ipswich folk strive desperately hard to be lively and "up to date," and they succeed admirably. They have their fashionable quarter near the Lower Arboretum, where wealth and culture are very much in evidence; they have a couple of good theatres, they go out a great deal in the evenings, they are nothing if not artistic, and they have a miniature St. James's Hall, which seats some two thousand persons, and to which the best musical talent is invited.

As a manufacturing centre it can hold its own against much vaster towns, though its products are chiefly confined to agricultural implements. To almost every small householder in England the name of Ransome, Sims, and Jefferies is familiar; but lawn-mowers and knife machines are only the trifles produced by this huge Ipswich firm, whose works cover eleven acres and give employment to eighteen hundred men. Here one may study the progress of modern farming in the wonderful machines turned out by thousands from this famous manufactory. Steam ploughs, combined reapers, binders and threshers are exported hence to all parts of the world, helping to spread the fame of Ipswich as the home of agricultural science. There are all manner of other manufactories in the town, too, chiefly of chemical manures and stationery wares; but ladies' corsets come in a good second to the agricultural machines; some two or three thousand men, boys, and girls, finding this industry the mainstay, so to say, of their existence.

A Sketch in the Dock, Ipswich.

Altogether it is a bright and light and pleasant place, which should, in the days to come, turn out some even better men than those already associated with it; for young "Gipp-ings," as, according to Professor Skeat, the aborigines were called, have everything within call to brace them for social and commercial warfare. They may slake to the full their thirst for knowledge and march abreast with the times in their municipal improvements and pursuit of art; but they have, too, a river at hand, unequalled in England for its picturesqueness, on which to row and make strong their thews and sinews.

Behind all these old streets, remote from the jingle of the tramcars and the sleepy thoroughfares, is the Promenade, a broad and leafy walk "down by the river-side," where the vessels are always to be seen going out and coming in, and the incessant clang of the shipwright's mallet strikes ever on the ear. It is from this point onwards that Ipswich becomes picturesque, and her sons are enabled to revel in the delights of healthy outdoor exercise.

On every hand, without the city, lie temptations to walk, to row, to ride, and to study nature as revealed in the quiet beauty of Suffolk scenery. Along the banks of the beautiful Orwell Gainsborough wandered for hours, finding material in abundance for his brush, and studying the exquisite effects of sunlight and shadow on its waters. Charming as it is to glide lazily along the stream, it is even more delightful to follow the river's course inland.

Ipswich, with its foreground of shipping, its houses rising among the trees above the level of the town, is an "impression" to take from the river; but what joys "on either side the river lie!" What wonder that the "Gipp-ings" boast of their town and its surroundings, and proudly vaunt their beauties! Walk down "Gainsborough's Lane," to which, if the weather be bright, an Ipswich host invariably hurries one with all convenient speed, and appreciative adjectives will be exhausted in less time than it takes to traverse it between the dog-roses and honeysuckle that overflow its hedges. Gainsborough has immortalised its quiet charms in "The Market Cart," but it should be still a happy hunting ground for the " simple landscape painter."

Why go seeking fresh woods and pastures new when such a wealth of material is at hand within two hours' ride of London? Hills, valleys, and streams, sleepy pastoral scenes, rutted roads full of colour, gorse-covered heaths, gleaming like gold in the sunlight, and leafy lanes, rich with wild flowers and ferns, help to make the scenery, with the useful addition of remarkably fine oak trees and some comfortable old halls, picturesquely situated on the wooded slopes to the river. One may fish or dawdle, paint or drive, with equal satisfaction about Ipswich, and return, like a giant refreshed, to the life and bustle of the town itself, certain of finding it always on the alert, and nowhere more so than at the railway station, one of the best served in all respects of the many excellent stations on the Great Eastern system.

CHAPTER XII.

UP THE ORWELL.

HAVING reached Ipswich, the obvious thing to do is to make the trip up the river of which East Anglians, and Ipswich folk in particular, are so justly proud. Somebody once called the Orwell "the English Rhine," others have likened it to Southampton Water, but surely there is no need whatever to compare it with anything. Its merits are self-sufficient, its beauties and its charms unquestionable, and whether it resembles this or that has, after all, nothing to do with the indisputable fact that it is the prettiest and most interesting river in the Eastern Counties, and one of the most picturesque, if not one of the most extensive in England. Even the first journey over its waters leaves a strong impression; but as acquaintance with it deepens, as its "points" become better known, its banks more familiar, and Freston and Chelmondiston, Wherstead and Woolverstone, develop from mere guide-book names into haunts hallowed by pleasant memories, then it is that the Orwell's fascinating spell is thrown over one completely, and it becomes easy to understand why the river is so dear to those who are natives of the delightful villages and towns by which it flows. Apart from its scenic attractions, great as they are, the Orwell may be said to almost overflow with interest. There are stories and legends and celebrities to associate with almost every inch of its banks, and one must be unimaginative indeed to sail by these picturesque shores amid surroundings ready-made for the romancist, and see only the trees and sloping lawns, the effects of sunlight and shadow, the parks and churches and mansions, that form an effective *mise-en-scene* for the tourist, and are to him that and nothing more. The officials on the excellent steamers running between Ipswich and Felixstowe seem to be never weary of supplying their passengers with the ordinary local information on each point of interest they pass. And there are doubtless some hundreds of good folks who sail the Orwell in the summer, and are quite content to be told about the Cat House, and Freston Tower, and So-and-So's works, without ever dreaming that they could, an' they would, find mines of interest behind the great masses of trees upon which they bestow a passing glance as part of "somebody's park." As a picture the Orwell is delightful, but it is doubtful whether, when one comes to think it all over, the river is not equally remarkable for its associations. Unfortunately these are caviare to the general, and all its glories are not unfolded like a panorama in the course of a cheap trip on a river steamboat. Picturesque as it is at all times, even when the odorous and leaden-coloured mud-flats are exposed by the receded tide, and the shipping in Ipswich dock looks gaunt against the factories and foundries on the river-side, it is naturally when the sunlight dances on its silvery waters reaching well to the level of the wooded shores, that the Orwell is seen to the best advantage.

It is a wonderfully fine picture that meets the eye as one looks back to the dock and Ipswich when a few hundred yards up the river. In the background there is the town itself set among trees; in the foreground

Chelmondiston, or Pin Mill, on the Orwell.

a mass of shipping, the huge grim warehouses, the mill chimneys rising above the trim gardens, sloping to the water's edge, of Ipswich magnates, and the wide, shining stretch of river through it all. It is truly an impression for the painter or the etcher to lovingly reproduce, and strangely different from any later one save that received at Harwich, which is far less effective, since the river view is hidden from sight round the corner as it were, directly the Quay comes into view. Ipswich has all the advantage in this respect, and, as at Yarmouth, its shipping, as seen from the river, appears to be mixed up

in some strange fashion with the trees that line the
promenade. It was a distinctly happy thought of the
"Gipp-ings" to make a boulevard of this piece of shore;
for not only is it an agreeable walk for the townsfolk,
but it is a pleasant retrospect from the river, while it
creates a favourable impression upon those who approach
Ipswich by water. The scene is always busy and bright and
gay. People certainly make the best of everything at their
command in this enterprising old town. They are fortunate
in the possession of a charming river, but they are not
merely content to let it run its course as best it may
by their shores. With its new dock-gates, its improved
river-bed, and its extended Quay at Ipswich, the Orwell has
become quite an important river, with no inconsiderable
steamship trade; and as one looks up the stream at the
effective picture in which the shipping is so important
a feature, it is easy to see that the craft lying at anchor
in the dock are not mere pleasure boats and smart yachts
and smacks. There are real vessels here of some two
thousand tonnage, manned by real swarthy sailors who lend
additional picturesqueness to the river-side that is here
delightfully free from the usual riparian squalor. Huge
machines and chemicals and much corn speed away down
the bright and beautiful Orwell, which is now considerably
more than ornamental to this district of East Anglia.
For that matter, the Orwell has done its duty to its sons
in the matter of fetching and carrying goods for many
a generation. But there was a time when the merchandise
borne by its bosom was not carried quite so openly as
now-a-days. A century ago, even, there were lurking
round the villages hereabouts plenty of the Will Lauds
and Luffs who figure so conspicuously in the favourite local
novel, "Margaret Catchpole." The quiet creeks between
the woods and parks on either side of the river have

been the scene of many little adventures in the old days, when wilder fowl haunted them than are now to be found there, and "pigtail" more often formed part of their cargo than pig-iron. The bold smuggler flourished mightily round the Saxon shores. He found them pleasantly adapted to his purpose, and the Orwell especially favoured his nefarious little plans. The land of Mynheer is within "convenient distance," and he had only to potter round the Dutch coast or even to wait a bit "off Harwich," till a Dutchman hove in sight, and the rest was comparatively easy.

Draughts as deep and considerably more potent than the waters of the rolling Zuyder Zee resulted from these little expeditions, and when the waves of the tidal Orwell ran high, and the trees of Woolverstone, Broke Hall, and the beautiful home of the celebrated Admiral Vernon dipped low to the water's edge, it was the easiest matter in the world to run a little cargo of kegs and other unconsidered trifles up one of these creeks and bestow them in the villages around. Everybody "did a little in smuggling" more or less. Life was tolerably uneventful and money inconveniently scarce, and to run in a few contraband articles occasionally with every facility at hand not only varied the monotony of existence, but, as the advertisements say, increased incomes "in an easy and pleasant manner." All along the Orwell, the spirit of the smuggler is very prevalent, to which, maybe, is due not a little of its fascination for the loiterer on its waters.

Bourne Bridge, which dates back to 1351, and the pretty river-side "Ostrich Inn," with its tea-gardens and old-time associations, are after all less interesting than Levington—once as famous for its roses as its smugglers—and Crane Creek to those whose tastes are for adventure and romance. But the interest of the river is thus admirably diversified. The woods and slopes and pleasant parks, the picturesque villages and interesting old churches, built apparently, as seen from the river, amidst clumps of trees, are as bread to the ham sandwich. When the strong meat of adventure has been tasted at one point, and the palate tickled

A Ford near Chelmondiston. Winter Evening.

with the pungent associations of smuggling and naval encounters at another, one is agreeably soothed and satisfied with the tranquil scenes that lie on either side of the stream. So, full of enthusiasm for Lord Gwydyr's beautiful trees in Stoke Park, and the slopes from the river-side to Wherstead, gleaming like gold with a mass of gorse, we begin to scent sport and adventure with Freston Hall in sight and Downham Reach at hand.

Wherstead, with its curiously prominent church tower surmounted by a black ball that has always been the cause of abundant mendacity on the part of the local boatmen, since everybody asks what it means and nobody can rightly explain, is, like most of the villages hereabouts, of some interest.

Close at hand is Nacton, where Suffolk "punches" are still to be seen as strong-boned and stout-chested as that which Margaret Catchpole bestrode when she first gave evidence of her equestrian powers; and the Priory Farm, built of the remnants of Alneshbourne, at which this remarkable and certainly undesirable domestic lived in service, is hidden away behind the wonderfully tinted trees that leave an indelible impression of a trip up the Orwell. All along the river, and inland in the surprisingly rich and varied country that lies between Felixstowe and the county town, the trees are magnificent in size and foliage, but here especially they strike one by reason of their abundance and colour. Beneath the shelter of some of these sturdy oaks and giant elms such daring spirits as are shadowed in the history of Margaret Catchpole might have disported themselves on Downham Reach.

It is from Freston, beloved for picnics, and by no means the most beautiful object in the varied and charming landscape of the Orwell, that the most romantic material is secured, and, according to the more prosaic folk, the best view of the river is obtained. Romance is, of course, all very well in its way, and has the advantage of being within the reach of all; but happily, it is also possible in this case to come down, or rather go up to the practical level, and "do" Freston Tower at will. One does not like in these latter days, when traditions and illusions are so ruthlessly mown down, to be

too accurate in dealing with these old places; but charming
as the Rev. R. Cobbold's romance about Ellen de Freston
and the gallant Latimer may be, there is little doubt as to
the original intention of the builder of Freston Tower.
Our forbears had a keen eye for the picturesque, and
recognised a good site when they saw one. Obviously,
it occurred to the de Frestons that this was the place
for a "look out," and they could not have chosen a
better one. Not improbably it was used, too, for other
purposes; but it is as well, perhaps, not to take the
utilitarian view of the building as one floats beneath its
castellated tower, to which, according to an old custom,
all "Gipp-ings" married in the month of May made a
pilgrimage.

> "No burgess on his wedding day,
> Which falls in white-thorn merry May,
> Shall happy be in house or bower,
> Who does not visit Freston Tower."

It certainly improves the picture to paint it in the
memory with a little "local colour," and to associate
with

> "Old Freston stern and grey,
> Looking o'er the watery way,"

the wily Wolsey and his patron's daughter, the fair
Ellen, whose hand seems to have been vainly sought by
every eligible young man in East Anglia, from Lancham
of Lavenham to Tendering of Tendring Hall, and from
Cove of Covehithe to Broke of Nacton. It is pleasant
to think of this fascinating Suffolk maiden in her garden
of roses—some of the earliest planted in England—
and to fancy her sailing past these same woods and
villages in her stately barge, whilst de Freston and
her two admirers, Wolsey and Latimer, pleasantly recalled

the sanguinary encounters with the Danes are associated with this part of the river. The historical and the picturesque are agreeably combined at this point of the river. It is opposite the glorious oaks that half hide from view the Freston Tower, which one naturally associates according to local tradition with good Latimer and my Lord Cardinal—the butcher's son of Ipswich—that Gainsborough's Lane lies, wherein the painter "so often sat to sketch on account of the beauty of the landscape, its extensiveness and richness of variety."

Woolverstone, just behind, the "show" place of the district, charming as it is, is less interesting than Captain Pretyman's beautiful Orwell Park. The obelisk, proudly pointed out to the river steamer tourist as an object

A Bit of the Bank opposite Pin Mill.

of interest, is, like that at Holkham Park, not altogether a thing of beauty, though its erection was prompted by the best of motives, the desire of a loving son to perpetuate the memory of a good father. With Woolverstone, moreover, is associated nothing more romantic than the well-known London street in which Theodore Hook perpetrated his famous hoax. That the Berners of Woolverstone can claim Berners-street as their own is doubtless a matter for considerable satisfaction on their part. It is true the dells of Woolverstone are pleasanter than the unromantic neighbourhood of the Tottenham Court Road, and the song of the nightingales sweeter than the shrill whistle of the London *gamin;* but after all, it is but cause and effect, and the effect in this case is a singularly charming one resulting from a very prosaic cause. Woolverstone is scenically most attractive when the silvery shades of evening fall over the trees, and the beautiful long-haired Scotch cattle wander to the very river's brink to give life to the picture. Sometimes, when the tide is low, the herons come down to dabble on the mud flats, while the soft-eyed deer peep wonderingly through the great masses of ferns that grow almost to the water's edge.

At Chelmondiston, or Pin Mill, just beyond, the old smuggling interest is again revived, this having once been a famous haunt of the wily ones, but its reputation now is wholly respectable. It is not the sound of the muffled oar nor the flash of the signal light that one expects here, but a series of beautiful landscape studies, as varied as if they were presented in panoramic form. The scene is always changing, but it is always effective, and Pin Mill will make the artist a good picture whether seen in spring or summer, autumn or winter, in sunlight or shadow, or whether the tide be high or low. Here might one spend half-a-dozen "sweet little summers or so," and find perpetual change of scenery if not of diet, for the Pin Millian is primitive in his ideas and his resources are limited; but these are details best left to the imagination. It is best to throw the shadow of romance over Chelmondiston and forget the rest. After all, one can consider eggs and fish and fresh meat in other places where the glories of this lovely little village are not obtainable.

Even Orwell Park, once the home of the hero of Porto Bello, Admiral Vernon, afterwards Viscount Orwell, cannot outvie its charms; though Orwell Park, both within and without the house, is a fascinating halting-place. There is a fine old breezy "Rule Britannia" air about the whole of this district, for next door, so to say, at Broke Hall, lived and died Sir Philip Broke, who commanded the *Shannon* when she won a victory for the British in Boston Bay; and the first Englishman who sailed round the world, Thomas Cavendish, having made a nice little fortune by more or less legitimate means, subsequently settled down to the life of a fine old English gentleman at Grimston hard by.

Admiral Vernon, however, secured the best situation for his house, which probably contains the finest collection of Old Masters in East Anglia, and certainly, the three best Murillos in the country. It is altogether a storehouse of treasures. The library is overflowing with rare old editions of which bibliophiles only dream; it has fine statues, delightful Van der Veldes and Titians, and not a few valuable modern pictures. Colonel Tomline, its late owner, who rebuilt the house, was an amateur astronomer, and from the huge observatory erected by him a magnificent view of the surrounding country is obtained.

It is curious how lively the river becomes again at this point. Just about here it suddenly deepens, and the festive oyster, which takes kindly to East Anglian waters, keeps the dredger in constant employment. Butterman's Bay is generally full of craft, large and small, and between here and Shotley the scene becomes picturesque again in a wholly different way. Presently, Harwich comes in sight, with its sea full of ships, its noisy, bustling steamboats and packets, its hideous Martello tower and busy pier.

Near Chelmondiston. (I in Mill.)

Harwich never looks better than it does from this point of view. It is a narrow-streeted, ugly, uninteresting little town, with all the unpleasant and none of the picturesque characteristics of the old Dutch ports it so closely resembles. Its inhabitants are proud of the many Royal visitors they have had, the ubiquitous Elizabeth, who evidently moved about her kingdom a great deal more than the present sovereign, despite the limited travelling facilities of her day, having of course been one of them. But certainly as one comes into Harwich from Ipswich, the scene is impressive. The Stour and the Orwell and the sea itself seem all to merge into one; the Dock, which the late Colonel Tomline of Orwell Park presented to the town, is always full of vessels; and Parkeston Quay, with its perpetual steamboat service to the Continent, is almost a town in itself.

Between Parkeston and Felixstowe, Harwich itself fades into comparative insignificance. Dovercourt, the residential quarter of the town, has made a brave but futile effort to establish itself as a watering-place. It possesses a Spa, said to have existed for over two hundred years, which statement anyone who is rash enough to taste its waters will have no reason to doubt; it has sands, and market gardens abound in the vicinity; but beyond these, the attractions of Dovercourt are not abundant, and it is upon Felixstowe, across the way, that the attention of the holiday-maker is now-a-days centred.

CHAPTER XIII.

HARWICH PORT.

IT is not until you begin to study Harwich from a traveller's and a business point of view, that its importance and advantages manifest themselves. It is not until the Continental express has whirled you down from Liverpool Street to Parkeston Quay to meet the steamer, on to whose deck it is almost possible to step direct from the train, that you are able to realise how completely and comfortably Harwich links the Continent with England. To run over from this little "village on the shore," as the name denotes, to Berlin, to Amsterdam, to sandy quaint Scheveningen, where Mynheer and his family take their annual seaside holiday —and sea and sands are vaster than anything on our English coast—takes but little longer and is every whit as convenient as going from London to York.

Harwich is about the last place in East Anglia wherein one would wish to linger, but it is a place for which one has a profound respect having travelled this way to the Continent. It is just one of those towns which were made to usefully serve as a stepping-stone to better things. This character it has always borne. Martin Frobisher evidently found it out, for he sailed hence to find the N.W. passage, and for centuries, even from the

The Orwell near Harwich.

Anglo-Saxon period, the port has been embarking and disembarking kings and queens and travellers of every degree. But it has certainly not been for centuries that the waters of the Scheldt have lapped by daybreak the next morn against the vessels that left the lights of Harwich behind but seven hours previously; nor that such luxurious vessels as those which now ply between Holland, Denmark, and this port, have sailed the hundred miles or so that lie between them.

Parkeston Quay.

Parkeston Quay is a very recent development of the "village by the shore," and at its present rate of progress there will surely come a time when people will speak of it and its traffic, not only as one of the most important features of East Anglia, but of England. Its growth has been marvellous; but it has been well fertilised with the money of the enterprising Great Eastern Railway Company, and almost every season, as the Continental traffic increases, Parkeston gains in glory. What would Elizabeth, who characterised Harwich as "a pretty little town, wanting nothing" say, could she find herself suddenly on Parkeston Quay any evening just before ten p.m.? Ablaze with electric light, it presents one of the most animated and amusing scenes that Sunrise-Land can offer. The train, just in, has discharged all sorts and conditions of passengers and every variety of luggage, from the humble handbag to the lordly travelling trunk; and not even the bewildered Dutchman on his way home again can help wondering at the completeness of the arrangements. For Parkeston is really a miniature town roofed in, and, Gulliver-like, one has only to stretch out one's hand, so to say, to

In the Saloon of the "Cambridge."

grasp at every need. Train, boat, hotel, refreshments, travelling comforts, all, everything are within immediate reach. It is a puzzle to find out where the platform leaves off and the quay proper begins, or which is hotel and which is quay; but there is no doubt whatever about the existence of the comfortable hostelry at Parkeston at this time of night. It pours forth a stream of passengers on to the deck of the finely-appointed steamer, just now panting to be off, and the electric light flashes from every window and shows up every varying expression of every passenger's face. If one went no further afield in Harwich than this wonderful quay, one would be firmly

The " Cambridge."

impressed with its importance, and, one might say, its exportance. And now that the new route to the Hook of Holland has been opened, and the "Chelmsford," the "Berlin," and the "Amsterdam"—the magnificent trio of boats—have been launched, the port, as represented by Parkeston alone, has more than ever become a centre of interest. For, by this new service, Berliners and Londoners have almost become next-door neighbours. One is shot from one city to the other as if by magic. This grand new conjuring trick is performed daily by the G.E.R. You quietly and calmly dispose yourself in a saloon carriage after dinner in London, you wink and blink a little at the dazzling brightness of Parkeston an hour

Great Eastern Hotel, Harwich Quay.

or so later, tuck yourself up in a luxurious bunk on the "Chelmsford," say, and at ten o'clock the next morning you are bowling along the Friedrichstrasse, as if it were but an adjacent thoroughfare to Liverpool Street. In these circumstances Parkeston is not a place to " laugh to scorn."

Harwich may not be a town of " sweetness and light," it may not be an ideal holiday resort, though, strange to say, there are persons who find it is something more than the Eastern—the Great Eastern, one might perhaps venture to say—gate to the Continent. There is certainly nothing else like it in this part of England. Even if the delight of making a cheap tour of the Ardennes, of poking about Bruges, with its beautiful old houses and famous belfry, of "doing" the Rhine, or any other of the good things it brings within reach in more senses than one, is not to be indulged in, it is worth while to journey to Parkeston just to watch the steamers go out and come in, to see John Bull *en route* for what Mr. Toole invariably calls the "continong," to see his unfeigned delight when he realises that he is back again where he is thoroughly understood, to study the Batavian working man and his wife, the foreign Jew, and the strange variety of tourists that East Anglia herself transports hence to see the sights in "foreign," as they loosely designate all places outside their own particular country.

Since these cheap—and they are wonderfully cheap—tours have been arranged by the G.E.R., even Hodge finds his way abroad in holiday-time. It is no uncommon thing to find in the villages that the young folks have been across from Harwich to Antwerp or Amsterdam, doubtless being far more impressed when their journeying is over with palatial Parkeston than with any of the more picturesque and instructive "sights" of Belgium or Holland. Still they do go, and there is therefore hope for them, and for this widening of their thoughts Harwich, otherwise Parkeston, has to be thanked. Now they will go still further afield by this new route, and more than ever will the quay be a centre of attraction. With miniature

Off Harwich.

Atlantic liners incessantly departing and arriving, and train loads of passengers being continually deposited on the mammoth landing-stage, it will be here, if anywhere, that perpetual motion will be discovered.

Sunrise-Land may boast of its river scenery, its flowery valleys and wild heathlands, its fine cities and sleepy, picturesque little villages, its magnificent coast, its Broads and vast tracts of corn; but it has every reason to vaunt with the greatest pride this ancient yet most advantageously modernised port.

CHAPTER XIV.

FLOURISHING FELIXSTOWE.

WITH Felixstowe just at hand it is small wonder that colourless little Dovercourt is fading into absolute insignificance. There is something almost pathetic in the genteel pretence of the latter to maintain its position as a watering-place in face of the indisputable fact that Felixstowe greedily gobbles up all the visitors and has all the attractions. Poor little Dovercourt! Its future can hardly be called promising, but it deserves an encouraging word for the excellence of its Cliff Hotel, its interesting old church, its safe sandy beach, and its desperate efforts to impart to itself an air of festivity by the erection of a monster Swiss Cottage, known as "Riggs' Retreat," which is consecrated to amusements calculated to appeal to those holiday-makers who see no reason why the sad sea waves should have the monopoly of the noise.

At Dovercourt they will tell you that it is to the golf-links Felixstowe owes its success. This is undoubtedly true in a measure. Mr. Arthur Balfour and his golfing brethren must have brought the pleasant little village into greater prominence than it would otherwise have enjoyed, and the enthusiasts who come down to the finely-situated Bath Hotel on the top of the hill to golf at all seasons, declare that the links here, which contain nine holes, are the finest in England. They are certainly less picturesquely situated than those at Cromer, though Bawdsey Ferry is a pretty enough little place, where sea-pinks and "thrift" and salt-lavender abound: but the many distinguished members of the Felixstowe Golf Club refuse to hear a word against the beauty of their favourite resort, and in order to prove their appreciation of and belief in Felixstowe, not a few well-known men have built for themselves smart villas on the bright yellow cliffs, to which they and their families come in the summer, and for that matter at all seasons of the year, for golfing goes on perpetually here whenever the weather permits. There is in consequence a decidedly smart air about Felixstowe if you keep severely away from the lower part of the beach, flooded all through the summer months with trippers, for whom refreshments, steam round-abouts, and other marine delights are provided with a prodigality that does not tend to enhance the beauty of the pebbly shore.

The beach under Bent Hill is altogether a snare and a delusion. It is devoid of sands, and abounds with small lodging-houses; but higher up and lower down, to speak paradoxically, that is to say on the top of the cliffs and beyond Bent Hill, past Mr. Cobbold's charming grounds in the direction of Bawdsey, sands put in an appearance, and here smarter Felixstowe does its bathing and its promenading. It was out here, in a couple of the new red-brick villas, that the Empress of Germany and her little sons stayed during their visit in 1891, and the small Teuton princes spent the greater part of their time on these excellent sands, riding on the famous donkeys of this part of the world, and digging and paddling to their hearts' content. The glow of that Royal visit has not yet faded from Felixstowe. The shops still display photographs of the Kaiser and Kaiserin, and the natives are full of stories of the Royal lady's charming simplicity, gentleness, and gracious appreciation of their little town.

Since then Felixstowe has greatly enlarged its borders. The well-planned residences of local magnates with golfing tendencies have increased in number, and Captain Pretyman, the new lord of the manor, who has promised a new church, and enlarged the Institute and Reading Rooms among other things, has been most energetic and successful in his endeavours to make Felixstowe "go." The roads are excellently laid out, lodgings are at a premium in the summer months, and the shops supply every need of visitors who are not content to "rough it" because they are at the seaside.

Altogether one takes away a pleasant impression of flourishing Felixstowe, always providing that one keeps well away from the cheerful but not always inoffensive tripper. Ipswich is at hand, it must be remembered, with its hundreds of factory operatives, and on high days and holidays they come here in their might and hold revels on the beach. It is glorious for them to fill their lungs with the keen exhilarating air that sweeps across from the North, and scarcely strange, perhaps, that the change from the close confinement of factories and workshops to the freedom of the shore with its lively seascape should provoke them to shout aloud with joy.

This same seascape, by the way, is a great feature of Felixstowe. By day the sea is literally "alive" with vessels and boats. There is much coming and going between the delusive "Pier," that is only a landing-stage, and Harwich Harbour; the Ipswich boat calls and leaves here many times daily in the summer; and further out on the highway to the Northern seas, huge vessels seem to be ever sailing away into space. At night, too, the sea still has its fascinations for those on land. The electric brilliancy of Parkeston is just visible across the waters, and far and near myriads of lights sparkle over the sea from outlying vessels, lighthouses, and lightships. Everybody walks out to Landguard while staying at Felixstowe. It is one of the places "to be done," and if the battery is not particularly interesting when it is reached, and the pedestrian is not duly impressed by the fact that the Dutch were repulsed

Landguard Fort, Felixstowe.

here in 1667 despite the fact that they managed to land three thousand men, the way thereto is very charming over breezy Langer Common; and three miles in this bright, crisp, East coast air counts for nothing even with the invalids.

Felixstowe may well be proud of its air. There is plenty of it, and no doubt about its invigorating qualities. It sweeps in from the sea, it rushes over the commons, it blows briskly, fiercely from the North, and sends one home with an appetite like a hunter; it braces up the nerves and blows away depression and languor; and when it has done all this for the summer visitors, it most obligingly deals gently with the natives, and treats them so mildly that they actually boast of their "winter season," and laugh to scorn the suggestion that east winds make the East coast impossible at some part of the year. They will point convincingly to their Convalescent Home on the shore— an imposing building that has lately been enlarged—and assure you that its inmates sit on the balconies and in the grounds in December, and bask in sunshine when their shivering friends in town are "frozen out." They will take you into the picturesque and beautifully-kept gardens of the Bath Hotel, and show you flowering shrubs and fig-trees whose fruits really ripen to the fall, and challenge you then to doubt the mildness and geniality of their "winter season ;" and if after this you are doubting still, the railway company will readily prove that it brings down trainsful of golfers and others to prosperous little Felixstowe when other East coast watering-places have, like the dormouse, rolled themselves up, and, to all intents and purposes, gone to sleep until summer days shall come again.

Taking Felixstowe all round, it is about as resourceful a marine village as any on this coast. If you do not golf—but almost everybody does here—you can fish. Across the ferry at Bawdsey, past the palatial Club-house, is the mouth of the Alde, famous for its boating facilities, and herein are excellent bass and mullet; while out Falkenham way, perch and pike and roach of excellent proportions may be angled for by those who obtain permission of the owner of Orwell Park, to whom the broadlike water belongs. But if the "gentle art" is not to your fancy, there is Harwich Yacht Club just over the way, and it is well-nigh impossible to stay here without taking some interest in yachting ; for between Harwich and Brightlingsea yawls and cutters, and smart yachting craft of every shape and size, are perpetually moving ; the latest products of the Wivenhoe yards being usually put through their paces here before they go to sail other and more distant waters. Furthermore, the boating possibilities are well-nigh endless. Visitors may make more use of the sea at Felixstowe than is commonly the case at marine resorts, and they have, too, a couple of rivers at command. They run over to Holland and back from Parkeston, they paddle about between here and Walton-on-Naze, they go backwards and forwards to Ipswich, they sail up the Alde, and if they like they can explore the Deben, on whose right bank is the picturesque old town of Woodbridge, the birthplace of Barton, the Quaker poet and chum of Charles Lamb.

The drive to Woodbridge, or better still, the walk there through quaint little Walton, the two Trimley villages with their picturesque ruined churches jostling each other, so to say, in a common churchyard, past the fine churches of Waldringfield and Brightwell, and the interesting old halls of Capel and Stratton, is one of Felixstowe's best excursions. But Nacton Heath runs it very hard. The walk over this wild, breezy gorse-covered common, shining like gold in the summer sun, past Captain Pretyman's house, is delightful, and gives one a most favourable impression of Suffolk scenery, which is not to be judged by the immediate neighbourhood of Felixstowe itself. But if complaint is urged against the "unbeautifulness" of the village and its vicinity, the loyal Felixstowian will promptly declare that its antiquity makes amends for all. It certainly can lay to itself the flattering unction that it is no mushroom place. That familiar figure of East Anglian history, Felix the Burgundian, is well to the fore, having been engaged in missionary operations here some twelve hundred and fifty years ago. At Dunwich, as we shall presently see, he was very active, but he seems to have "got through" with a considerable amount of work at this place since he gave his name to it, and built a church on the site of which old Felixstowe church now stands. He was, however, by no means first in possession. The Romans had been before him, and even to this day excavators turn up coins and pottery and other relics of their occupation. They built unto themselves a strongly-fortified castle at Walton, which village, until quite recently, was the centre of life hereabouts. But that East Anglian tyrant, Roger Bigod, who, like the other members of his family, was for ever squabbling either with the King or his neighbours, brought about the demolition of the castle in 1176. He had previously endowed Felixstowe with a priory, dedicated to the Burgundian missionary Felix, but when he showed rebellious tendencies some years later, Henry II. swept down upon his castle as he did later on in the case of Sir Hugh Bigod at Bungay, and nothing now remains of the fortress but a few stones scattered elsewhere in the village. When Henry VIII. was dealing with Wolsey's College and other buildings in Ipswich, he swept away Roger Bigod's Priory, the revenues of which Wolsey had applied to the foundation of his college.

But though robbed of these antiquities, Felixstowe can still show at least the foundations of its whilom palace, in which Edward III. once stayed. There is not much of it, but enough to give it an antiquarian air and dissipate any idea that it is a brand-new watering-place, with the latest modern improvements—and drawbacks. Felixstowe disclaims any such suggestion, and bravely holds its own with Colchester and Dunwich as an ancient institution and a Royal resort.

Before passing hence to Aldeburgh, the next "point," Hollesley Bay, has to be seen, for here is the Colonial

College, most admirably designed and charmingly situated. The lads in training here for colonial life must have what Americans call "a real good time," and when the time comes for them to seek their fortunes across the seas, they must often think regretfully of their pleasant sojourn in this Suffolk nook.

CHAPTER XV.

ALDEBURGH—ANCIENT AND MODERN.

COMING straight into Aldeburgh as a stranger and a pilgrim from other more fashionable and apparently more picturesque Eastern resorts, the impression received is distinctly unfavourable. As a rule the stations of the Great Eastern Railway, ever most mindful of the comforts of its passengers, are not calculated to depress the spirits of waiting travellers to a lower degree than is inevitable; but about Aldeburgh station there is a peculiarly forlorn and disconsolate appearance that chills one at once. And the finer the day, the deeper seems its gloom, so that the entry into this quiet, breezy little Suffolk watering-place, if effected by train, can scarcely be said to be made in favourable circumstances. Nor, as one journeys down the road, past the snug residences and the large though not architecturally beautiful sixteenth-century church to the shore, do its attractions—for they do exist—force themselves upon the notice.

It is, however, a pleasant surprise to find the door of the church open, as a natural pause is made at its gates. Suffolk is almost, but not quite, as bad as Norfolk in the matter of keeping its church doors locked. Except on Sundays, or by routing out the sexton, the chances of seeing into the beautiful and interesting ecclesiastical buildings for which this county is famous, are small indeed. Here and there, though, one meets with a more enlightened vicar, who, like the parish priest of this town, leaves his church unbarred and unlocked for visitors and others to enter as they will.

Within S. Peter and S. Paul they find a finely-carved pulpit, bearing the date 1638, some good brasses, the bust of Crabbe—" the poet of nature and truth "—and a replica of the medallion tablet erected in Westminster Abbey to the memory of the late Henry Fawcett; but otherwise there is no particular interest about the church, a fact the more to be regretted as it is happily made so easy of access.

The influence of the Garretts, with whom the blind states man was closely allied by marriage, is strong in the town. In the churchyard the name is repeated again and again. Almost one of the first houses one notices in Aldeburgh is Alde House, where the late Mr. Newson Garrett, father of the well-known lady-doctor, Mrs. Garrett Anderson, M.D., who also has a house here, and of Mrs. Henry

Leiston Abbey from the Road.

Fawcett, resided; and on the golf-links in the summer one may be sure of meeting the two clever descendants of the

Leiston Abbey.

late owner of Alde House, the brilliant Miss Philippa Fawcett, and her young cousin, Mr. Cowell, both of whom are Senior Wranglers. Even in journeying to Leiston's famous Abbey, the name of Garrett pursues one, for here there are huge ironworks belonging to Messrs. R. Garrett and Sons, and as they employ something like six hundred men, and their buildings cover at least ten acres of ground, Garrett and Leiston are almost synonymous terms. But these are not first impressions of Aldeburgh, nor are its Mayor and its Town Council, its Jubilee Hall, its river, and its quay. It is with its two straggling streets, admirably described by Wilkie Collins, its pebbly, sandless, untidy, uninviting beach and sea-front, that acquaintance is first made; and it is not strange in these circumstances that dismay should fill the soul of its explorer. Picturesque the shore may be, and most assuredly is when the eye becomes accustomed to its most admired disorder; but it is scarcely attractive, especially if viewed as a possible holiday-haunt for little folk. The sea laps against the stones in the roadway, and has that dull, hueless appearance that is characteristic of the waters washing the lower Saxon shores. A kind of marine gaiety is imparted to the beach by the flying of many red-and-blue flags from very aggressive bathing-machines, and by the perpetual presence of groups of regulation seaside sailors, who pessimistically romance about the weather and apparently spend more time ashore than afloat. And on the whole there are rather more boats hauled up on the beach than are in the sea. One has almost to climb them to get along, and certainly to steer one's way carefully over the old masts, anchors and chains, coils of rope, fish-baskets, and all manner of flotsam and jetsam with which the shore is strewn.

Thus it comes that Aldeburgh disillusions one at first sight. It is as the song says, charming when you know it, but you have got to know it first; and, in any case, its beach and its sea are not its strong points, although, paradoxically, it is on the former that one of the most interesting features of the town is found. This is the ancient Moot Hall. All who can paint, and many who cannot, at once make a picture of this picturesque old building, which architecturally and archæologically—even though it is restored—is the only object worth attention in Aldeburgh. How old it is cannot exactly be discovered, but it was standing, unquestionably, early in the sixteenth century, and was probably built long before, though it is generally loosely described as Elizabethan. Still used by the Petty Sessions and Town Council, it was doubtless once a vastly important building when Aldeburgh was a borough of some size, sending two members to Parliament, and its ancient constitution consisted of thirty-four burgesses. Round about here clustered the town, and all business was carried on; for, originally, a Saturday and a Wednesday market were held, Elizabeth granting the former and Edward VI. the latter. Where there is now only shingle a market cross once stood; but in those days this was the centre of the town, which then possessed no less than eight hundred fishermen, while fifty or sixty ships plied the North Sea betwixt here and Iceland.

Later on a wool-spinning industry was established here, but by degrees, slowly but most surely, the cruel sea crept in and grasped at poor little Aldeburgh, which vanished bit by bit, till whole streets disappeared and the industries declined. Eleven houses, in one of which Crabbe was born, were engulfed in a single day, when the waves roared and thundered on the shore with special vehemence, while but a few years previously an entire street disappeared in an equally short space of time. Violent storms, now happily less prevalent, were once, it would seem, unpleasantly frequent in this borough; for in 1642, according to a pamphlet, curiously enough published by one Thomas Fawcett, an elaborate account is given of a wonderful thunderstorm, which broke over the town "on the 4th Day of August, at five of the clocke," in that year, when "so fearful and terrible a noise was heard in the Ayre," that the terrified inhabitants thought the town besieged.

Within the Moot Hall, by the way, there are some curious old municipal treasures to be seen, and the fact that they are displayed by no less a person than "Mace," enhances their importance in the eyes of the awe-struck visitor.

Wandering along the beach, where goats and donkeys are tethered, past the Reading Room, the handsome houses in Brudenill Terrace, and the life-boat—which has had much service since it was presented by Mrs. Hounsfield—one becomes more and more favourably impressed with Aldeburgh. Gradually it is made evident that it has a quiet charm of its own, though it is true one has to acquire the taste for it. It is altogether quaint.

The Moot Hall, Aldeburgh.

Fringed by the shingle, which here serves as a beach, there is a kind of informal—very informal—parade, extending for nearly two miles to Slaughden Quay. It is along here that young Aldeburgh has set up its smart houses, with their trim gardens; but this "fashionable quarter" is curiously leavened with the store-huts of the fishers, and the funny little wooden watch-tower, the admiration of the boys. Altogether, just about here, the sea and land seem to be somehow mixed together, till one almost expects to see the vessels come sailing right into the front gardens, where, as Wilkie Collins pointed out in "No Name," the "staring figure-heads of ships do duty for statues among the flowers." The scene becomes lonelier presently, and thoroughly Dutch. A huge white mill rises up suddenly from the flat meadows, grazed by red and white cows. Trees become scarce and stunted, the setting sun turns the meres into crimson pools, and land and sky and sea are all one. Then one discovers why folks come here year after year, why the fathers and the boys love Aldeburgh, and why the artistic soul hankers after its flatness. It is to Slaughden that folks turn again and again when staying in Aldeburgh, and it is never disappointing in its effects. On the contrary, this weird, treeless, "forlorn outlying suburb" in the marshes is ever supplying new and beautiful "impressions." Its native poet, in picturing this desolate quarter of the town with its quaint quay and fishers' cottages tumbled together, has painted the scene with almost terrible realism.

> "Here samphire banks and saltwort bound the flood,
>   There stakes and sea-weed withering in the mud;
>   Lo, where the heath with withering brake grown o'er,
>   Lends the light turf that warms the neighbouring poor,
>   From thence a length of burning sand appears,
>   Where the thin harvest waves its withered ears;
>   Rank weeds, that every art and care defy,
>   Reign o'er the land and rob the blighted rye."

Nobody could better describe the country hereabouts

than Crabbe, who was so perfect a word-painter, and whose early days were passed on Slaughden Quay, where he helped his father, a salt officer, to pile up casks, before he was bound to an apothecary near Bury. Perhaps his fellow-villagers distrusted the skill of the erstwhile Slaughden labourer; but, at all events, he did not succeed in his native place when he came back to practise on or among them, and he then took to versifying, and finally to Holy Orders, returning once again to Aldeburgh, where he this time officiated as curate.

The deserted Martello tower, which is Aldeburgh's most costly if not most useful or ornamental building, lends this part of the town a further attractiveness in the eyes of the boys, and of those who appreciate the effective forlornness of the whole scene; but it is the Alde, especially, which makes Slaughden to be highly esteemed. Aldeburgh is justly proud of its river. It is one of its features, and everybody who loves boating, and is acquainted with the waters of East Anglia, knows the Alde. It is always alive with little craft of all shapes and sizes, and though the sea may be running ever so high, and the wind "blowing great guns," the enthusiastic oarsman or amateur sailor need never be cheated of his boating here. The Alde is always accommodating, and if you tire of boating, there are plenty of fish in its waters and fowl on its banks. From here, too, one may sail down past old-world Orford right away to Walton-on-Naze and Felixstowe, where, as we have seen, it empties itself into the sea.

Orford Castle is one of those places in which the "sympathies" revel. It is delightfully romantic, it is most effective in the moonlight, and it is just sufficiently far off to deter chaperones from making the journey with the young people, while the prospect of descending the rickety ladder at Slaughden Ferry is not alluring to them.

A Sketch on the Sea-Front, Aldeburgh.

But not to have seen Orford is to have but half enjoyed a visit to Aldeburgh, and to have missed one of Suffolk's most interesting and most picturesque ruins. Like Dunwich and Aldeburgh, Orford was once a thriving town and extensive borough, but the ruined castle keep, standing grey and solitary on the lofty mound—from which one may look across the trees of Sudbourne Park, and Orfordness with its two fine lighthouses—is now its only glory. One can little imagine Orford as a flourishing port, nor picture a town spreading round the castle, which with the castle at Norwich was once under the constable-ship of Hubert de Burgh; but it was evidently a place of importance, and the castle must originally have been a very large building. At present it is a village of ruins, dear to the artist, professional and amateur, and a perfect paradise for picnics and lovers. Some of its lanes are still called "streets," and the imaginative may romance here to their hearts' content, while the more practically-minded find refreshments, plentiful and excellent, by-the-way, at the "Crown Inn." But though Orford is "first favourite" as an excursion from Aldeburgh, and certainly out-distances, in every sense of the word, busy Leiston, there is plenty of interest to be found here. Leiston is, from a picturesque point of view by far the more attractive place, and historically its superior, though its records date from 1439. But Leiston was a flourishing place when Edric of Laxfield, in Saxon times, ruled over extensive domains in these parts, and at all periods of history from that time till the sixteenth century Leiston was regarded as a place of some importance.

The remains of the beautiful Abbey, built on the site of a much older one in 1389, are most charmingly situated on the summit of a hill just outside the smoky townlet which is now chiefly inhabited by ironworkers in Messrs. Garrett's foundry. Although the ruins are disfigured by the presence of farm buildings erected in their very midst, one is still impressed with their grandeur and beauty; and it is easy to imagine how magnificent the structure must have been before the hand of time and the vandal fell upon it. Still, its brickwork—and especially its remaining tower—is splendid, and its whole appearance most picturesque. That it should have been suffered to fall into such decay is a thousand pities, for East Anglia could scarcely have possessed a finer abbey than that of Leiston. Its history is an interesting one. Ranulph de Glanville, its founder, is a prominent figure in the ghostly crowd who hover round these relics of the past. He was, for one thing, an extensive builder, and evidently a man of considerable substance, for to him not only this abbey but the Priory of Butley, now also a ruin about five miles from Orford, owed existence; and he was moreover a legal and official luminary of no mean order, since he was at various times Sheriff of Lancashire, Yorkshire, and Westmoreland; ambassador to Flanders; and subsequently Chief Justiciar. Leiston eventually passed from the hands of his heirs into the family of the Earls of Suffolk, and at one time it was in the possession of handsome Charles Brandon, Duke of Suffolk, whose marriage with young Mary Tudor is chronicled in the romances of Ipswich. Again and again the names of this young couple occur in the course of rambles through Eastern England. Just as the Pastons become quite familiar friends to the student of Norfolk history, so do the Brandons engage one's interest in Suffolk. Here, at Leiston, we find they must once have had a home, though it was but a temporary one, for by-and-bye it transpires that the gallant young nobleman exchanged the manor and Abbey for Henham Hall, near Southwold. The Marquis of Buckingham in James the First's reign, and the Harvey family in that of Charles I., held Leiston, which eventually passed to the Montagus and the Vannecks.

Breezy Aldeburgh has one decided advantage over most little watering-places of its size along the Eastern shores. It is unusually sociable. Tennis, golf, and boating are not its only attractions, though such liberal and excellent provision is made for the enthusiasts who find these sports sufficiently soul-satisfying, that if there were no other means of killing time here, at least abundant out-door amusement would be provided. But Aldeburghers are not content to rest either figuratively or literally on their oars, or, for that matter, on their racquets or clubs where amusement is concerned. The private residents are numerous hereabouts, the visitors include many well-known folk, and so they have set about providing a form of subscription entertainments, pleasantly dubbed "socials," which keep little Aldeburgh gay enough in the season.

The late Mr. Newson Garrett, in 1887, together with the lord of the manor, added to the existing reading room a large public hall as a memorial of the Jubilee, and herein during August and September there are many pleasant gatherings. Concerts and dramatic entertainments provided by well-known artistes, dances for the little people on wet afternoons and for the "grown ups" in the evenings, are surely attractions enough to lure holiday-makers to this cheery little corner, even had it no natural features to recommend it to notice; so "taking one consideration with another," young men and maidens are about as well provided for at Aldeburgh as at any place along the coast. Golf, tennis, boating, dances, and romantic ruins ought to satisfy the most exacting seaside visitor, especially when he or she has in addition so charming a variety of drives as are offered hereabouts, although Aldeburgh only possesses two means of egress. Drive over the heathery common, and with the blank sea space in view all the time, you will come to Leiston; or take the other road past Friston and Hurt's Hall, and sleepy Saxmundham will be reached, whence onward to lovely Yoxford, the "garden of Suffolk," the land of flowers and exquisite lanes overhung with magnificent trees, behind which are hidden such fine mansions as the Elizabethan Cockfield Hall, the home of the Blois family; Carlton Hall, belonging to the Garretts; and Thorrington.

It is pure delight to wander in and about this ideally lovely village, to revel in its wealth of wild flowers and its beautiful parks. Peaceful and picturesque and restful above all the many other pleasant Suffolk villages that could be named, Yoxford is a place to visit, not once, but many times. Its charms are not to be described in half a dozen sentences. It is the centre, as it were, of a district as beautiful as it is interesting. Mr. Clement Scott, the prince of holiday-makers, has called it "Lazy-land"; but in truth one is never idle here, being far too tempted on all sides to walk over the glorious heather-clad moor of Westleton, or through the grove-like roads on either side of which the gardens of the picturesque old cottages make brightness for the eye with masses of flowers. This is the place to see roses. They seem to grow everywhere. The air is laden with their fragrance; there are literally "roses, roses all the way." One may almost fancy their scent is wafted across the brilliant purple heath to Blytheburgh, which, with Dunwich, is one of the most attractive of the many excursions from cheerful, untidy little Aldeburgh.

CHAPTER XVI.

A CITY OF THE DEAD, AND SUNNY SOUTHWOLD.

AND so we come to Dunwich, across the wild stretches of gorse-covered heath, weirdly impressive in that strange sunset glow peculiar to flat countries where marshlands abound. Dunwich the desolate, the city of the dead: once the most populous, the most important seaport of these Saxon shores, the home of kings, the centre of ecclesiastical and commercial activity—for it was the capital of East Anglia—now a heap of ruins, a handful of crumbling grey stones, "where sharp the sea bird shrills his ditty flickering flame-wise through the clear live calm." The sea alone holds sway, swirling and beating against the cliffs that bit by bit have been engulfed with the lordly pleasure houses, the fair buildings, the stately churches that were once the glory of this buried city.

Here truly is a paradise for the dreamer. The ordinary "every-day" visitor, who drives hither from busy sunny Southwold, bringing materials wherewith to picnic under the shadow of the ruins whose roofs once echoed with "holy chant and psalm," sees nothing but decay and desolation in the scene. Sight-seers come in parties as a matter of course from Aldeburgh and Southwold, and are languidly interested in the fact that in these grassy cliff-side fields "a King's court, a Bishop's palace, a Mayor's mansion, fifty-two churches, and as many windmills" once stood; but for those blessed with poetic fancy there is much more here than a mere heap of ruins on a dreary cliff. Here all day long in the summer one may dream the hours away, peopling the palaces and the streets of this buried city with priests and traders and pilgrims. Its fascination becomes greater and greater as one traces out the plan of this stately

An Old Well Southwold.

A "Bit" at Southwold.

town, and recalls its historic traditions that will endure even when the last remnant of ancient Dunwich has been swept away. Maybe the historians who have written of the city have been tempted to give undue freedom to their pens; but after taking their descriptions with a very large grain of that famous local production,

Southwold salt, it is clearly seen that Dunwich was no mean city.

The inhabitants seem to have had at all periods a fairly uncomfortable time so far as the sea was concerned, for even in Edward the Confessor's day Dunwich had suffered the loss of a royal and an episcopal residence; but about the reign of John things were more flourishing. It had been strongly fortified against the marine as well as other enemies, and eventually at least six parish churches, dedicated respectively to St. Leonard, St. John Baptist, St. Martin, St. Nicholas, St. Peter, and All Saints, as well as municipal and extensive domestic buildings, a fine harbour, and a Franciscan monastery—part of which, with the ruins of All Saints and a fragment of a hospital still stands—made up the city.

There is plenty of information to be had about ancient Dunwich. It has had its historians and its great men, and so recently as 1886 it preserved some of its old importance by electing a Mayor and Corporation. It still has its corporation plate, its funny old silver mace, sergeant-at-mace's shield, and its three seals, all preserved in the Town Hall.

One may literally lose oneself in the mists of antiquity, wandering here on the cliffside within these ivied ruins as the history of Dunwich is recalled. For here nearly *thirteen hundred* years ago Sigeberht, King of East Anglia, established a palace for himself and a church for the first bishop of East Anglia, Felix the Burgundian. This same Sigeberht, as one finds at Bury St. Edmund's, founded a church and monastery there, and as a road led direct from Don-e-wic to Bury there were doubtless many pilgrimages between the two cities. It is interesting, too, to trace the history of Norwich Cathedral back to this heap of ruins by the sea; for it was here, of course, that the first Bishopric of East Anglia was established, fifteen subsequent Bishops holding the See, which a few years later was merged with that at Elmham, thence removed to Thetford, and finally established at Norwich.

So here, among these few remnants of past glories, one may rest, and in imagination listen to the chanting of the monks and the tramp of the soldiers, and conjure up visions of the pageants and processions of kings and prelates, courtiers and burghers, that once filed through its streets. In these grassy fields the drama of life has been played for centuries. Burghers have bargained and traded in the busy market-place where the barley now waves, love's young dream has disturbed the peace of many a Dunwich maiden whose ashes have long ago been scattered on the winds, and centuries have rolled by since the old monks listened to the confessions of reckless Saxon soldiers and unscrupulous traders. Of what hundreds of romances, bloody deeds, noble sacrifices, and saintly lives, sorrows, hopes, fears, and successes these crumbling walls could tell!

Reluctantly one turns back from them to little Southwold, with its fashionable visitors, its golf-links, and many evidences of social and commercial activity.

> "So the dreams depart
> And the fading phantoms flee,
> And the sharp reality
> Now must act its part."

Not that Southwold is a smart seaside resort of the regulation pattern. Like Aldeburgh it, too, is innocent of a pier, and the nigger does not find favour here; but it is an enterprising little town, and above all things quaint in the extreme. It is a place of which one speedily grows very fond. In or round it there is a wealth of interest, and as a holiday-haunt in the truest sense it stands unrivalled on this part of the coast till Cromer, the most beautiful of all the Eastern resorts, is reached.

Southwold Church.

Of artists it is beloved, and they are to be found here by the dozen, of all degrees, from the strangely-garbed, tousled-haired female art student, to the Royal Academician in search of "low tones." Southwold, and the surrounding and fascinating villages of Wangford, Blytheburgh, and Walberswick, have pictorially appeared again and again upon the walls of the Royal Academy and other art galleries, and there is no reason why they should not continue to provide a wealth of material for landscape painters as yet unborn. Whether they stray through the funny little town itself, or wander over the magnificent surrounding heaths, where yellow broom and purple heather outvie each other in luxuriance and richness of colour, temptation lies in the way of wielders of the brush.

Southwold, to start with, possesses a church like a miniature cathedral, rich in colour and interest, and accessible at all times, moreover, to the visitor. St. Edmund's, Southwold, is one of the five remarkable churches, all within a walk of each other, for which this little corner of Suffolk is famous; of these the church at Blytheburgh is undoubtedly the finest, but its condition, unfortunately, is lamentable.

> "All roofless now the stately pile
>   And rent the arches all,
> Through which with bright departing smile
>   The western sunbeams fall.
> The choir is hushed—and silent now
>   The organ's thrilling sigh;
> Yet swells at eve from many a bough
>   The linnet's lullaby,"

wrote Agnes Strickland, whose grave is within the churchyard of Southwold. St. Edmund's, which almost equals it in magnificence of proportions and richness of decoration, is happily in an excellent state of preservation and worthily appointed for worship by its present vicar. Supposed to have been completed during the reign of Henry IV., his emblems and those of his consort, Joan of Navarre, occur frequently on the doors and in the beautiful windows, all of which are profusely decorated with badges and emblems and arms, such as those of its patron saint and the town corporation. The windows are one of its glories, chief among which, however, is the beautiful woodwork of the interior—rood-screen, pulpit, choir stalls, roof and font-cover all being of old oak—most of it of the same date as the church, and either richly carved or elaborately painted. In its "palmy days," before it was so scandalously mutilated, the church must have been remarkable for the extreme beauty of its interior painting and carving; but Dowsing, the Suffolk iconoclast, did his worst here, and has left his miserable mark to perpetuate his name in shame upon the building. There is, beside the vestry-door, a curious old carved wooden figure, known as "Jack Smite-the-Clock," which doubtless has for generations served to keep children quiet, and most certainly to amuse those of an older growth; for by some arrangement of his internal economy this quaint little armour-clad figure, who in one hand bears a sword and in the other an axe, announces the approach of choir and clergy, when the bell ceases tolling, by striking on a contiguous bell. There is a similar but smaller figure in Blytheburgh church, but it is much mutilated, and not in working order.

The unfinished tower, which is a hundred feet high, looms over the town, and bears aloft a memorial, in the form of a clock, of one of Southwold's leading spirits, the late Mr. Debney, the "universal provider" of the town. "Debney's" is still, under the guidance of his sons, the centre of commercial activity in the town, and attracts not only the anxious materfamilias, catering for a huge and hungry family, but such men-folk as care about curios; for here among the dress materials and the groceries one may be sure of finding a few pieces of antique furniture, one or two handsome eight-day clocks, works of art, and bits of old china, as well as all the latest information on every local subject.

Though naturally unequalled in beauty and size and interest, St. Edmund's is by no means the only place of worship in Southwold. On Sunday mornings there is a veritable babel of religious tongues in the little town, Churchmen, Wesleyans, Congregationalists, Baptists, and Salvationists vieing with each other in calls to service. At all times the Southwoldians make themselves heard tolerably well, for if they are not crying their wonderful shrimps and soles—the like of which are not to be met with elsewhere, either as regards size or quality—they are lustily announcing drives, or vending produce from neighbouring farms and gardens. In their sunny little market-place they are peculiarly active and energetic, especially on Thursdays, when, as if by magic, fruit and vegetables, new-laid eggs and oaken chests, old brass work and all manner of odds and ends appear to spring out of the ground, and completely transform the usually severely neat little square with its village pump in the centre, its miniature Town Hall, two-manned Police-station, imposing banks, solid-looking residences, and the comfortable "Swan Hotel." In the Town Hall, by the way, one is required to believe that municipal business is transacted; but this statement demands a certain amount of credulity on the part of the visitor, until he discovers that a Mayor undoubtedly exists, and that there are likewise four aldermen, twelve councillors, a town-clerk, mace, a high steward, a crier, and a fen-reeve, who evidently do their duties well, for Southwold is keen on improvements, and is nothing if not ambitious.

It is justly proud of its gas and its fine new waterworks, its well-planned streets, the scrupulous cleanliness of the town, and its excellently-kept roads. It even boasts a suburb with a lighthouse in its midst—though neither the one or the other owe their existence to municipal enterprise; and at its present rate of progress this suburb on the north cliff bids fair to make Southwold into a very extensive town one day. They evidently do not let the grass grow under their feet here, except on the "greens," which are such a delightful feature of the town, for less than six years ago there were only fields where there are now handsome terraces, smart villas, and excellent shops. These "greens" pop up unexpectedly in all quarters of this unconventional little town, like oases in the desert; so that however much they may build up sunny Southwold, it will always be free from the objectionable stiffness of the regulation seaside town.

Just outside the churchyard, on St. Edmund's Green, the stocks and whipping-post—relics of the "good old days" when they dealt with tramps and beggars and other misdemeanants in summary fashion—still stand. They had a delightfully original way of checking epidemics and scares in those times, for whipping-posts appear to have been brought extensively into play for persons suffering from small-pox. Perhaps if the same drastic method were now employed for influenza patients, we should hear no more of that dread disease. But besides St. Edmund's, or Tibby Green, there are Church Green and East Green, Bartholomew Green, North Green, and South Green; "greens" enough in fact, for the whole population, altogether leaving out of the question the magnificent common, unbounded by hedges, where the cricketers and golfers and lawn-tennis players may make themselves thoroughly happy. What a glorious playground it is for the children! As they shout and scamper among the gorse, the strong air blows in on one side from the rolling

Southwold Church and Stocks.

sea, and on the other from the sweet-scented pine groves, the only remnants of the woods and forests once covering this district. Small wonder, truly, that Southwold grows apace when it possesses such a common as this, such magnificent air, such ruins—and such soles.

This common, by the way, is a grand vantage ground for

sunset effects. Not here, as at Cromer—pre-eminently Sunset as well as Sunrise-land—can one watch the sun depart in a blaze of light, dyeing sand and water with dazzling hues; but hardly less effective in its way is the glow of the sinking sun over these great flat stretches of land and water, "the wide-winged sunset of the misty marsh," the mills and ruined church towers looming large against the sky. Every object is magnified and sharply outlined, and the white horses on the common stand out like monster silver models against skies of copper and orange and palest grey. This, too, is the time to see Walberswick—the artist's happy hunting ground—which lies across the ferry at Blackshore Quay. The ivied tower of its stately church is the "show" ruin of this part of Suffolk, and is, in sunlight and moonlight, the delight of Southwold's visitors. But at no time is the quaint little picturesque hamlet more effective than in the fading light of a summer sky. Across the river the beautiful Blythe, that flows through Laxfield, becomes a "broad" at Blytheburgh, and, creeping by meadows and commons, half concealed by reeds and rushes and yellow irises, here finds an outlet to the sea. The bracken on the common is tipped with gold; great patches of copper light brighten the reedy pools and the dark river; the handful of red-roofed cottages and the stately tower stand sharply defined against a leafy background. Then suddenly haze steals over the picture and daylight dies, leaving one the memory of an exquisite "harmony" in gold and grey.

The "cliffs" of Southwold are not easy to discover. It is considered courteous to refer to the slight elevation of the land by the seashore here as "cliffs," and one airily speaks of strolling along them; and as it is by comparison that most things are judged, Southwold is certainly perched high above the foaming waves if compared with Aldeburgh, where land and sea are on a level. But though at no point do these "cliffs" by courtesy attain a greater altitude than that of a fairly high bank, it is by no means easy walking along them when "the stormy winds do blow." The sea rages and the wind blows with terrific violence just here, and the quaint little bungalows and queerly-shaped cottages almost overhanging the shore are fitted with an arrangement of double doors in consequence. How

Walberswick Ferry.

they must rattle and the windows shake when the land is swept with winds from the sea. At the charmingly-named "Centre Cliff" Hotel, always gay with flowers, one is safe enough from blasts and torrents, as it is set back just far enough to protect it from the full force of storms; but on the grassy Gun Hill one stands a very good chance of being blown away, not by the battery, but by the wind. This, in calm weather, is Southwold's promenade, and its six guns, captured at Preston by "Bonnie Prince Charlie," and presented to Southwold by "Butcher Cumberland," give it quite an air of importance. Ask any of the natives about these guns, and you will hear the most conflicting accounts of them, the general impression among the marine population, being, apparently, that they were captured in the great fight between the Dutch and English fleets in Sole Bay in 1672, when, as the old ballad says,

> "Well might you hear their guns, I guess,
> From Sizewell gap to Easton-ness,
> The show was rare and sightly;
> They battered without let or stay
> Until the evening of that day,
> 'Twas then the Dutchmen ran away,"

but not, however, until the famous De Ruyter had been wounded and Vice-Admiral van Ghent killed, a fate that likewise befel the gallant Lord Sandwich, who made a brave fight against a powerful fleet, and whose body, still accoutred with the insignia of the Garter, was found floating in the bay.

It is odd to sit in the curious and not too well-provided Casino on the Gun Hill and think of this naval engagement in the peaceful bay, where the succulent sole and sprightly shrimp abound. Greater prominence still has been given to the Gun Hill by the erection of the new baths adjoining the primitive salt-works, with which Thomas Gardner, the Dunwich historian, was once connected. When all the buildings are finished it is anticipated that the town will possess baths outrivalling the famous ones of Droitwich, since the additional advantage of magnificent sea-air will be lent to them.

If there were only sands instead of shingle along its beach, from which one has so fine a view of the German

Ocean, Southwold would be an almost ideal little spot. It is a place for old and young. The little ones love these wild stretches of bright heath "rounded about by the wavering sky;" they enjoy the endless panorama of ships a-sailing the sea; the marshes gay with strange blooms and many-tinted grasses, and haunted by teams of bright-breasted mallards, oxbirds, and other wild-fowl with which this coast abounds. And, for the seeking, what botanical wealth is to be found in these marshes, where

> "On its wiry stem, in rigid bloom,
> Grows the salt lavender that lacks perfume;
> Here the dwarf sallows creep, the septfoil harsh,
> And the soft slimy mallow of the marsh;
> Low on the ear the distant billows sound,
> And just in view appears their stony bound;
> No hedge nor tree conceals the glowing sun,
> Birds, save a wat'ry tribe, the district shun,
> Nor chirp among the reeds where bitter waters run."

What glories there are in the quiet leafy lanes and on the beautiful heaths, rich with vivid heather and gorse and bracken, as one rambles or drives to Reydon with its fine church and Elizabethan mansion, to sleepy Wangford, to the picturesquely-situated Henham Park, now in possession of Lord Stradbroke, but once the home of young Charles Brandon, Duke of Suffolk, to decaying Blytheburgh or quaint Covehithe, to beautiful and interesting Wrentham, whence Benacre Park may be visited, or to Lowestoft which lies beyond, through lovely, leafy lanes, and past "broad"-like lakelets, fringed with silver birches and glistening with myriads of water-lilies—Lowestoft the lively, where the peace and quaint picturesqueness of Southwold are perforce forgotten.

CHAPTER XVII.

FISH AND FASHION.

IKE some other resorts that could be named, Lowestoft begins in fish and ends in fashion. On a bright August morning, when sea and land are bathed in sunlight, and the town is seen in its gayest and busiest mood, one may stroll in five minutes from the midst of millions of silvery but odoriferous herrings to one of the finest esplanades in England, where some of the prettiest girls in the county, in their smartest gowns, are to be seen. Lowestoft is to Yarmouth what St. Leonards is to Hastings, with this difference, that the "metropolis of Bloaterdom" is ten miles away from noisy, roystering, but withal quaint and ever-fascinating Yarmouth. It is a little expedition to visit one from the other; a pleasant rest to seek out Lowestoft, with its smart suburbs, its air of county respectability and fashion, from "tripper-" haunted Yarmouth; and delightful, on the other hand, to drive over from Lowestoft to the picturesque old town, immortalised by Dickens, with its red-tiled houses, its mass of shipping, its narrow streets and Dutch-like quay, and its marvellous beach, crowded with myriads of "'Arries and 'Arriets" in all stages of existence and of gaiety, the like of which is not even to be seen at Margate itself.

No properly constituted visitor to Lowestoft would dream

of leaving the town without making acquaintance with
the huge mackerel and herring market, built by the
Great Eastern Railway Company, who annually dispatch
throughout the country from this port about fourteen
or fifteen thousand tons of fish, including soles, plaice,
and haddocks, as well as the famous herrings. It is
a wonderful scene in the morning, when the smacks
come in and discharge their cargoes on the quay. There
is a veritable babel of tongues; for the fishers are of
all nationalities, as may be inferred from the fact that
there are vice-consuls for Russia, Spain, Denmark, and
Belgium, and that Norway and Sweden, France and

Fish Market, Lowestoft.

Germany, have likewise their respective representatives in Lowestoft. Ton after ton of the glistening spoils of the sea are piled upon the quay, and almost as speedily borne away again, when

Types in the Fish Market, Lowestoft.

the fish merchants have completed their transactions, to undergo the curing process, which converts them into "bloaters," "paste," and other breakfast dainties.

When the fish is not actually *en évidence*, there are always active indications, to say nothing of the ancient and fish-like smell pervading the whole of this quarter of the town, of the great trade done here. As we stroll through the markets, when the smacks are all out, and comparative calm reigns instead of the noise and bustle of unloading, the shouting of sailors and the clamour of the salesmen, it is

A Lowestoft Smacksman.

through a maze of barrels that we thread our way. Hundreds of kegs and casks of various sizes are piled on high, some empty, some full, either of the bright scaled fish or of the rough salt, which the men are rapidly shovelling into them from the great trucks in the sidings. Maybe, too, if it be the right season, huge, giant blocks of ice, hauled this way and that way by powerful, golden-bearded Norsemen, fill up the quay, whence they will be presently carried to the Ice House without the Market, where thousands of tons are stored away for summer use.

At almost all times the basin is full of "luggers" and trawlers, so that, like the sea itself, the vast market is ever restless; but, even if they are at their quietest here, this great centre of the fishing industry is always briskly plying the trade at Woodgers', or in the huge Raglan Works of the famous firm of Messrs. Maconochie, where four hundred men and women are employed in "curing" the lively herring of his original freshness, turning out in the course of the year many a "last" in salted, kippered, and potted forms.

FISH AND FASHION.

The temptation to explore becomes irresistible when once the way is found into this part of Lowestoft, where, by the way, it is very curious to note how the native goats self-divide themselves from the visiting sheep. For between the "old town" and aristocratic Kirkley, between the "Beach" and the Esplanade, there is not only actually the river, spanned by a swing bridge, but a great gulf of class distinction.

In the smart shops in South Lowestoft, the fine pier, the yachting community, the hotels, and glistening sands,

The Harbour Basin, Lowestoft.

gay and lively enough with children and barking dogs, barrel-organs, itinerant photographers, vendors of lollipops and fruit and seaside toys, the fishing folk apparently have no interest. They dwell, a race apart, in an atmosphere of tarred ropes, tanning, dried and drying fish, in the cobbled, hilly "scores" that run down to the Beach, conservative as to their fashions and their customs, and apparently better pleased with their quaint little "scores," across which one might stretch the arms and touch the houses on either side, than with the broad handsome new streets of fashionable Lowestoft. For them, the band on the pier, the beautiful mile-long Esplanade, the smartly-dressed visitors, have no attraction. They work hard, both men and women; they have their own occasional amusements, marry and intermarry, and live their lives out generation after generation in the same houses and "scores," and concern themselves not a whit with the modern improvements of their picturesque old town.

From the Beach, Lowestoft, regarded from an artistic point of view, looks its best. The sea, like a great hemisphere of silver in the bright sunlight, is crowded with ships and boats with glittering sails. In the sailmakers' yards the eye is dazzled with a dozen different hues of red, extraordinarily vivid in the white light; and glancing up the "scores," over which the town itself appears to rise, one catches further ruddy gleams in the slanting roofs of the cottages, strangely tumbled together on the slopes; the white High Lighthouse starting up, apparently, from among the trees which crown the height, in sharp contrast to the colouring around.

Belle Vue Park, above the "Beach," has been well-named, for the view up here is charming. This is not because, as the guide-book naïvely tells us, the Nelson Column at Yarmouth is "a prominent feature in the landscape," though it is not at all improbable that this may be regarded by many who find their way hither as a great attraction, but because the seascape is so fine from here, and the "impression" of the town and country round so thoroughly characteristic and unblurred.

Here the calm of summer evenings is often disturbed by the banging and fizzing of fireworks, the strains of a band, and other sounds of revelry. "Fairy lamps" and Chinese lanterns glow among the trees and flowers; and on such occasions the hilly glades are any but secluded spots, and the gentle murmur of the sea is completely outdone, as an aid to the utterance of lovers' vows, by squibs and wind instruments. However, the wild and breezy Denes lie just beyond, secluded and quiet and romantic enough. This is by far the finest walk in Lowestoft, but it is not found out all at once. It has to be "discovered" and, maybe, is all the better in consequence. In many ways these Denes somewhat suggest the beautiful Cromer cliffs, for the air is sweet and keen and colour abundant. Now down in heathery dells, now on gorse-covered hillocks, below which lies the sea, one may wander undisturbed among the russet bracken with the silvery-throated larks for company. Mr. Colman's charmingly situated house, "The Clyffe"—the view from which so delighted Mr. Gladstone—is just beyond here, and further still are Corton and Gunton, a couple of quaint quiet little villages.

So one would fain linger in older and quieter Lowestoft. But some irresistible spell always draws one back pierwards, to study Lowestoft as she is best understood of the holiday-

In Belle Vue Park, Lowestoft.

maker. Her town hall, clubs, free library, convalescent home and churches concern the inhabitants rather than the visitors, though it is true the latter show no small amount of interest in the fine old parish church, which

St. Margaret's Church, Lowestoft.

contains memorials of some ancient "sea-dogs," most of them native productions. As an ecclesiastical building, St. Margaret's is well worth a visit, though this entails the usual hunt after the keys; but those who like good services betake themselves on Sundays to the beautiful church in smart red-brick Kirkley, to which trim suburb all fashionable Lowestoft flocks for its accommodation.

Nobody set down at Kirkley, which is at one end of the famous Esplanade that has Lowestoft's curious but comfortable pier at the other, would doubt the fact of Lowestoft being a fashionable resort of the Eastern shores. Prosperity is stamped upon it from one end to another. It abounds with smart villas, its terraces plainly bespeak the payment of many guineas a week for accommodation therein, its gardens are trim, its inhabitants unmistakably fortune's favourites. From Kirkley Cliff come streams of smartest maidens, who make of Lowestoft pier at all hours a veritable "garden of girls," and it supplies the beach with all the most bravely-arrayed babies.

From the Royal Hotel along Wellington Terrace and the Marine Parade—where, as a well-known journalist once pointed out, the houses are so aristocratic that they have actually turned their backs on the sea, leaving their gardens only to the gaze of passers-by—to this prosperous suburb, a long line of handsome houses extends, and on summer evenings, when the sands are deserted and the time has not yet come for the excellent band to make its third and last appearance on the pier, and shadows are beginning to clothe the great forest of masts in the harbour, there is a veritable fusillade of knives and forks heard through the open windows of these trim pleasure-houses by the sea, and light laughter floats out on the warm still air, with the odour of flowers and savoury dishes. There is nothing at such a time to suggest the "tripper" in Lowestoft, but everything to indicate the presence of county families. Presently, when the pier is lighted, and the well-worn "Intermezzo" from the "Cavalleria Rusticana" and lively popular airs are borne inland from the pier-end, fashionable Lowestoft goes forth again.

Pier and Reading Rooms, Lowestoft.

The elders find after-dinner enjoyment in the excellent reading-room on the pier, and for the juniors, who are weary of watching the glow of the lights on the ships at sea, the gleam of the phosphorescent waters and the ghostly vessels, there is the charming promenade that leads them beyond Kirkley to Pakefield, high up on the cliffs, whence they can look down on the brightly-lighted town and the grand sweep of sea.

Comparative calm reigns in the town during the afternoons. The sands are, of course, always more or less lively. The children desire nothing better than to burrow in the deep, glistening beach, and the excursionist never slumbers or sleeps; but Lowestoft visitors of the approved pattern go elsewhere after luncheon. Oulton Broad, alive with yachts of all sizes, lures one to its beautiful waters, to enjoy a scene of wonderful brightness and animation. The tiny steam-yachts and wherries form a positive fleet on this great curving sheet of deep green water, and one may be almost as certain of meeting with friends here as in the Row when the London season is at its height. Everybody seems bent on aquatic pleasure. There are small rowing boats ever darting in and out among the larger craft, perky little steam yachts, making more fuss than if they were Atlantic liners, solemn wherries gliding noiselessly along like marine ghosts, grimy colliers and fishing smacks in picturesque confusion on this great mass of water.

For those who are piscatorially inclined, Oulton is a great attraction. The gentle angler is well looked after hereabouts, especially at the Wherry Hotel and at Mutford Bridge, where tackle, bait, and punts are supplied in profusion; of water, fresh and salt, there is certainly no lack, and those who know their way about, and recognise how much more easily fish will rise " for a consideration," may discover the whereabouts of fair-sized roach and perch.

There is, a mile or so distant from Oulton, an exceedingly pretty, though small, piece of water called Flixton, which the more adventurous spirits seek out; but it is Fritton Lake that is the chief centre of attraction to all within reach of its beautiful waters. Of all the broads this is by far the most lovely, for not only does it cover an area of sixty acres, but its surroundings are of exceptional beauty. Fringed by birches on either side, and enclosed by the woods and groves of Herringfleet Hall and Somerleyton Park, it is, on a hot summer's day, the most dreamful retreat imaginable. To float under the overhanging trees and lazily angle for the golden-scaled rudd, or to ramble along the banks to Somerleyton—an ideally beautiful village —are methods of idling away the hours that can be strongly recommended. Somerleyton can be by no means missed, for the drive along from Lowestoft is one of the pleasantest that can be taken. "Long fields of barley and of rye, that clothe the wold and meet the sky," glisten in the sunlight, and alternate with the heathery commons and sweet Suffolk lanes, luxuriant with foliage and flowers and overhung with wild apple trees. The ubiquitous mill is always well to the fore and in perpetual motion, and the little village, when it is reached, is "quite a picture" in itself.

Sir Savile Crossley throws his house and grounds open to visitors on certain days, and there is much to be seen without and within. The Hall of Somerleyton, which has been rebuilt and is a very fine building, has had many owners. Lord Sydney Godolphin Osborne held it in the first part of the century, but he found it worth while to part with it, in 1844, to Sir Morton Peto, who greatly enlarged and beautified the park, which possesses one of the finest lime-tree avenues in England.

But of excursions from Lowestoft one might write indefinitely, for in every direction there is something to be seen either by land or water. One may potter up the Waveney to Beccles, one of the most charmingly situated towns in Suffolk, with a fine church and some interesting old manors in the vicinity; altogether a quaint old town, with richly-

Kirkley Cliffs, Lowestoft.

tinted buildings tumbled together by the water side, sleepy, and peaceful, and picturesque, or go further along to sleepier little leafy Bungay, almost hidden in trees.

There are the remnants of a once famous castle here, that belonged to the turbulent Bigods, Earls of Suffolk. They seem to have been always warring with somebody, and were tolerably sure of their power and the resisting strength of this particular castle, and that of Framlingham according to the old song.

> "'Were I in my strong Castle of Bungay,
> Upon the waters of Waveney,
> I would not care for the King of Cockney,
> Nor all his braverie.'"

But Henry II., whom Hugh Bigod thus contemptuously defies, was not easily frightened, for

> "He marshalled his merrie men all,
> And through Suffolk they marched with speed;
> And they marched to Lord Bigod's Castle-wall,
> And knocked at his gate, I rede.
>   'Sir Hugh, of the Castle of Bungay,
> Come doff your cap to the King of Cockney.'"

At the sight of the king and his "merrie men" the boastful Bigod appears to have behaved like the bold baron of burlesque.

> "He trembled and shook like a May Mawther,
> And wished himself away.
>   'Were I out of my Castle of Bungay,
> And beyond the River Waveney,
> I would not care for the King of Cockney.'"

> "Sir Hugh took three-score sacks of gold
> And flung them over the wall,
> Said he 'Go your ways in old Mischief's name,
> Yourself and your merrie men all,
> But leave me my Castle of Bungay,
> Upon the river Waveney,
> And I'll pay shot to the King of Cockney.'"

Coming back from Beccles, on the way to Yarmouth, there is another and more interesting castle, familiar to all explorers of the Broads, and a favourite haunt of all Yarmouth visitors. Burgh Castle is a splendid specimen of Norman flint work, and is weirdly picturesque, standing on the dark marshy shores of the oozy Yare, with great broad-bosomed Breydon, joined by the junction of the Yare and Waveney, stretching before it. Yarmouth must be seen, but Breydon water tempts one sorely to sail on through the lovely string of lakes that constitute "Broadland," whose beauties and delights are not unveiled to the hasty excursionist.

CHAPTER XVIII.

THE SAINT'S SEPULCHRE.

IN an early autumn, as the train puffs lazily along the little branch line from Mark's Tey to Bury St. Edmund's, Bishop Hall's description of Suffolk as "a sweet and civil county," seems to be a trifle bald and unconvincing. It might have been equally said of tranquil Essex, since it conveys to the mind no idea of the varied scenery, the pleasant prospects, the fertile valleys, the great breadths of corn fields and rich woodlands of Constable and Gainsborough's country. Just here, on a bright September morning, when the autumn tints are beginning to flush the groves of Long Melford and Lavenham and Bradfield, the birthplace and last resting-place of Arthur Young, this episcopal commendation of the country seems to err decidedly on the side of moderation. Perhaps the good Bishop of Norwich, who, when he was rector of Hawstead, must have known this tract of country well, was not an enthusiast on the subject of scenery; but it is, of course, only fair to his descriptive powers to take into consideration the changes that must have taken place in the landscape in the four hundred years that have almost elapsed since Lady Drury gave him the living of the village that lies under the hills between Whelnetham and Ixworth.

Through the winding valley of the Stour, as the train creeps leisurely from station to station, apparently urged forward to Bury by no consideration of time, one has a succession of charming pastoral scenes, even more beautiful now than in early spring, when the tenderest tones are on the trees, and the ground is bright with the green and gold of acres of cowslips and king-cups. Then nature, like a young beginner, seems to be only dabbling with primary colours, now she is sure and prodigal of her tints. Yellow and red and green and orange are splashed recklessly on everything and with excellent effect. The hedges are gay in gold and red. On the ridges of the bare, brown fields stand the rich, new stacks of corn; and the pheasants, in full plumage, gleam in the sunlight as they rise from the ground, startled by the passing train. Presently there is a patch of vivid green where the turnips are coming on, then a great mass of golden oaks, glittering against the dark firs in the background; the white sheep graze peacefully on the hillsides, the rabbits scatter in all directions at the sound of the whistle. Suddenly the scene changes, the colours fade, and here is a study in grey and silver. The low-lying meadows in the valley are flooded already with early autumn rains, and the geese, heedless of the approaching feast of St. Michael, and the sage and onions in the neighbouring cottage gardens, dabble and "sossle" in the silvery pools.

It is tantalising to think of the churches and the old halls that are hidden away behind these trees, to know that across the meadows and fields lies the way to some of the most interesting of all the villages in this "sweet and civil country." Here are Bures, where Edmund, King and Martyr, the Patron Saint of Bury, was crowned; Sudbury, with its three old churches and memories of

Gainsborough; and picturesque Long Melford, in the
fifteenth century "the seat of a flourishing clothing
trade," and now famous for its magnificent flint and
white stone church, built by the wealthy clothiers. It is
hard indeed to get further than Melford, for besides
its fine church, its attractions comprise the moated Hall,
where, in 1578, the Speaker entertained Elizabeth, "as
virtuous and regular a house as any in the land;"
Kentwell Hall, one of the most perfect specimens of
Elizabethan architecture in England; and Boxted Hall,
a grandly picturesque old Tudor mansion, enough to
keep the antiquarian and romancist busy for a week.
And beyond is Lavenham, another centre of the woollen
trade in the fifteenth century, of which a splendid
memorial exists in its church, chiefly built, like that of
Melford, by rich merchants. And, further on still, the
magnificent ancestral home of the Rushbrookes, another
well-preserved and moated Tudor hall, where, too, the
ubiquitous Elizabeth, who must have been on a perpetual round of country house visits, was entertained
"two several times," with the French ambassadors, by
Sir Robert Jermyn. Through Bury are Culford and
Euston, Hengrave and West Stow Halls, Ixworth and
Ampton and Ickworth, houses and parks of extreme
interest and beauty; and thus the "bright little town"
lies sandwiched between fine old country seats and
picturesque villages.

Bury is one of those places that have not to wait to
make their effect on the stranger. The bright, cheerful
aspect of its broad, clean streets and pleasant old houses
at once creates a favourable impression, but its spick-and-spanness is never aggressive. It is counteracted by
the ruins, the historical churches, the time-worn
buildings, the associations of this most interesting old

town, sleepy and quiet enough now, but once the chief centre of religious life in England. Kings and bishops have rattled under the old Abbey gate, parliaments have been held here, and so magnificent was the Abbey church, that Herbert de Losinga, for ever appearing in the pages of East Anglian ecclesiastical history, made desperate efforts to remove the See from Thetford hither, but its abbot was not prepared to let his position slip away from him. An appeal to Rome settled the matter in the abbot's favour, and Herbert de Losinga, as we know, moved on to Norwich, "taking it out" of the lord abbot of Bury, however, by borrowing the land tax given to his monastery for its further enrichment, and building Norwich Cathedral with the funds, which, it is needless to say, he never repaid. They had splendid quarters, these old monks, in this cheerful little corner of Sunrise-Land; for the town stands on a hill, looking straight into the face of the rising sun, and on its eastern slope, at the foot of which flows the peaceful little Lark, and its tributary, the Linnet, are the remains of the famous monastic pile which Sigeberht founded in 631. From Bury to Dunwich there led a Roman road, and having provided for the spiritual needs of the latter city when he held his court, Sigeberht turned his attention along "the King's Highway" to Bury, and dedicated to Our Lady the beautiful church, afterwards to be the shrine of the saintly Edmund, and the wealthiest and most richly-decorated monastery in England, Glastonbury alone excepted. Hither to pay their vows came the Confessor, Henry I., Henry II., and Richard I., who made a pilgrimage to Bury before starting for the Holy Land. John was here in 1203. Henry III. contracted his fatal illness whilst holding a Parliament in Bury. Edward II. spent

The Norman Tower, Bury.

the Christmas of 1326 here. More than a hundred years later, another Parliament was held in the town by Henry VI., the scene being commemorated by Shakespeare in the third act of "Henry the Sixth." It has still its royal visitors, for the Prince of Wales is a frequent guest at Culford Hall, Lord Cadogan's seat, just without the town, and Bury was one of the last towns to entertain the young Duke of Clarence before his death in 1892.

Of the grand old monastic buildings, the Abbey Gate, a beautiful specimen of decorated work; St. James's; the splendid Norman Tower, erected as an entrance to the cemetery of St. Edmund; St. Mary's, and the picturesque old Abbot's Bridge over the Lark, alone remain. Within the Botanic Gardens, on the site of the great court of the Abbey, where the nurses and children of Bury's smart residents take their daily airing under the beautiful trees, there are still a few grey fragments of walls, the Abbot's Bridge close to the East Gate of the town, and the indications of the great church of St. Edmund, in which were discovered and re-interred, in 1772, the remains of the Duke of Exeter, second son of John of Gaunt. It was in this church, too, that the great meeting of the barons took place in 1214, which has for ever made Bury sacred to those who value the liberty of the English race. Langton and the barons, weary of John's tyranny and tricks, met here at Bury, on St. Edmund's day, November 20th, under cover of paying their annual devotions at the Saint's shrine. In the church, the Archbishop read to the eager multitude a rough draft of the charter of liberties he had drawn up, and standing before the high altar, he received the oaths and protestations of the barons to maintain their confederacy until the king should, by sealed charter, ratify these articles. Thus it came about that Magna Charta was signed at Runnymede, and that the Saint's sepulchre has become, as it were, a shrine of English rights. The names of the twenty-five daring baronial spirits who were appointed to keep John up to the mark, are inscribed, with the following, upon a tablet affixed to one of the piers which remain of the eastern transept of the old church :—

> Where the rude buttress totters to its fall,
> And ivy mantles o'er the crumbling wall;
> Where e'en the skilful eye can scarcely trace
> The once high Altar's lowly resting-place—
> Let patriotic fancy muse awhile
> Amid the ruins of this ancient pile.

Six weary centuries have passed away,
Palace and Abbey moulder in decay;
Cold Death enshrouds the learned and the brave;
LANGTON, FITZ-WALTER slumber in the grave.
But still we read in deathless records how
The high-souled Priest confirmed the Barons' vow;
And FREEDOM, unforgetful still recites,
This second birthplace of our Native RIGHTS.

The Abbot's Bridge, Bury, from the Gardens.

A soothing air of peace and piety pervades the gardens and the surrounding walks. Even the children, playing in the long avenue of ash trees over the graves of the royal and prelatical sleepers, seem subdued and awed. The grey towers of St. James's and St. Mary's solemnly guard the scene, which is curiously impressive and picturesque in its way. From yonder red-brick building, just seen through the trees, come the recipients of Clopton's bounty, in their quaint, old-fashioned plum-coloured coats with gilt buttons and high-crowned hats, to potter about under the trees, and give an old-world touch to the picture. But there are ghosts enough within these holy precincts to bear one company if one but seeks them out.

In St. Mary's, the roof of which beautiful church is perhaps the finest specimen of open timber work in the world, sleeps Mary Tudor, in whom one cannot but take a romantic interest, as she appears again and again to the rambler through Sunrise-Land. At Ipswich, we live with her, as it were, in the early days of her marriage with Charles Brandon, Duke of Suffolk. We can picture her still quite young and full of life, proud of her gallant young lover-husband, who had won her heart when sent by her brother, Henry VIII., to fetch her from the French court after the death of Louis XII., her doddering old spouse. We can imagine the little scenes which ensued between her and the irate Henry when her marriage with the handsome young ambassador was declared, the journeyings to and from Henham and West Stow, and the last scene of all, when she came to be laid here at St. Edmund's shrine. At the dissolution of the monastery, the remains of Mary Tudor were removed to St. Mary's church, where they now lie beneath an altar-stone, and under the window erected by our present

Queen to the Royal lady's memory. In the Athenæum opposite, some of the hair clipped from her head when the tomb was opened over a hundred years ago may still be seen.

If one went no further than these precincts, but wandered in and out of St. James's and St. Mary's, the cemetery of St. Edmund, now a favourite walk of the townsfolk, where formerly miracle plays were performed, and in which the Chapel of the Charnel yet is to be seen, Bury would be still one of the most delightful old towns in East Anglia; for here within these few grey walls and shady gardens are more historical memories and antiquities than half-a-dozen other towns could offer. But it has attractions without. There is Moyse's Hall, a former "Jew's House," or as Dr. Margoliouth thinks, a synagogue of the period of Henry I., and, until recently, used as the Police-station; there is the Guildhall, which has a fine Early English porch; the remains of the old St. Saviour's Hospital, where, says tradition, the Duke of Gloucester was done to death; the modernised Grammar School, founded by Edward VI., and famous for the number of bishops it has produced.

Bury, too, has dear associations for the lovers of Dickens. In Abbeygate Street, now lined with smart shops, was the ladies' school, familiar to all readers of Pickwick; and with the excellent "Angel Hotel" opposite the Abbey Gate, Mr. Pickwick and Weller were well acquainted. The pump is gone under which Sam had his "half-penny shower-bath," but the spot where the sanctimonious Job Trotter sat is still pointed out.

It is curious to note the strong Reformation flavour still clinging about the little town where in the three last years of Mary's reign no less than twelve martyrs blazed "for the Faith." The names of Ridley and Hooper and Latimer recur again and again; indeed, Ridley and Hooper's Tannery confronts one at the eastern entrance to the town, and every other family seems to possess a small Latimer or Ridley among its boys. Evidently the old Bury folk did not stop at half measures in any of their undertakings. Down ~~Eastern~~ Street, on the old bridge, there formerly stood a ducking-stool, where they brought to book any ladies whose tongues were abnormally long, or fingers light; and according to the old records it was used with tolerable frequency. And the Bury men were apparently well kept in check too, for one reads of one lady who regularly beat her lord when he differed from her on political questions. On the wall of the Chapel of the Charnel is a tablet setting forth how one Sarah Hodge, suffered death by *hanging*, in 1800, for the terrible crime of admitting her young man into her mistress's house, and "becoming the instrument at his hands of the crimes of robbery and housebreaking."

Save on market day, when round the old Jews' synagogue in the great market-place there are the usual signs of provincial life, a glorious stillness reigns in these bright old streets. Bury is proud of its nobility and gentry. There has been no period in its history when kings and nobles have not been frequently within its gates, and even now it basks in aristocratic favour; for the Marquis of Bristol at Ickworth, Lord Cadogan at Culford, the Duke of Grafton at Euston Hall, are all within hail; and the peace of these old-fashioned thoroughfares is only disturbed by the rumble of well-appointed broughams, and the simple-looking little "traps" of the county families of the neighbourhood, except on market day, when the farmers' boys and the thick-shod country folk wake the echoes. The days have gone by when Bury had its fairs, "where used to assemble a great concourse

of ladies and gentlemen from various parts of England."
Mary Tudor is stated to have held quite a court within
the abbey grounds on the occasion of "Bury Fair,"
which, according to other authorities, literally partook
of the nature of a matrimonial market. The knights
and gentlemen's daughters of the whole of East Anglia

In the Gardens, Bury.

who came hither in "infinite number," must on the whole have had "a real good time"; for the fair "seldom concludes," says the "Magna Britannia," "without some considerable matches," and in addition to the "comedy, which is acted every night," there were assemblies each evening in the neighbouring houses. The daughters of Sunrise-Land

and its knight-errants certainly do not now depend on Bury Fair for the arrangement of their matrimonial little plans, nor are assemblies and comedies frequent. Bury is bright and interesting, but extremely decorous. An occasional visit from Mr. Toole, a meeting of the Antiquarian or Archæological Association, a concert, or a Primrose League entertainment, are now its chief excitements; and it is probable that Mary Tudor and the old Abbots now at rest within the Abbey precincts would find the town rather slower though not less select than in the days when minstrels and mountebanks performed on Angel Hill to a goodly company, and kings held parliaments within its walls.

CHAPTER XIX.

CAMBRIDGE.

TO see Cambridge as it deserves to be seen, to appreciate to the full its stately buildings, its beautiful leafy avenues, its antiquities, its uniqueness—for there is no other English town like it—it must be actually lived in, not for a week, but for months. To rush through this famous University town is to waste splendid sight-seeing material, and to receive but a blurred impression of what should be, and is indeed to those who know it well and love its ancient stones, its turrets and chapels, its towers and narrow courts and historic buildings, a most beautiful and enduring picture of a town which has no parallel in the world except Oxford. Yet it is this hasty impression of Cambridge that many have to obtain, thankful that they have even thus been permitted to take a fleeting glance at such buildings as the imposing Fitzwilliam Museum, and the grand Chapel of King's College, and to fall but for a few hours under the spell that overhangs this centre of learning. Cambridge is not to be lightly nor unadvisedly described. Many volumes are needed to fully tell of its glories, and even such a minute descriptive work as Cooper's "Memorials of Cambridge," but partially deals with this vast subject. It is therefore but a photographic view on a small scale, an impression at best indistinct, that can be gained by a brief survey on an autumn day when the town is waking up again after its long summer sleep, and the colleges are once more alive with their "men."

Cambridge station is one of the very best on the G.E.R. system. Always remarkable for their speed and accurate time, the G.E.R. trains which come hither seem to run into the ever-cheerful station from all parts of England

King's College.

with astounding rapidity and punctuality. And not only is Cambridge station famous for its train service, but it enjoys moreover the enviable reputation of having one of the best refreshment rooms to be found in the kingdom, a reputation which keeps green its memory in the minds of many travellers. It is at all times more or less sprinkled with parsons and undergraduates; but when the "Long" is over, and Regent Street echoes with the rattle of cabs bringing "Sophs up again," and the usual stock of "freshmen," this most attractive station becomes a splendid observatory from which to study John Bull, junior, his pastors, masters, and parents. It is generally under the parental wing that "freshmen" nervously make their entry into the University town, and under the same guidance that they make a tour of the "sights," which, a few months later, they so proudly show with much display of knowledge of "'Varsity" history and manners to their fond and duly awed relations. Their sisters and "cousins," only just released themselves from the strict surveillance of girl-school-life, are amazed to see the way the "men" stroll in and out of each other's colleges, and to find that they know almost as much about them as if they were at each and all of the seventeen. It is not, perhaps, so much a matter of surprise to the elders, though, that Tom's and Dick's and Harry's bills are long, when they see the Cambridge shops, which seem at a first glance to be occupied chiefly by tailors, outfitters, and bootmakers. Presumably the sweet girl-graduates of Newnham and Girton on the outskirts of the town, who so frequently outrival the undergraduates in the "Little-Go" and Tripos, both mathematical and classical, do not run bills at the local dressmakers and drapers and livery-stable keepers. In this, as in respect of work, they are decidedly a force for good in a University town, as the authorities readily admit.

Though the day be gloomy and the glory of summer departed, yet an impression of brightness is gleaned on the very threshold of the town. There is colour of a kind in the grand old buildings and churches and in the streets. Trumpington Street, the first point to be made for, since there is the famous Fitzwilliam Museum

The Entrance, Trinity College.

— with its splendid marble staircase, its "old masters," and famous library—is full of it. For opposite King's College, whose magnificent Chapel dominates the town of which it is decidedly the most beautiful building, is King's Parade; and here it is the "custom of an afternoon" of Dons' wives and Proctors' pretty daughters to promenade in their smartest attire, while the lads in their college "blazers" of various and frequently vivid hues, mingle with the crowd on their way to and from the river, and fill the scene with movement and colour. And by-and-bye, when the college walks are reached, it becomes almost dazzling. Cambridge is very proud of the trees in these gardens. The country round, fen-like in character, is so bare and flat and treeless that the magnificent chestnuts of Trinity, and the limes, yews, and elms on either side the Cam are doubly dear to the dwellers in the town. And how indescribably beautiful they are on an autumn morning, when, tinged with gold and red and orange, they make a background for the grey bridges and colleges of Magdalene and St. John's, Trinity, Clare, King's, and Queen's. To Wordsworth, devoted as he was to nature, they were a great joy, and Gray has sung of them in his sweet and simple fashion in the beautiful "Installation Ode."

> "Ye brown o'er-arching groves,
> That contemplation loves,
> Where willowy Camus lingers with delight;
> Oft at the blush of dawn,
> I trod your level lawn;
> Oft woo'd the gleam of Cynthia silver-bright,
> In cloisters dim, far from the haunts of folly,
> With Freedom by my side, and soft-eyed Melancholy."

Is not the garden of Christ's, too, another of the sights of Cambridge by reason of its trees, and more especially of the famous mulberry which Milton, who was at Christ's for seven years, is said to have planted? Here the trees make a leafy screen to the ancient fish-pond, now converted into a bath, wherein, with the busts of Milton and that eminent Platonist, Cudworth, looking amiably down upon them, the undergraduates disport themselves in the early morning in company with the few remaining carp, one of whom enjoys a reputation for antiquity that varies according to the veracity or mendacity of one's cicerone. The "college groves and tributary walks" of St. John's with their magnificent elms, seen to perfection from the picturesque bridge, and the equally beautiful and, maybe, even more fascinating avenue seen from Clare Bridge, make an everlasting impression upon the sight-seer. Having but once stood on Clare Bridge, or on that of St. John's, one is never likely to forget the calm beauty of the scene that lies in view. And how often in after life must it recur again and again to the memory of the lads, who, during that happy period when they were "up," learned to note its every aspect?

It is small wonder when the staircase and the art treasures of the Fitzwilliam have been seen that it is to Trinity everyone hastens on coming to Cambridge; in whose quadrangles, Bacon and Dryden, Isaac Newton, George Herbert, Byron, Macaulay, and Tennyson, among other distinguished men, have conned their books as students within its famous walls. If one went no further there would be enough here to delight and interest for a whole day. Its magnificent Great Court, in which statesmen and poets and great divines have walked, and "Master Herodotus," whose father is the Master, and whose mother was the Senior Wrangler of a recent year, is now daily aired in company with a couple of baby brothers; its fine Chapel full of memorials of Trinity alumni, whose organ is perhaps the finest in England, and chiefly its

Clare College and Bridge.

superb library are its "sights;" but like the Chinese
puzzle boxes, wherein one is enclosed within the other,
so here, at Trinity, are there treasures and interests and
"sights" within "sights." In the library, for instance,
at whose threshold one pauses in wonder and admiration, who shall determine when its interests have been
exhausted? Naturally, it is to Thorwaldsen's beautiful
statue of Byron, to the original manuscripts, written in
Milton's own clear hand, of that beautiful threnody,
"Lycidas," and of "Paradise Lost," sketched out as a
tragedy, to the Tennysonian manuscripts written, too,
with exquisite neatness, that one first gravitates; but
there are as well, it must be remembered, Byron's first
letter, in cramped, boyish hand; Newton's correspondence
with Cotes, his hair, his compasses, and other relics.
There are Elzevirs and Aldines, before which the true
book-lover stands in lowly reverence, while even the
book-shelves themselves, carved by Grinling Gibbons,
claim attention. It is difficult indeed to get further on
a tour through Cambridge when Trinity is reached and
time is short. But if your guide be an undergraduate,
he will not suffer you to pause here. He is certain to
hurry you to the cloister to play upon you the old trick
of the knocker on the bottom door, which may be knocked
by stamping on a certain flag-stone at the top of the
court; he will have the "billiard table" plot to show,
Tennyson's and Byron's rooms, the hall and the vast
kitchen. And there are still St. John's beautiful Chapel
and Hall to be visited, the Senate House, where honour
and glory or "plucking" awaits those who enter, and
Queen's, the most picturesque and mediæval of all the
colleges, founded by Margaret of Anjou. Here, in Erasmus
Court, the great scholar lived in the rooms in the tower.
In the secluded elm groves whence one looks back on the

quaint old Lodge of the President, in the long, silent galleries and cloisters, time seems to have paused, and were it not that from out the dwarf doorways of the smartly-decorated old rooms, lads in " blazers " and football jerseys, riding boots and other modern attire come bounding out with the strange low cry uttered on two notes, which is

Part of St. John's College and Bridge of Sighs.

the regulation "'Varsity" call, it would need no great effort of imagination to fancy that one were living back in the fifteenth century, and that Erasmus might at any moment descend his turret stairs and come for a walk on the terrace, and grumble to Fisher, as yet possessed of his head, of the quality of Cambridge beer. In each and every college one might thus linger to revive memories of the past and live again with ghosts of pious founders and famous scholars; but when a "snap-shot" of the University has to be taken it is only possible, when thus much has been seen, to visit each hall of learning for its special feature only, thus seeking out Magdalene for its Pepys' Library, Jesus for its chapel, the Cromwell portrait at Sidney Sussex, the Christopher Wren Chapel at Pembroke, and the library at Emmanuel.

It is when the shadows are beginning to steal through the oriel windows of the old buildings, and the lads in their gay coats who have been canoeing under the golden chestnuts and purpling elders that overhang the river have gone into their rooms again to brew tea and read awhile before dinner, and King's Parade and Trumpington Street are less lively, just before choral evensong is sung, and the bright-faced little choir-boys quaintly garbed in tall hats and gowns with which their broad Eton collars look so strangely incongruous, have passed through to prepare for service—that King's Chapel, dedicated to Our Lady and St. Nicholas, by Henry VI., its founder, is best seen. Then there is that solemn stillness in the air, that beautiful softening light of the gloaming that best attunes the mind to a just appreciation of the beauty and magnificence of the chapel in which one involuntarily keeps silence. Presently the myriads of tapers glimmer against the dark choir stalls, the perfectly trained voices of the boys rise to and die away in "that branching roof

> "Self-poised, and scooped into ten thousand cells,
> Where light and shade repose, where music dwells;
> Like thoughts whose very music yieldeth proof
> That they were born for immortality,"

Boys of King's Chapel Choir.

the pictured stories of saints and holy men in the magnificent windows grow wholly indistinct, and one steals away awed by the impressiveness and solemn grandeur of the scene.

One goes but a very little way in Cambridge before Hobson becomes a prominent feature. Hobson, indeed, may be said to pervade the town. The celebrated old Cambridge carrier appears in all directions, and whatever "Hobson's choice" may have meant, there is very little choice now about Hobson in Cambridge. One encounters him first, so to say, in Trumpington Street, through which the springs run from the picturesque conduit erected chiefly by the public spirit and generosity of this curiously progressive old carrier of the sixteenth century. Hobson was a man born out of due season. If he had lived now-a-days, he would probably have been a millionaire peer, and Cambridge would probably have been the richer by another College. He saw his chance, however, in the sixteenth century, and having taken the tide of his fortunes at the flood, and amassed a neat little sum by letting out saddle-horses to the lads, he applied it to good uses. It is to Hobson the Spinning-House owes its foundation, and the Corporation of Cambridge as well as the poor of several neighbouring villages have reason to be grateful to him. Taking all this into consideration, we can forgive his prevalence, though he is apt, truth to tell, to become a trifle of a bore in the course of a walk through the town, where streets and tavern signs, portraits and inscriptions, keep his memory green.

There is a general tendency to repetition in Cambridge. It is only necessary to mention Caius in the way that it is commonly pronounced to produce the time-honoured "chestnut" about "Bunch of Caius," a story probably told at least once in every one of the three hundred and sixty-five days of the year. "'Varsity" slang and "'Varsity" stories are soon acquired; the "men" are so free with the former, and the latter are so very limited. Down by the boat-houses at Commencement one may learn it all, when the banks of the Cam are brightened by the presence of gaily-dressed girls, who are easily infected by the one and amused by the other. They think it immensely clever when somebody explains that All Saints is generally called "St. Opposites," because it faces Trinity and Christ's, and they are duly impressed by the importance of the "men," and their self-coined diction. "St. Opposites," by the way, is one of the new churches of Cambridge. For ecclesiastical antiquities, one must go to the funny round St. Sepulchre's, to Saxon St. Benedict's, the burial-place of the irrepressible Hobson, with its most remarkable Romanesque tower, to the University Church of Great St. Mary's, or drive out

On the Backs, Cambridge.

to the scanty remains of Barnwell Priory or Sturbridge Chapel. In the matter of drives and walks, the Oxonians have a decided advantage over the Cantabs. Cambridgeshire is not the most beautiful of the Eastern Counties. In a county which can dignify the Gog-Magogs with the name of hills much cannot be scenically expected. The camp of the summit of these "mounds" is of interest, however, as having been in occupation of the Romans and the scene of the legend re-told by Sir Walter Scott in the "Host's Tale" in "Marmion," just as Trumpington, which is, however, not wholly unpicturesque, figures in Chaucer's "Reve's Tale." "Trompynton," not far from "Cambrigge." past the Botanic Gardens, and the St. Neot's Road with Madingley Hall as the bourne, make pleasant enough walks for the lads on summer evenings; but when the services of Hobson's successors are called into requisition, and saddle-horses and traps are out, it is Newmarketwards through Cherry Hinton, a colony of fruit-farmers, and Fulbourne and Bottisham and Six Mile Bottom, that they take their way. Or, maybe, to picturesque Audley End, where Elizabeth found her way, and was, in 1578, visited by a deputation from Cambridge, who presented her with "the New Testament in Greek," and a "pair of perfumed and embroidered gloves," which evidently were much more to her fancy, since it is specially recorded that "Her Majesty smelling unto them, put them half waie upon hir hands."

Near to the Botanic Gardens (mentioned above) are the handsome buildings of the Leys School. Its many departments, its numerous athletic associations, its fine architecture, ought to interest all visitors to Cambridge. The school was opened in 1875, and it has admirably maintained the object for which it was formed, namely, to provide a superior education on the most liberal and broadest Christian principles.

To do Cambridge justice, it is not a place from which one desires, as they would say on the other side of the Atlantic, to "excurt." Its interior fascination and attractions are great. It has its theatre to which excellent companies come in term-time, its streets are broad and electric lighted by night, its shops are attractive, and where will finer or more interesting buildings be found?

CHAPTER XX.

A FANE IN THE FENS.

WHEN journeying from Cambridge to the "City of Eels" by way of the road, the wonderful fen country, of which Ely has been called the fortress, is seen to the greatest advantage. The turnpike road lies through the most famous part of this remarkable district of England, which, unless the sun be shining over the tracts of corn, that flourishes mightily in this rich, peaty soil, has, as Carlyle said of it, "all a clammy look, clayey and boggy," and anything but cheering to the eye. But withal there is a vast amount of interest in it. It is marvellous, as one bowls along the firm road, with rich pasture lands and fertile corn-fields on either side, to think of these 680,000 acres as an inland sea; to picture it all a noxious swamp, infested with wild-fowl and poisonous insects, overgrown with rank weeds and reeds; a weird dark waste of waters, whirling and swirling muddily in and out the channels, through the whole of this great province.

The wonderful transformation that has been wrought can only be realised by driving through Fenland, the richest pasturage in England, and seeing it as it is, with its well-tilled fields, its green meadows filled with sleek, handsome cattle, and its prosperous little villages; and thus comparing it on the spot with the vast morass that it was when the gentle St. Etheldreda, taking the largest of the islands that rose here and there above the dismal waters, founded thereon the monastery, which eventually became in some respects the most beautiful of all the English cathedrals.

Even in those days—the date of St. Etheldreda's first building is A.D. 672—the monks indifferently struggled to grasp the land from the clutches of the waters that were ever rushing over and "drowning" the district, and, after the fashion of the "holy friar," they managed fairly well to increase their revenues by their farming operations. The haggard, half savage, stunted little "yellow bellies," amphibious creatures, who dragged out a miserable existence by damming up the waters and catching the fish and fowl with which they abounded, were not "in it," of course, with the monks, and rather resented than otherwise any attempts

Ely from the North-East.

to retrieve the swampy land from the waters, whence they derived their subsistence and a liberal supply of rheumatism, ague, and low fever.

There is no more interesting reading of its kind than the history of the ultimate reclamation of the fens. Successive generations of engineers, from the time St. Etheldreda, with her nuns and her monks settled here even unto this day, have had a hand in the work; for even now, when the waters have been rolled back for three centuries and the land flourishes, it is only by constant care and scientific thought and skill that Fenland is still kept within the grasp of her sons.

The dissolution of the monasteries, however, brought about the dissolution of the Fenlands, and their condition was so lamentable that James I., who, like the rest of his family was given to taking from rather than giving to the country, declared that he would drain them at his own expense rather than suffer them to remain as they were. This desperate resolve was not carried out, however. Instead, he called in the great Dutch engineer, Vermuyden, stirred up the Commissioners of Sewers of Norfolk, who could not come to terms with the Dutchman, and finally excited the landowners of Fenland, chief among whom was Sir Francis Bedford, to undertake the drainage of the Level. There were no leading articles to criticise the scheme, no evening or local papers to find fault with it and predict its failure; but Vermuyden met with plenty of opposition all the same. The "fen-slodgers" reviled him; the whole county revolted against the employment of foreign labour, and, finally, Cromwell, then member for Cambridge, and living at Ely, in the little house still standing by the side of St. Mary's Church, set his heel down on the work; and it was not until after the Civil War that Vermuyden was able to carry his scheme to a successful close. There has been a great deal done since. Rennie, Talfourd, and others, have followed in the Dutchman's wake; but to him will ever belong the greatest glory of this vast undertaking.

Of Ely it may almost be said that there is nothing but the Cathedral. This magnificent church, the largest, the most varied, and perhaps the most beautiful in England, is Ely *tout seul*. One feels, indeed, that nothing else is needed here. Towering, as it does, over the surrounding district for miles, it of course completely dominates the mere handful of houses and village shops that constitute the "city," and nestle, as it were, beneath the shadow of the great grey pile. Everything is dwarfed beside it; there is literally nothing to distract attention from the great object of all tourists' visit to the city, of which St. Etheldreda is the patron saint.

Ely Porta, by which the park leading to the new precincts is entered, is not, of course, to be overlooked, for it dates back to the latter end of the fourteenth century. The aggressively new red-brick Theological College and Hereward Hall, nearly opposite, must keenly feel their position, in face of this grim and grey old structure, that has held its own for centuries, and trained within its walls generations of boys. It was bluff King Hal himself who founded the famous King's Grammar School, held within the rooms of this ancient gateway; but the scholars long since outgrew the accommodation provided in its fine old vaulted rooms, whence the *raison d'être* of the modern Hereward Hall, opened with the Theological College in 1881. Within the precincts the Deanery, the quaint dormer-windowed and richly-toned residences of the canons—once part of the monastic buildings—and the peaceful old-world gardens thereto attached have a fascination of their own. They attune one, so to speak, to the Cathedral.

The Bishop's Palace, a good example of the Tudor style,

is likewise too interesting to be passed by, though its position opposite the striking west front of the Cathedral, and in face of the wonderful Galilee Porch, renders it liable to merely passing notice. Of that porch whole chapters might be written. It has been said that there is nothing

West Front of Ely Cathedral shewing the Galilee.

like it in the world, and this is certainly true of the Octagon within. If there were nothing else to see here, save this porch and the Octagon, Ely would still be a corner of Eastern England to which all lovers of the beautiful would find their way; but in the Galilee we take but the initial step towards the architectural glories of this most beautiful

Cathedral. When on a bright summer afternoon the western doors are open, and, standing in the sunlight on the Palace Green, one looks through the porch's richly-moulded arches that spring one from another up the vast Norman nave, is there anything that can compare for grandeur and perspective effect with the view? If only it were possible to take away some of the hideous stained windows from the transepts there would be not a single jarring note from end to end of this vast and marvellous building. But though this discord has been irretrievably made, there is much for which to be really thankful as one surveys the modern work within the cathedral. It underwent restoration at a dangerous period; for the work of rescuing it from its deplorable state of neglect began in 1847, yet there is nothing but praise to be given to the late Sir Gilbert Scott and his successors for its present rich and reverent condition.

Somewhat of the glory that has been added to it is at once apparent on entering the western tower, the ceiling of which was painted by the late Mr. Le Strange of Hunstanton Hall, to whom the interior beauty of old Hunstanton Church is likewise due. Death, unfortunately, prevented him from finishing the finely-conceived painted ceiling of the nave, which forms so striking a contrast, by reason of its magnificence, to the simple grandeur of the Norman arches below; but his memory has been perpetuated by the worthy completion of the work he began, and to him belongs the chief honour of having largely helped to still further beautify this grand old church. It is not from below that this ceiling and that of the Octagon can be fairly seen. From the clerestory a much finer view can be obtained. It is, indeed, only from the far end of the clerestory that one fully realises the enormous extent and the varied beauties of the Cathedral.

The vergers and the picturesque but garrulous old bedesmen will "run on" illimitably about Alan de Walsingham, the designer of the wonderful Octagon, whose beauties it is impossible to describe; they will descant on the varied styles of architecture to be seen here; they will leave you in no doubt about all the modern improvements, and carefully point out the attractions of the fine brass gates; the handsome oak lectern, given by the recently deceased Dean Merivale; the carved pulpits and splendid reredos, presented by Mr. J. D. Gardner; and they will not suffer you to miss a single monument; but it is only by pottering round by yourself, by spending a lonely day in the cathedral, when the American visitors who flock here in crowds in the summer time are not about to set the tongues of the vergers wagging, that you can really appreciate all the splendour, the harmony, the variety, of this—in some respects—unique building. Better far to go alone into the Lady Chapel, now used as the parish church, which must once have been a splendid specimen of Decorated work. Then, uninterrupted, it is possible to picture what this building must have been when its niches and its richly canopied bays were filled with statues, its superb tracery gilded and ornamented like the arcade behind the altar. Then one can see how much damage was done here by the Lord Protector, and how fine an architect the world lost when Alan de Walsingham was laid to rest beneath the beautiful monument he himself erected in the Octagon.

Here, too, with the beautiful choir on one side, the vast, impressive nave on the other, how much more one appreciates the marvellous design, the beauty of the tracery, the majesty of the whole conception, when standing alone beneath this great tower! It is with a sigh of regret that one turns even to pass within the choir itself, where there is so much to admire and to awe one. Fine as the work of

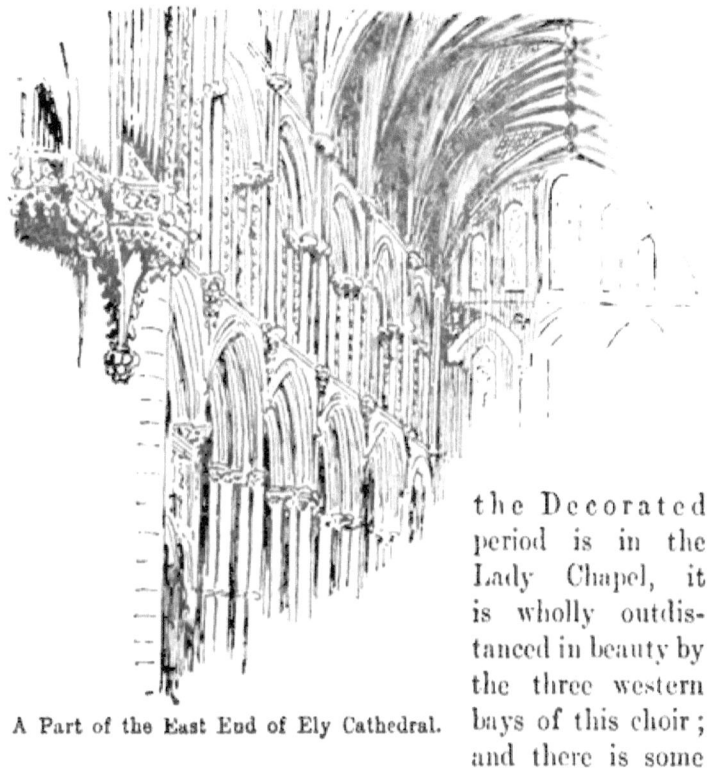

A Part of the East End of Ely Cathedral.

the Decorated period is in the Lady Chapel, it is wholly outdistanced in beauty by the three western bays of this choir; and there is some beautiful Early English work on the western side.

Coming straight into the choir from the nave the contrast between the different styles of architecture is most strikingly marked, while the reverent care bestowed upon the sanctuary by those in authority can hardly fail to impress even the most unthinking sight-seer. They are not content at Ely that their high altar should be an insignificant object amid beautiful surroundings. Every effort has been made to render it worthy of the church and of the beautiful choir in which it stands. Situated behind the present altar was the shrine—part of which is still to be seen in the cathedral —of Ely's foundress, St. Etheldreda, whose whole history is set forth in the sculptures of the Octagon. Her translation into the cathedral was celebrated by the establishment of a fair, at which the pilgrims, as a pledge of their visit, purchased certain silken chains known as St. Audrey's (abbreviated to T'Audrey) chains, whence it is stated was derived the word we use to describe any flimsy, showy article. Happily, there is a better specimen of stained glass at this end of the cathedral, Bishop Sparke having left a sum of money for the purpose of providing an east window. This worthy bishop, together with the late Bishop Woodford, sleep in the south aisle beside other of their episcopal brethren, of whom no less than thirty-eight have, it is said, been interred within these walls. From among the twenty-three whose monuments still exist, Bishop Hotham (1316), once Lord Chancellor, stands out as a shining light of Ely, for it was during his episcopate that part of the Octagon was finished and the Lady Chapel begun. There is Bishop Northwold, too, who built the east end of the cathedral; there is that distinguished prelate, Patrick, and Bishop West, who strangely links "Ely's stately fane" with Putney, his native village; for in this cathedral and in the parish church of that well-known metropolitan suburb, he built chapels almost identical in design. Barring these episcopal monuments there is not much to claim attention in this direction in Ely, neither are there cloisters to lure one without, for these have disappeared with the extensive conventual buildings of the cathedral. Had they still existed, and had Ely been rich in monuments, it would have been an almost Herculean undertaking to have ever fully seen its glories. Already it overflows with interest; for has not Ely been said to be "a complete epitome of English architecture," while its beautiful Octagon, its Lady Chapel, its Galilee porch, its hanging organ in its golden case, its nave, have no compeers in the whole of England. They are absolutely unique.

This sleepy miniature city has had a varied and interesting history. It is difficult now to realise, as one strolls along the two or three still streets of this city by courtesy, that it is a great historical centre of England ; that it was here Hereward fought the Normans ; that its monks and priors and abbots here held mighty sway ; that it has ever been other than a drowsy corner of a dreary county. There was a holy calm around it even in the old days. Etheldreda found it a haven of rest : Canute came here frequently to seek peace. It inspired him to write one of the earliest ballads of our land.

> "Sweetly sang the monks of Ely,
>   Knut, the king, rowed nigh :
> 'Listen how the winds be bringing
> From yon church a holy singing !
>   Row, men, nearer by.'
>
> Sweetly sang the monks at Ely,
>   Knut, the king, rowed nigh :
> 'Listen to the angels bringing
> Holy thoughts that seem like singing !
>   Row yet nearer by.'"

If, however, Ely is diminutive and sleepy as a city, it is fully equal to any gastronomic demands made upon it, and its pilgrims need never go hungry away. He has lost a fine sight and a delightful experience who has not spent a morning in the famous market-gardens lying under the shadow of the great solemn minster, or tasted some of the products of the Isle. Here one may see acres of asparagus being cut on an early summer morning, that beautiful dark-flowered Cambridgeshire "grass," so highly prized in the London markets. Here fruits of all kinds, and strawberries and raspberries in particular, are gathered by the ton. From Ely station they send daily truck-loads of luscious "berries" to the north and south. It is a land literally overflowing with strawberries and cream—and asparagus! What a Lucretian feast they can offer you in the comfortable "Lamb Inn" after Sunday morning service in the cathedral; for ducks thrive amain on the swampy fen-farms round about, and lambs fatten freely on the rich pasturage; and with asparagus as plentiful as potatoes, illimitable strawberries and cream, and Cottenham cheeses from the birthplace of the famous old Pepys, it is possible to dine both unwisely and exceedingly well.

CHAPTER XXI.

IN FENLAND.

A Corner in
Peterborough Cathedral

T is early morning. The cuckoo, who has been up since daybreak, monotonously repeating his imbecile cry, which unfailingly suggests that some other sound is to follow, has flitted from tree to tree with the evident determination of waking every living creature in the neighbourhood. Awhile ago he seemed to have tired of his self-appointed task, and from the far distance, which in this case certainly lent enchantment to the voice, only a faint " oo—oo" fell occasionally on the ear. Now he has returned again to the tree, whose branches shade the window, and with a persistency worthy of a better cause he has cuckooed so loudly that sleep has become impossible, and one by one the drowsy inmates of the farm have roused themselves to action. Moreover, his successful efforts to disturb the neighbourhood have been supported by the clacking and clucking and quacking of innumerable geese and fowls and fine Aylesbury ducks in the yard below, where just now the "gangs" of women and children are waiting to be drafted to work in the far-off fields.

It is a quaint scene. "Twitching" to-day is to employ their time, and the women are already armed with the huge forks with iron tines wherewith they will be presently heaping up the couch-grass, or as it is botanically known, *triticum repens*, which infests the fenlands, and necessitates the constant weeding of the fields. The women are decidedly in the majority. A few men have joined them, and there are some children in the "gang;" but these presumably are those whose quicker brains have enabled them to pass the required "standard" in good time, so that the School Board can no longer restrict them from adding to the weekly income at home. There are plenty of stout, mottled-armed lasses among the number, whom one would expect to find engaged in the dairy or household work of the farms and dwellings of the district. They are young and strong, and would be invaluable surely as domestic helps; but here they are instead, up with the sun, waiting like labourers of the other sex to be sent about the hard field-work, and apparently quite happy and well accustomed to the task. A couple of brawny men are making ready the huge waggon-horses for the day's labour, and when the brown-faced maidens, as soon as this is done, swing themselves into the heavy vehicles, it is clear enough that they are to the manner born. They look picturesque enough as they stand chatting and laughing among themselves, some with their implements across their shoulders, others with arms akimbo in true feminine fashion. Yet, there is no diversity of costume, and they give little or no colour to the picture, for their raiment is of the soberest shades, and even the cotton sun-bonnets, which young and old alike wear,

In the Fens.

are dull in hue. But withal they make effective studies that harmonise well with the scene in which they figure. The key of colour is a low one in Fenland. Brightness and glow are rare indeed. Even at this hour, when the sun is flooding the flat landscape and turning each field into a veritable lake of light, there is but little colour in it all. The land is patched with green meadows, threaded as it were with the roadways that wind about and yet all lead in the same direction; but one misses the wild flowers, the mellowed tints of old mossed and ivied farms, the varied shades of the woodlands, the blossoming hedgerows, and even the brownness of the fields of other counties.

Fenland is bare and colourless, and these women-workers attune their dress to the surroundings. It is well suited to their occupation, however, and as they presently file out of the yards with the barking dogs about them, they look quite as well equipped for the dirty, arduous labour before them as the men. Even the most ardent reformers of feminine attire could find little fault with them in their short kirtles, their high leather-top boots that meet the abbreviated petticoats, and the sensible headgear that protects them equally well from rain and sun. They are tanned, of course, a fine rich brown, and their arms and hands are as rough and as sinewy as those of the husbands, fathers, and brothers; but, by-and-bye, when the day's work is done, when the horses are groomed and stabled, and the great heaps of twitch have been duly burnt, these sun-burnt agricultural labouresses will come home and discard the rough boots for fashionable buttoned ones, and lay aside the kirtles and the sun-bonnets for gaudy stuff gowns with high sleeves, and hats of more or less fashionable shape, adorned with bright ribbons and plush and impossible flowers. To be at liberty to parade the village all the evening in their finery is their reward for the long hours of labour in the fields. It is better to rise up early, they argue, to toil all day beneath the sun, to drive the cart across the hard fields in harvest time, than to go to "sarvice," where the hours of work are longer and those of freedom so limited.

They are off now, plodding heavily down the "drove" that leads from the farm, and though their work lies some distance away—for the lands hereabouts are often far from the homesteads—we can see them distinctly the whole length of their journey by reason of the flatness of the land. The figures are curiously distinct in the clear light which brightens the blackness of the peaty soil and flings down before one an absolute unblurred impression of the unbroken tracts of country, so that a horse and cart coming down a "drove" some two miles distant, appears as clear to us as if it were but a couple of hundred yards away. *À quelque chose malheur est bon*, and there is some compensation even for the flatness of these surroundings. Life is very dreary in these isolated fen-farms; but though the inmates may not be able to visit each other when

Ready for Shearing.

in the winter months the soft black earth of the "droves" reaches to the hubs of the wheels, and it is only possible at all to get on to the made roads by attaching three or four big cart-horses to the traps, and so pulling them out of the sloughs into which these "droves" degenerate in bad weather, the fen-men and their families may at least sit within doors and see every horseman and chariot and pedestrian on the high roads. Almost the whole of one village may thus be taken in at a glance. Like a map it is spread out before one. To paint the picture this sunny morning of early summer, looking from out the honey-suckled porch of this typical Fenland farm, is an easy task. In the foreground the shepherd is clutching at the fleecy wool of a fat, panting sheep, while its companions, huddled together in a corner of the pen, look on at the shearing operation with wondering, startled eyes; the background is a very forest of black mills, that, turn as one will, stand gaunt and spectral, for some of them are but skeletons, like sentinels in the fields.

"Where is the corn to keep these mills in perpetual work?" the stranger to Fenland is at once prompted to ask, as these eternal mills whirl round and round before him and nothing else breaks the monotony of the landscape. There are acres of potato-fields, and asparagus almost covers the land; but surely there is never corn enough grown to supply these endless mills with work. The fen-men are proud enough to explain their presence. It is the ubiquitous mill that has drained their country and turned the great wastes of water, the meres and the fens, into rich arable and pasture land. Where once boats plied and fish abounded the corn now waves and the cattle browse. Whittlesea Mere, one of the largest of the fens, is now a tract of valuable land, over which towers one of the finest Perpendicular church spires in England, that serves as a land-mark for miles around. And so throughout the whole district. Marshy grounds, dykes and ditches, dulness, web-feet, and unredeemed flatness, are the visions

Shorn.

conjured in the minds of those who think of the Fen-country, and in some respects the pictures are not unreal. But as one journeys further and further through this most interesting portion of East Anglia, it is found that so far from its being the dismal swamp, the desolate waste of waters, the unpicturesque and uninteresting district imagined, there is in Fenland not only an impressive sense of vastness and restfulness, but an amount of interest which is not made apparent by a hurried scamper through the county which boasts the most beautifully situated University and the most stately and varied Cathedral in England.

The hills and valleys, the streams and woods and shaded lanes of other more picturesque counties are not more dear to their sons than are the low fertile corn-fields and rich pastures, snatched by toil from the clasp of the waters that once flooded the land, to those who live their lives in this curious corner of England. The modern artist finds unquestionable charms in these unbroken tracts of corn and market produce, from amidst which the farmsteads, the mills, the churches, and the piles of black peat that is here, as in Ireland, the fuel of the poor, stand sharply against the skyscape like the toy-villages the children set out on the nursery table. It is a complete change to find oneself on an absolute level, to look over twenty miles or so of county at a glance, to see one vast plain of rich grain, to feel, so to say, like Gulliver in Lilliput, not because the scene is small or aught is in miniature, but because the spectator stands over all and looks down from his own height, as it were, on these extended and withal picturesque flats of dark soil. There is even a certain grandeur in Fenland. Its beauty would most assuredly not attract the mere holiday-maker, the seeker after "scenery," the idler who likes pretty walks and rustic lanes and conventional country attractions. But as a change from undulating landscapes—from the hill-countries and the wooded districts—the artistically-minded find joy in Fenland. No one can deny its interest.

Seek you a new experience of country-life, a set of new character types? There, far away from a railway station, round about Thorney with its remnants of a once famous abbey, let us say, or in sleepy Benwick, from whence trains are distant in every direction at least seven miles, discover a fen-farm. When once the "drove" is entered that leads thereto, and the clouds of black dust that rise from the dusky land as the horse plods through it have settled again, the world lies behind you, and kings may lay aside their mortal state, Governments change, and Society be shaken to its very foundations, but life will go on in the Fenland farm as usual, and you will be pretty sure to be blissfully unconscious of the national or social excitement for at least one day after the rest of the United Kingdom. That "drove" is the great gulf that is fixed between the world, as townsfolk understand it, and the dwellers in the farm. Once a week they may emerge from their isolated retreats when Wisbech or St. Ives—where presumably dwelt the proud possessor of the seven wives mentioned in the famous "catch"— or the justly famous Peterborough Market are in progress. But for the remaining six days they are absolutely in retreat. Herein lies the charm of this quaint district to the stranger. It is delightfully restful to lean over the farm gate, and looking across the dykes and the patches of green where the sleek cattle are browsing or the corn waving, to realise how far away are the daily newspapers, the rush and roar of trains, and even the highways that lead to "civilisation."

Against the horizon there are rows of pollards and black water-mills, ofttimes seen through the mist that rises from the low-lying land, and occasionally a church stands outlined on the plain. Up and down the river that flows through Benwick and Ramsey and the ecclesiastically famous Doddington, the very heart of Fenland, to Lynn, the barges are always passing with their cargoes of grain and straw and mammoth potatoes, and one may almost fancy as they sail slowly past the almost treeless shores of the fields and meadows that it is upon an expanse of water the eye is gazing.

In one of these small hamlets, where the "droves" are characteristically long and it is particularly "bad going" for the horses, there is almost a colony of bachelors. They are successful breeders of the fine, sturdy mares and stallions that win them renown at the "Shows," and their land flourishes, so that they seem eligible enough for the matrimonial market; and one at first is led to wonder whether they are members of some Fen Society which enforces celibacy upon its sons. But the suspicion dawns at last that the fen-maidens favour the lovers who are not of the shires, dreaming of the life that for all of us always seems to be gayer and fuller of possibilities in the great elsewhere; while, not unnaturally, the hearts of the girls in other counties fail them when wooers from Fenland picture or introduce to them the lonely, isolated homes beside the meres, the solitude and bareness and " unbeautifulness," as Mr. Oscar Wilde would say, of their land.

Doubtless, as a change from the dulness of Fenland farm-life, Peterborough presents itself to the agriculturists, their wives and daughters, in the light of a gay centre. After all, it is by comparison that we judge all things, and though Peterborough and Paris commence with P., just as Macedonia and Monmouth are both spelt with an M., the one is to the other as moonlight unto sunlight, and as water unto wine; but compared with Benwick or Somersham, Whittlesea or Wimblington, Peterborough is in truth a city of a thousand sights, a veritable modern Athens. It is not viewed, however, precisely in this aspect by the pilgrim in East Anglia. That he knows not the magnificent west front of Peterborough Cathedral is a confession not lightly to be made by him who would boast of acquaintance with the architectural and antiquarian glories of the Orient of England; yet, low be it spoken, it is for this and nothing more that the unfenny one forsakes the quiet pasture, the stillness, the quaint pictures of the villages for the quasi-excitements of pretentious Peterborough.

Once or twice a year, when the famous cart-horses of the district are on view and the annual show is held, Peterborough does waken to some semblance of life. "Horsey" folk make their appearance in the dull streets and jostle the clergy, who at all times pervade them, and the Cathedral Close is not then the centre of attraction, as at all other seasons. For the Law-courts, the County Training School for Schoolmasters, opened thirty years ago by Justice Jeune's father, who was then Bishop of the Diocese, the Infirmary, and the many banks, which at least indicate its commercial prosperity, being visited, the architectural sights of Peterborough are exhausted; then the Cathedral alone claims attention. Having previously become acquainted with the glories of the almost bewilderingly beautiful Ely, one is tempted to awe the garrulous and unusually mendacious verger— who obligingly adapts his history and description of the Cathedral to the religious views of the sight-seer, cautiously

ascertained in advance—by treating the building as a somewhat poor "show." But Peterborough Cathedral promises at no distant date to present a striking contrast to its former forlorn and neglected condition. To its penultimate Dean, now Bishop of Worcester, belongs the honour of setting on foot the work of restoration, so sorely needed; and some marvellous improvements have been completed within the interior this year. Already the Italian mosaic pavement of the choir, dedicated by the Primate in 1892, has been laid at a cost of three thousand pounds by the generosity of the late Dean Argles, who likewise presented the beautiful new pulpit and throne; and beautifully carved stalls, each bearing effigies of the Deans or Bishops of the Cathedral from its foundation to the present time, have been fixed at a cost of one hundred and twenty-five guineas apiece by the Freemasons of the diocese, in addition to some handsome sub-stalls, given by the women of Peterborough. The family of the late Dr. Saunders, too, have contributed a magnificent white alabaster reredos of baldachino design; and the organ and case, the gift of an anonymous donor of four thousand pounds, is now complete; while, as a public memorial to Dean Argles, who was himself so generous to the Cathedral and so active in its restorations, iron sacrarium screens have been placed in the choir. Careful excavations have been made, and the outlines and remains of the old Saxon church revealed; the Eastern chapel, with its beautiful fan tracery ceiling, has been opened for service, and a handsome recumbent effigy will shortly be added to the monuments as a memorial to the late Archbishop Magee, translated from Peterborough to York in 1891. But it now devolves upon the Restoration Committee to very earnestly turn their attention to the fabric of the Cathedral, which is

West Front of Peterborough Cathedral.

unquestionably in a serious condition. The magnificent west front, its great glory, has long been threatened, and the Eastern chapel imperatively needs underpinning if it is to be saved, while both transepts, unless speedily taken in hand, will, like an unsound tooth, go too far to be satisfactorily stopped. Mr. Pearson, R.A., has not yet diagnosed the case of the west front, but he suspects grave trouble and a consequent outlay of many thousands. The present building, for Peterborough had been destroyed no less than four times before this Cathedral was built, was commenced in 1117, and the choir belongs entirely to this period; but the beautiful west front, the ecclesiastical glory of the city, is not supposed to have been added till nearly a hundred and fifty years later. Strangely enough it is Henry VIII., whose name has certainly not been handed down to posterity as that of an earnest Churchman, to whom the preservation of the Cathedral is due. Here, in 1535, Catherine of Arragon was buried by the famous old sexton, Scarlett, who subsequently laid another unhappy royal lady, Mary, Queen of Scots, to rest within these walls; and for his first wife's sake, Henry spared the Cathedral while engaged in the work of spoliation. Poor Catherine! "So good a lady that no tongue could ever pronounce dishonour of her." Henry's respect for her was somewhat tardily shown; but after all, what there was of it was at least enduring. Some time since, a tomb of one of her maids of honour, who slept beside her, was opened, and some silken finery found intact within it. Mary Stuart's corpse was removed from Peterborough to Westminster, after being interred a quarter of a century, by request of James I., and his letter to the Dean, asking for his mother's remains, hangs in a frame above her now empty tomb. Of the "Grand Old Man," Scarlett, who interred these two hapless Queens as well as a couple of generations of his townsfolk, Peterborough is very proud. It was not until within two years of completing his century that he furnished another Cathedral sexton with the job of digging his grave, and at the west end

"YOU SEE OLD SCARLETT'S PICTVRE STAND ON HIE,
BUT AT YOUR FEETE HERE DOTH HIS BODY LYE."

Judging from this portrait, he was a truculent old person, for among the "tokens" referred to in the inscription is a formidable whip, wherewith it is assumed this "first grave-digger" kept the curious at bay when he was at work.

CHAPTER XXII.

THE METROPOLIS OF THE TURF.

THIS is essentially the place for the "early worm." In more senses than one it is necessary to get up betimes in the morning in this "natty" little town, for as a journalist of a sporting turn once said, "Horses are taken out and somebody is taken in long before breakfast in the 'metropolis' of the turf." And indeed, by the time most folks are beginning to think about a morning walk—and those who know not the ways of the astute trainer and his merry men, innocently imagine that the beautiful four-footed creatures, who are practically the leading lights of the town, are out for their matutinal gallop—a great ca!m has fallen over Newmarket, and outwardly and visibly it might be a cathedral city, so still are the beautifully-kept roads and streets. It is before the morning newspapers have come in and the telegraph office is open, long before the odour of ham and eggs is in the air, that the regiments of horses in their gay hoods and cloths file up the hilly street that leads to the famous heath ; and from the spick-and-span double gates and newly-gravelled stable-yards with which the town is riddled, dapper lads and muffled-up lightweights in their short drab covert coats are seen to emerge. At this time of day Newmarket is very wide-awake indeed.

There is a mighty tramping of horses and jingling of snaffles as stable after stable turns out; the men are all as trim and alert as if it were midday; the lads look keen-eyed and healthy; the horses sniff the fresh air and neigh joyously; and presently when the great stretch of magnificent elastic turf at the top of the town is reached business commences in real earnest. Off they all go, some

Character Sketch at Newmarket.

through the gap in the famous "Devil's Ditch," some backwards and forwards over short courses that look but half a mile or so long.

Away down the town, too, on Warren Hill, much the same scene is being enacted. On the famous Bury Hills a hundred or more gaily-hooded creatures are being "put through their paces," their owners and trainers may be determining the great question whether this one or that one shall be entered for coming races, and consulting as to their prospects of success. An hour later Newmarket, so far as the horses go, might be any ordinary country town. They have all been taken home to the exquisitely-kept stables attached to the various trainers' solid and imposing-looking houses. Here they have been carefully washed and rubbed down, their delicate fetlocks tenderly swaddled in soft bandages, their sleek, satiny coats covered with fresh cloths, the toilet process being almost as elaborate as that undergone by a new-born baby. Whilst watching the grooming of the descendants of such equine heroes as Robert the Devil or Merry Hampton, it is impossible to help remarking the astounding orderliness and exquisite cleanliness of all the arrangements, and this characteristic of every stable is the characteristic of the whole town. It is absolutely spotless and as neat as the proverbial "bandbox." Every knocker shines, every stone is white and polished, the little traps that rattle through the streets all look as if they had just been driven out of the maker's show-rooms, even the tradesmen's horses are groomed like ladies' park hacks, and men and women alike have a trim, taut air about them that one never sees elsewhere. About the men there is a curious sameness. Like soldiers, they all have the appearance of having been cast in a mould of one pattern. They are all more or less diminutive in stature, they all wear very short, drab coats, thickly seamed, they are "queer about the legs" and clean-shaven, and to a man they wear horse-shoe pins. The "lads" are miniature replicas of the same pattern, and like their elders, they, too, seem always to have been just washed and brushed up.

Before one goes very far in Newmarket it becomes evident that its men, women, and children are "horsey" to the back-bone. It would not be in the least surprising to hear that the babies learn to say "gee-gee" and "whoa" before anything else, or that they knew the names of the last twenty-six Derby winners before they had mastered the letters of the alphabet. For the "stable mind" is literally cultivated in Newmarket from the cradle to the grave. In the toy-shops the only playthings to be seen are whips and reins, horses, stables, and race-games; and in the jewellers' windows every article is in the form of or ornamented with a horse-shoe, a whip, or a snaffle. But they are never trumpery goods. When sporting folk spend the money that changes hands with such startling rapidity and in such large sums in this seemingly quiet little country town, they spend it freely, and like their money's worth in return. It is on this principle that everything is organized and maintained here.

Newmarket is famous for its pretty houses and for the neatness and completeness with which they are kept. The big houses are elaborate within and without, their lawns are absolutely perfect, their gravel paths as smooth as glass, no weed is ever suffered to grow apace within their borders, and flower-beds, always horse-shoe in shape, are as trim as if their owners had nothing else in the world but gardening to occupy their attention. And it is the same with the less ambitious establishments. They are all marvellously exact and smart, and all seem to have had money freely spent upon them in a greater or less degree. The hospital just beyond the railway station—hideously suggestive of the perils of the field—is a smart red-brick building that would do credit to any town. It never stands in need of funds, and its wards are models of cheerfulness and neatness.

A little further in the town, facing the hill that leads to the Heath, is the town clock, presented as a Jubilee memorial by "Charlie" Blanton, the owner of Robert the Devil, and this again is an evidence of racing folks' love of doing things well; while, but a short distance away, the Stablemen's Institute, opened in 1893 by the Prince of Wales, and built at a cost of £3,000, is a handsome

Character Sketch at Newmarket.

addition to the public buildings of the town. It is most handsomely fitted up, and is specially designed to provide a bright recreation resort for the stable-boys. The owners and trainers and successful jockeys are ever anxious for the welfare of their "lads." They are not permitted to skulk round at night, and if they care to read there is a fine reading room, duly furnished, of course, with sporting literature for their use.

Very curiously, the "Rooms," where during his frequent visits the Prince of Wales always stays, are in outward aspect the least imposing building in Newmarket; a quiet modest-looking structure, which, unless any of the meetings are imminent—when there is evidence enough about its door that it is no ordinary place—might be easily passed by the innocent stranger. But not so the houses round about it and on the way to the Heath. It is plain enough to be seen that these are not the residences of ordinary country townsfolk.

High Street, Newmarket, when the shops are passed, is in appearance a kind of miniature Piccadilly. It bristles with mansions within whose doors during the July meeting or in Houghton week the "smartest" portion of Mayfair is gathered together. Lady Stamford for years has had the huge white house on the left that seems to have been transported straight from Carlton House Terrace: almost on the edge of the heath is "Bridlemere," the aggressively red-brick "cottage," built unto himself by Sir Edward Lawson, of the "Daily Telegraph:" and he has for neighbours the Duke of Devonshire, Lord Bradford, and Baron Hirsch. Out at Cheverly Green, Lord Randolph Churchill entertains his friends, and at Sefton House, on the Bury road, the "merry duchess," Her Grace of Montrose, has been wont to hold court at every meeting. Lower down the town, at Heath House, surrounded by beautiful ivy-clad trees, the Duke of Portland is to be found, literally next door to his trainer, Mr. George Dawson, whose favourite and most successful pupil was poor Fred Archer. And but a few paces distant, close to the church of All Saints, which, by the way, these racing folk are very proud to keep in good order, and in whose yard is the tomb of Frampton, "keeper of the running horses" of William III., Anne, the first and second Georges, and the "Father of the Turf," stands the modernized Royal Palace of Charles II., in convenient proximity to the house occupied by Nell Gwynne.

Now-a-days, Newmarket could hardly be described as a quiet place when the fancy of its visitors and inhabitants have lightly turned to thoughts of stakes and handicaps; but it is unquestionably "slow" at such times as compared with corresponding periods of the year in the "good old days" when Charles and "poor Nelly" graced it with their presence. Mr. Evelyn, who had probably been invited down by the king, was horrified at the revelries in progress during his visit in 1671, in what is now "Houghton" week. "I found," says he, "jolly blades racing, dancing, feasting, revelling, more resembling a luxurious and abandoned rout than a Christian court." Mr Alfred de Rothschild now lives in the Palace, part of which is also an Independent Chapel; and it is to be hoped that the shades of the "jolly blades," or of "the merry monarch" and Mistress Gwynne, do not disturb any of the present occupants of this royal residence, which stands, by the way, conveniently near to the almost equally historic "Rutland Arms." Within the quadrangular yard of this famous inn, celebrated alike for its associations and the excellence of its food, have been, and are still, at the duly appointed and faithfully observed seasons of the turf, gathered together most of its familiar figures. It is just as well maybe that its walls, if possessed, as the saying goes, of ears, are not gifted with speech, though its reminiscences of leading turfites would certainly be entertaining if not always instructive. Like all else in Newmarket, it is wonderfully smart and "natty"; but its neatness and smartness are tempered by age. There is an agreeable mellowed flavour about the picturesque old house and its well-known yard that is likewise observable, say those who know, in its port and spirits.

One is disposed to think always of Newmarket as the scene of life and luxury. And maybe, if it were visited only when the flowers in the well-tended gardens were all abloom, and the owners of all the big houses were in residence, when the Cesarewitch was within measurable distance and the streets were crowded "from early morn

The "Rutland Arms," Newmarket.

to dewy eve," it is this impression that would be received of the "metropolis" of the turf; but when the season is over, and there is time to view Newmarket more leisurely, it is, somehow, the pretty little cemetery on the very verge of the heath that stands prominently out in the picture of the town sketched on the mental canvas. Just past the smart collegiate school, where presumably the youths entrusted to the care of the Newmarket dominie are not engaged with the same kind of "books" as those used a few yards distant, there is a corner of the heath in which those who have run the last race are laid to rest, where "they can still hear the horses gallop." Here there is never any doubt about the betting. The odds are always on the pale horse, and he wins in a canter. It is a spot sacred enough to those who have the history of the turf at their fingers' ends; it is the skeleton at the feast, the most solemn warning to the noisy heedless crowds of gamblers who, "flown with insolence and wine," or dejected and ruined, pass by its gate on their way from the course. Here among others rest Hayhoe and Godding and French, Sam Rogers and Tom Aldcroft; and, nearest of all to the beautiful downs, which so often thundered with applause as he rode to win, sleeps poor Fred Archer beside the young wife, on the anniversary of whose death he terminated his life. He had "the income of an ambassador and the treatment of a gentleman"; but the "pace was too good to last," and the poor, gentle, modest "Tinman" fell a victim to popularity, the slave of the sporting public he served with such courage and fidelity.

CHAPTER XXIII.

WHITECHAPEL-SUPER-MARE.

THERE are still some old-fashioned folk who, remembering the days when they drove along the old turnpike road through Brentford and the curiously-named Billericay—whose etymology has proved a stumbling-block to the most learned—by Rayleigh and Rochford to Southend-on-Sea, speak of that hybrid watering-place in terms which amaze the younger generation. We have now-a-days grown fastidious about our seaside resorts. Cheap fares, and luxurious travelling facilities have rendered us independent of the once favoured haunts. We run up to Cromer while we read the morning papers, and sneer at Southend as being little better than an East-end suburb. While it is so easy to get sixty miles away we see no reason for exploring the country which we loosely describe as "near Gravesend." The cheap excursionists frighten us. Shrimps and "Aunt Sally" loom large before our eyes, and in imagination we picture noisy crowds of moleskin-clad costers, with their fearfully and wonderfully arrayed womenkind, indulging in that peculiar form of salutation whereby they generally display their exuberance of feeling when holiday-making. Southend-on-Sea is certainly not alluring when seen from this point of view; but there is, happily, another side to the picture, in which the shrimp is of infinitesimal size, and the coster and

"'Arriett," possibly otherwise engaged in the mysterious exercise of "knocking 'em in the Old Kent Road," are insignificantly represented. It is not well to seek it, if one would see it at its best, at such times as are conducive to merry-making. Southend on a Bank Holiday, for instance, would not be exactly the place wherein to spend "a happy day," unless the tastes of the pleasure-seeker ran in the direction of roundabouts, steam-horses, nigger-minstrelsy, and open-air dancing; but the habitués of this popular resort are not always in a position to indulge in the marine and other delights of their chosen watering-place. So there are times, therefore, when comparative calm reigns, and the fast and furious fun which characterises it on summer Saturday evenings and festive occasions generally is not manifest. The "fat baby" may perchance be seen for the modest sum of twopence, but its massive limbs are not displayed every half-hour as on "fashionable days," and the steam-horses gallop riderless, even when occasionally set in motion just to keep up the town's reputation for gaiety. The showmen lounge idly round their booths and caravans, and indulge in political discussions with the facetious flymen; the ladies attached to the troupes seize upon the opportunity to do the family washing; and trade being slack, the donkey-boys gamble away their profits in sulky silence by the shore.

Southend labours under many disadvantages that are not shared by other watering-places, for it is judged from many standpoints, and opinions vary considerably in consequence. There are those who went there years ago, and know nothing of its gorgeous villas, its charter, and its modern improvements; there are those, perhaps, who, like Mr. George R. Sims, went once on the occasion of a band and banner fête, when the tide was out and brass instruments were rampant, and mud and beer flowed, so to say,

Southend Pier.

through the streets; and some again who have never yet seen it, but who picture it as a squalid, dirty, uninteresting miniature Margate, and are prejudiced against it by the mere fact that it is possible to get there and back for half-a-crown, and to reach it by boat after a short journey down the Thames. But let us avail ourselves of the cheap fare, and seek out Southend on a bright summer day not consecrated to the use of the "tripper." The journey thither is an inviting one. It does not take us by the old riverside route, through East-end suburbs and malodorous and riparian villages, where the outfall of sewage, bone-boiling, and soap-making combine to thicken and pollute the air. The way now lies through a pleasant pastoral and ofttimes exceedingly picturesque district, which will surprise the stranger to Essex, who has been accustomed to hear that county described as flat and unbeautiful. When the line branches off at Shenfield, in which village, by the way, there is a fine thirteenth-century church, the scenery is unquestionably redeemed from the charge of flatness brought against the county, which an old writer describes as the "Englishe Goshen, most fatt, frute full and full of profitable things." Billericay, suggestive of Hibernian tours, and one of the first halting places, is itself perched high whence one can look across the Thames and lift one's eyes to the Kentish hills beyond; while within a walk is the beautifully picturesque Laindon range, from which the views are as charming as they are extensive. Here, therefore, at the very outset of the excursion, a fair impression is made, which deepens as Rayleigh, likewise set upon a hill and surrounded with smiling scenery, Hockley, almost encircled by the high lands which overlook the Crouch, and Prittlewell are passed. Almost within sight of the latter village is Southend, and no sooner is the fine station, which would do credit to many a larger and more fashionable resort, left behind, than the conviction is borne in upon one that poor Southend, long the butt of the jester, is, like the rest of Essex, a much maligned place.

Where is the dirt? Are these smart villas, with their well-kept lawns and carriage drives, the evidences of the squalor? The roads are broad and leafy, the newness and brickiness of the average seaside town is agreeably conspicuous by its absence. The jerry builder is not too aggressively in evidence; indeed, a comfortable, mellowed air pervades the town, at present rejoicing in newly-acquired corporate privileges and the possession of a comparatively brand new mayor. So far, too, the enterprising seaside landlady has not put in an appearance, and bowling along this pleasant avenue with a church at one far end and the sea at the other, one ponders upon the kind of residents who occupy these comfortable, handsome-looking villas. Prosperity shines through every window, and their aspect considerably tempers the surprise that might otherwise have been expressed at the palatial shops in the business part of the town. Curiosity is soon allayed as to the occupants of the pretty houses. They are mostly prosperous business folk, who, since Southend has been brought within convenient distance of town, have made homes for their families where they can breathe the air which, as it has ever been, is still famous for its bracing effect upon children. The daily morning and evening trains are full of fathers and sons journeying to and from town, and apparently paterfamilias finds that the decrease in doctor's bills balances the railway fare and time—it is only an hour—spent in travelling from the City to Southend.

Hadleigh Castle.

The children hereabouts, whether residents or visitors, all look very brown and bonny, and do full justice to the reputed salubrity of the air. Even the pallid-faced little urchins, whose speech bewrayeth them as natives of the populous East-end, assume a bronzed and healthy tint after a few days' stay down here, despite the fact that their consumption of cockles and flaccid buns is on a scale calculated to alarm careful and wise mothers, who recognise the fact that the infantile digestion does not correspond with that of the camel.

Cockles, by the way, are a delicacy presented to one at every turn in Southend. Huge stacks of bottles, of the pickle variety, filled with these molluscs, are exposed on the fishmongers' slabs, and seemingly enable numerous stall-holders to carry on a thriving trade. Costliness is not a characteristic of the cockle. For fourpence it is possible to obtain a goodly quantity, though judging from the rapidity of the sale and the number of bottles purchased at one time by the ladies apparently catering for the members of their party, the appetite of the Southend excursionist for this particular delicacy is peculiarly keen. Moreover, the cockle is regarded as a mere *hors d'œuvre*; it is evidently not taken seriously as an article of food, but is regarded, rather, as a whet to the appetite, a toothsome amusement for idle moments. The gallant young coster presents "'Arriett" with a bottle as they stroll together towards the pier, and while gazing over the waters to the shore, or enriching their store of knowledge by visits to the numerous "shows," they dreamily consume the cheerful cockle, which with pleasing simplicity they lure through its narrow-necked receptacle by means of the inamorata's bonnet-pin. Mere infants may be seen freely partaking of them, and no Southend tea would be considered complete unless they duly appeared in company with the less-favoured shrimp upon the board. Visitors of a sporting turn, who pursue the more or less gentle Waltonian art from the pier's end, employ the cockle as bait; but in this capacity it does not seem to be quite so successful, an occasional crab, considerably under the regulation standard, being the usual "catch" after the loss of about half a pint of cockles.

It is as the "front" is approached that Southend begins to assume its most cheerful aspect. But, contrary to expectations, not even here, where the swing-boats are found and the ear-piercing cornet greets one at every available corner, is this Essex resort the uninteresting spot that has been imagined. There are, in fact, the decided "makings" of a picture, as the Irish say, directly the corner at which stands the handsome and comfortable Royal Hotel is reached. A glance at this establishment is in itself reassuring. It has the appearance of being patronized by others than trippers, and indeed the visitors'

At Southend.

list here includes the names of not a few famous brain-workers who frequently run down to ferret among the quaint old scenes that many an artist and writer has immortalised. There are those who derive much more enjoyment and food for imagination from sitting on the covered balcony of the Royal Hotel at Southend, watching the ever-passing sails and the busy traffic of the water, with Gad's Hill in the distance where Falstaff and his merry men were put to rout by the rogues in buckram, than they would ever get from a visit to a more fashionable resort.

The shipping is a great attraction at Southend. Full-rigged vessels, river-steamers, yachts, and trading barges crowd the waters and animate the scene. There is always much coming and going, and even the London boat is in itself a daily excitement. Excursions by sea from the pier-end are always in progress. For trifling sums one may sail away over the main to Herne Bay, or explore the North Sea as far as breezy Clacton, where the real sea rolls over the sandy beach and health is borne in on every wave. There is an element of adventure in embarking on these sea-trips that lends them additional attraction, for, as a rule, one has to reach the pier end, which at Southend is not a few yards distant, but a mile and a quarter from shore. As far as the well-appointed pavilion, where theatrical entertainments, concerts, excellent refreshments, and other solaces are at hand, all is well. One may pause and look back at leafy Cliff Town by the Royal Hotel, or note the suggestiveness of the chain-pier end of Brighton in the Eastern part of the shore; but the distance that then lies between you and the boat is appalling, and Hobson's choice is presented of tramping out to the extreme mouth of the Thames, or of submitting yourself to the tender mercy of the electric tramway,

which whisks you over the very green water in an alarming
fashion, and unpleasantly suggests the "switchback"
railway. When one is brave enough to devote attention to
the study of fellow-passengers, it is vastly funny to watch
the agonised expression of the anxious mothers with many
olive-branches, and the timid young ladies in convenient
proximity to strong arms, as they find themselves literally
overhanging the sea. The amphibious Southender, who is
half landsman and half sailor, is very ready-witted upon
such matters as these, and is altogether somewhat of
a humorist, purveying his wares, whether they be "sails"

Southend at Low Tide.

or "drives," with much *persiflage*. And what wonderful
sails and drives the outlay of a shilling will secure! By
road or water one may go to Hadleigh and back at the rate
of a penny a mile, and a more interesting and charming
excursion could not be well imagined. Constable, the
artist, painted many scenes about here, and his picture of
Hadleigh Castle is one of his best-known works. It is
a fine old ruin, finely situated, picturesque in itself and in
its surroundings. Its date is 1231, but it has been in
ruins since the middle of the fifteenth century, and during

the centuries that have elapsed the mosses and ivy have been deepening on its walls, until the latter has become one of its sights by reason of the thickness of its stems and foliage. The artist will linger long in Hadleigh, for the view across the Kentish Hills, and of

> "The briny deep,
> Seen from the pointed promontory's top,"

and of Canvey Island, is not its only attraction. The church, a finely-restored Norman structure, is full of interest, and fresh colour and fresh interest has been given to the place of late by the establishment of General Booth's farm in this fertile district, the red-coated Salvationists making bright spots of colour in the scene. As a contrast to the peace of Hadleigh, Shoeburyness is offered as one of the many Southend excursions, where the belligerently inclined may revel in batteries, targets, artillery, and gunnery practice, under the guidance of the smart artillerymen who are always prepared to give explanation and agreeably romance for the benefit of the curious.

At Shoeburyness one may learn more about Armstrongs and Whitworths in half-an-hour than technical books would teach in a couple of volumes, and it is only by a visit to these wonderful "works" that the progress in modern gunnery is at all realised.

In the other direction, at Leigh, one may fight over again, with the "shades" of the many old sea-dogs who have been born and lived and died here, the naval battles of the "good old days," and eat its famous shrimps until it is time to stroll back past the Crow Stone, where the jurisdiction of the Thames Conservancy ends, along the shady, well-kept terrace walk that leads to salubrious Southend and an excellent dinner at the Royal Hotel.

CHAPTER XXIV.

CHELMSFORD.

STRANGELY enough, towns are both rare and insignificant in East Anglia. It is a land of smiling fields, of woods and streams, of meadows and small hamlets; rich enough, it is true, in ancient buildings, in beautiful old churches, castles, and priories, in remnants of past glories, civic, social, and ecclesiastical, but poor indeed, as compared with Northern and other counties, in the matter of towns. A few handsful of houses and shops, a church or two, a meagre population of ten or fourteen thousand, suffice to make up an East Anglian town. Colchester, the largest town of Essex, can boast of little more than thirty thousand inhabitants; and, as compared with this, modest little Chelmsford, its capital, is a mere village. Historically, Essex with its neighbouring Eastern counties has, by a long way, the advantage over more advanced and more pretentious divisions of England. Colchester was a flourishing town when Cymbeline, King of Britain, whom Shakespeare has immortalised for us, held sway and warred with the savage tribes that then ruled over the petty kingdoms into which the wild and trackless country was divided, and a little later on Chelmsford became of some importance. The Roman road had passed

The Shirehall and High Street, Chelmsford.

it by, but the town had always been in possession of the Bishops of London, and when, after the conquest, Maurice, a predecessor of the present occupant of the Episcopal chair of London, built over the river Can, which shares with the Chelmer the fluvian honours of the town, the traffic was somewhat diverted, and Chelmsford was at once brought into greater prominence. Thus its antiquity is indisputable, if it can lay claim to no great points of interest.

Unlike Colchester, it is not a place in which the tourist

immediately craves to linger. There is little to raise
the spirits or satisfy artistic hunger in the old town;
yet its quietude has a pleasantly soothing effect, and
soon tempts one to perambulate its singularly clean
streets, and explore the neighbourhood, which surprises
and delights those who, having fallen under the spell
of peace hovering over the Essex capital, have not
hurried thence, dismayed by its apparent slowness and
lack of interest. A general air of somnolence pervades
all country towns in a greater or lesser degree. Except
on market days, when everybody and everything suddenly
starts to life, like the Swiss figures at the Crystal
Palace which are set in motion by the insertion of a
coin in the slot, inhabitants and animals seem to exist
in a semi-lethargic condition. One is always tempted
to wonder where they hide, what they do, and how they
divert themselves on the days when they have not the
wild excitement of the market.

Going into Chelmsford on any day save Friday, when
the lowing of cattle, the grunting of fat swine, and the
plaintive bleating of the sheep proclaim the fact that the
weekly corn and cattle market is in progress, it would
be easy enough to fancy, without any great stretch of
imagination, that the indispensable wicked fairy of juvenile
fiction had cast its inhabitants into a trance. The streets,
which resound with the heavy footsteps of farmers, the
rattle of the dog-carts and "traps," the wagons and
carriers' carts, on this one day of life and activity, are
silent enough for the six remaining days of the week.
Now and then a carriage rolls through, for Chelmsford
and its environments boast plenty of inhabitants amusingly
classified by a local estate agent as " soup and fish families,"
the provincial mind apparently regarding a menu in which
these two courses are of daily occurrence as the highest

expression of prosperity and opulence ; but silence reigns supreme, as a rule, in the wide, prosperous streets of this spick-and-span town. Even the amateur photographer may bring his camera to bear upon the picturesque old church of St. Mary, set back from the High Street in a veritable grove of standard roses, or upon the imposing bronze statue of Lord Chief Justice Tindal, erected by the proud inhabitants of the town before their Shire Hall in Tindal Square, in memory of their illustrious townsman, with little fear of attracting the crowd which almost invariably congregates so soon as a photographic apparatus is set up. Frivolity of any kind, is, however, not a characteristic of the capital of Essex. A severe, solid, eminently respectable and prosperous air pervades it from end to end. The old, red-brick residences, mixed up after the fashion of most county towns with banks, public halls, and shops, are even stern in aspect, and the more modern buildings have apparently been erected to correspond with them in tone.

Here and there is an outbreak of flowers in old-fashioned balconies ; the gardens, which are seen sometimes about the older houses, are gay, too, with bright blossoms ; and occasionally, a more daring spirit has ventured to adorn the narrow-paned, old-fashioned windows with "Art" curtains and blinds, of which one may almost fancy the severe old flat house fronts look a wee bit ashamed. Yet Chelmsford is decidedly progressive in its ideas. Progress indeed seems to be struggling very hard with conservatism, and, on the whole, to be getting somewhat the best of the tussle, despite the obviously somnolent and old-world air that clings to the town and its people. Evidently, the Chelmsford town councillor is wide-awake, however sleepy the rest of the inhabitants may seem to be, for the electric light illuminates these quiet, well-kept streets and the fine shops, that, judging from their appearance, do a thriving trade, although, except on that red-letter Friday, when "the models work," nobody ever seems to enter them.

. Other evidences, too, are not wanting to prove that the thriving little town is striving its utmost to keep abreast with the times, though, like the poor gentlewoman, who, being driven to hawk water-cresses for a living, called them in a whisper, "lest anyone should hear her," it seems so terribly afraid of losing the air of distinction and old-fashioned, sober refinement that has so long been one of its distinguished features, that its modern improvements are undertaken in as unassuming and quiet a manner as possible. Vulgarity, noise, and rowdyism could

Tindal Square, Chelmsford.

never be associated with this town; yet its jail, pleasantly situated among the rustic old residences of Springfield, where, in trim gardens, surburban Chelmsford takes its pleasure, is so spacious as to suggest that a severe strain is made upon its accommodation. It is true that the grosser offenders against the law, who find board and lodging within its walls at the country's expense, come from various parts of the county, which measures no less than fifty miles in one direction, and sixty-three in another; so that the proportion of prisoners with which respectable Chelmsford supplies its jail would probably be very small as compared with the size of that grim building, even were the inhabitants less peaceably disposed and less Quaker-like in demeanour than these good folk, whose chief delight seems to be the scrubbing and cleansing of their streets and dwellings.

Another pleasing peculiarity of the town is the directness of its routes. Try as you will it is impossible to lose the way in Chelmsford, and the local flymen must find trade anything but flourishing, by reason of the facility wherewith the stranger may explore it. Everything lies straight ahead when once the railway station is left behind. One street leads from another, so that coming down the road from the station, Tindal Square is reached. Here, with the Corn Exchange, a building described in local guide-books as "imposing," and doubtless deserving of the description so far as the prices quoted within it by the wily merchants are concerned, on one hand, and the impressive Shire Hall on the other, stands a carefully preserved cannon, whose history appears to be shrouded in mystery so far as the inhabitants are concerned. They know all about the comfortable hostelry of the "Saracen's Head" just opposite, however, where the county magnates hie them when the meeting of the Assizes, a time of festivity

for Chelmsford, a county ball, or some other visit of special
importance brings them to their capital. Having mastered
the geography of Chelmsford thus far, it is "plain sailing"
enough to the other objects of interest in the town; for the
High Street, with its excellent shops, is the broad way that
happily leads not to destruction, unless a header be taken
into the Can, flowing beneath the bridge that bisects the
street, but to the Shire Hall and hospitable "Saracen's
Head."

Passing through this, and other streets of the town,
and noting its houses and its buildings, one is first
fascinated by the eminently solvent-looking banks, which
absolutely seem to invite the farmers to confide their
monies to their charge; and then amazed at the number
of solicitors who practise hereabouts. Doubtless the
services of all are in constant demand. The farmer is
nothing if not litigious, he loves "to have the law of his
neighbour," and so, for that matter, does every country-
man. It is possibly owing to the fact that so many of its
inhabitants are learned in the law that Chelmsford conveys
an impression of being exceedingly proud of itself, and
most anxious to preserve its dignity. There is nothing
specially interesting about its church, which has some
Perpendicular remains, but has been practically rebuilt,
yet there is an almost cathedral-like impressiveness about
it which is obviously cultivated; the Museum, too, an
excellent institution, founded by the enterprising towns-
people, could never be mistaken for any building save
one devoted to a serious and improving purpose. It is
almost forbidding in aspect, and the most staid of all
the Chelmsford residences surround it. No flighty,
giggling youth would ever dare to venture through its
portals, but maybe quiet, peace-loving Chelmsford possesses
no such juveniles. The visitors who inspect the antiquities,

A Bit in Chelmsford.

which from time to time have been unearthed in the neighbourhood and deposited within the Museum, are all sober-minded, knowledge-thirsty folk, who appreciate the grimness and the air of repression brooding over the Museum and its neighbours.

Young Chelmsford, however, is fond of out-door sports. Cricket, in the season, is always in progress, and the Chelmer, which meanders through the town, and past Beeleigh Abbey, is a favoured haunt of youth on summer evenings. The river is unpretentious, but the trees overhang its banks in tempting fashion to those who do their boating in couples, and there are pleasant views and parklands as it winds in and out. As a driving and walking district, Chelmsford can certainly boast of its attractions, and it is as one begins to explore it in this direction that its hitherto unsuspected charms are revealed. That there are fair country seats, and fine parks like Hylands and Writtle within immediate reach of the town, a great many people are aware. The latter place is especially familiar as a fine Elizabethan mansion and a tolerably interesting church, a curious combination of Norman, Perpendicular, fifteenth and sixteenth century work, are to be seen here. It may even be, too, that the fame of Great Baddow has sometimes lured the stranger to Chelmsford, for not only is the Essex race-course here, but to this village belongs the distinction of being one of the pleasantest and most picturesque hamlets in the county, while it bears the name of the founder of Clare College, who was born here at the close of the thirteenth century. Situated in a well-wooded district, and amidst undulating, heath-like scenery, it forms, with Danbury, one of Chelmsford's most favoured resorts.

Danbury, part of the forest of ancient Essex, is, however, the place of which the county town has reason to be most proud. As yet its glories are unknown except to the dwellers round about the pleasant capital of Essex. The holiday-maker knows it not, the "tripper" will never spoil its beauties, for it lies far beyond the reach of the railway. But what an ideal spot it is for a restful holiday! Who, seeking absolute repose and calm after the noise and tumult of town, could find a haven of more perfect peace than this wee village, nearly four hundred feet above the sea-level, in the very heart of Essex, where one may roam all the day through, knee-deep in heather, across the commons, where the browsing, gentle-eyed cows are often the only living creatures to be encountered for miles? Dwarf oaks and hollies, trimmed into shapes by the cattle, like the funny little toy-box trees of Holland, are thickly studded over these commons, and hereabouts are to be seen, too, some of the finest and oldest trees in the kingdom.

Except about Cromer, there are no lanes in England which compare so favourably with those of Devonshire as the beautiful, ferny, flower-bedecked lanes that lead to Danbury Hill. On either side the hedges, overflowing, according to the season, with sweet hawthorn and trailing vines and bracken; dog-roses, and honey-suckle, and convolvuli

The River, Chelmsford.

stretch across the path, high over the head, till almost meeting midway, they make veritable groves of these picturesque lanes, that lead, first to "the Rodney," and further on to the church, and the supposed Danish camp. A glorious panorama lies below. On one side, the sea may be distinctly seen, though the coast is many miles away; on the other, there are wide stretches of rich harvest fields, green meadow lands, and grey church towers and ruins. Just below are the remains of Bicknacre Priory, founded in the reign of Henry II.; Boreham Church, where the Earls of Sussex lie encased in lead in its Elizabethan Chapel; and New Hall, a fine Tudor mansion, now used as a convent School, built by the Earl of Ormond, grandfather of Anne Boleyn, who with her Royal consort visited the hall in the spring of 1524, after which Henry VIII. spent a considerable sum of money upon it. Elizabeth, into whose possession New Hall eventually passed, must often have sorrowfully thought of her fair but frail young mother's youth when she came here; perhaps its associations were too sad for her, for she subsequently gave it as a prize to the Earl of Sussex, having previously had her arms and the following modest inscription placed over the entrance hall:—

> Vivat Elizabetha.
> En terra la piu savia regina;
> En cielo la piu lucente stella;
> Virgine magnanima, dotta, divina,
> Leggiadra, honesta e bella.

Later on, New Hall fell into the hands of the unhappy Duke of Buckingham, and, later still, Cromwell lived here awhile. Among the oaks to the west is the Palace, purchased by the Duke of Argyle on the death of his father-in-law, Bishop Claughton. To the end of his life, the late Bishop loved nothing so well as a drive over the beautiful heaths that surrounded his secluded home in picturesque Danbury, in whose ancient but restored church a beautiful reredos has recently been erected to his memory.

There is, for those who have time to linger in peaceful Chelmsford after they have revelled in the quiet joys of Danbury, much else to interest them. This portion of Essex is rich in historic associations, and no centre from which to visit the old houses and churches and ruins that abound in the neighbourhood could be more agreeable than the cleanly county town, from which the drives in all directions are pleasing, if not always strikingly picturesque, and which, if it possessed no other attraction, would surely be deserving of honour in that it leads to the charms of healthful, peaceful Danbury, perched high above all.

CHAPTER XXV.

BOATS AND BIVALVES.

SINCE the days when Alfred drove the Danes into Brightlingsea, the oyster, which flourishes in the shallow "rays" about St. Osyth and the creeks lying betwixt here and Mersea Island, has, so to say, held sway in the Essex waters, and brought fame to the immediate town of Colchester. "Colchester natives," like "Dundee marmalade" or "Banbury cakes," has become a household expression, though Whitstable is now regarded as the great oyster-producing district of England. Like most popular beliefs, however, this is fallacious. It is, as a matter of fact, down here, almost under the shadow of St. Osyth Priory, and in this enterprising little village of sea-farmers and able yachtsmen, that the largest fishery of the esteemed mollusc is carried on. Although, low be it spoken, it is not every oyster that finds its way from Brightlingsea waters to the markets who can say "I am native here." The beautiful smooth-shelled, delicately flavoured product that can honestly claim this proud distinction is, certainly, found here in abundance, and is not to be easily mistaken, by those who know, for the intruders who come to fatten on the fare that makes our natives of such worth; but, side by side with them, are Portuguese and coarse Americans, which are imported in large quantities every season to be laid in these famous waters for a few weeks in order to acquire something of this local flavour.

As St. Osyth is redolent of flowers, so is "Brickelsea" of the appetising odour of the bivalve and of tar. The combination does not sound agreeable, but it has to be known to be appreciated. Like the sweet girl graduates, in "Princess Ida," "we've tried it and we know," and there is no better place to become acquainted with it than in Brightlingsea, one of the brightest, busiest, bravest little hamlets in all Essex. Oysters are not naturally obtrusive. Over their shallow beds sail the yachts that are ever coming and going, and, save that the beacon-poles roughly bound about with dried grasses mark their residential quarters, they are not very much in evidence in the land of their birth. That they are "round about" is, however, manifest enough. Everybody's garden is paved with their shells, and so soon as the water's edge is reached it becomes apparent that the oyster is not afar off. In truth the channel is densely populated with them, and when the water is clear they may be seen on the muddy slopes at the bottom of the creeks, lying in dark-green slimy ridges, snugly tucked up in their "beds," so to say, ready to be dredged when their time shall come.

Oyster-farming appears to the unprofessional eye to be the simplest business in the world. One might almost say that the golden rule of the merchants is "take care of the 'spat' and the oysters will take care of themselves;" for, as a matter of fact, there is nothing else to do towards the culture of the "native." In the summer time, when the "spat" floats on the water, it may sometimes be thought advisable to move it to richer "layings," and by-and-bye some of the young oysters may be "pitted;" but beyond this there is nothing to do but to hope for the best and await results. The oyster-farmer is spared a great deal of unnecessary anxiety in this way, for he cannot watch the gradual failure of his enterprise nor tell beforehand whether his neighbour will do better than himself. Their chances are equal, as are their shares in the carefully-prepared "layings," which are worth as much as four, five, and even seven hundred pounds an acre; the Colne "spat," that in due season develops into the famous Colchester natives, being worth something like twenty thousand pounds while it is, as it were, in its "long clothes" stage of existence.

It is a busy and exciting time down here when the fourth of August has passed. Then in the early morning the blue-jerseyed dredgers may be seen at work in their white-sailed boats, rowing in and out of the winding "fleets" and "rays" that lie between the "Hard" and the hilly little island of Mersea; and later on in the day the men, in the huge boots that reach well-nigh to their waists, standing up to their middle in the creek, sort out the useless and the "foreigners" from the hauls with a rapidity that is amazing to the onlooker. But Brightlingsea does not depend alone on its bivalvous business. There are no idle days in this enterprising little limb of the Cinque Ports. For its fame is not merely ostreal. When the inland hedges are blossoming, and the trees round the beautiful grey church tower that stands high above the village are putting forth their first green shoots, the yachtsmen make them ready for the work that lies before them, and the tap, tap, tap of the builders' hammers is heard incessantly in the ship yards. The sail-makers have their hands full, the ship chandlers' stock is at high water-mark, and so soon as the warm summer days come, away go the gay, newly-painted, newly-fitted little yawls, the smart cutters and the flat-nosed racers with their crews and captains recruited from the ever reliable "Brickelsea" men, and then the village is practically depopulated of its masculine inhabitants, and the oyster men alone hold sway. But as the days draw in again and the autumn winds blow chill, and the waters grow less and less calm, the "docks" once more show signs

Brightlingsea Church.

of life. By degrees the dark-faced, cheery sailors come back to their waiting little ones, the noise increases again in the builders' yards, and all day long the yachts are seen creeping home again round the "Point," till at last in the winter quarters there grows up a very forest of masts.

There are a couple of hundred little "docks" into which for the most part the yachts enter, though some, of course, are hauled into the yards to undergo thorough repair. Ofttimes there are as many as three hundred of these smart craft lying up, and then the creek, as viewed from the park, presents all the appearance of a great shipping centre. Hence one looks right across to the German Ocean which lies round the "Point," and would wash the shores of Brightlingsea if Mersea were not in the way.

But though the busy little village has thus been prevented from laying claim to the usual seaside attractions, it year by year grows in popularity as a resort for those who are interested in yachts, yachtsmen, and yachting; and in the long summer days, when the sun flashes all over the Hard and one may almost scent the sweet odour of the St. Osyth flower-farm across the creek, Brightlingsea is, so far as its visitors go, a very colourable imitation of Cowes. It has lately added to its public buildings the smart new Royal Hotel, where oyster luncheons are a speciality and the Brightlingsea Sailing Club has its head-quarters, and there are rumours that its guests often include personages whose names as inscribed upon their bills are less exalted than they are when figuring among the list of visitors at fashionable yachting stations. Boniface flourishes elsewhere in Brightlingsea, too, than in this imposing new structure. There is a comfortable old-fashioned hostelry, known as the "Swan," where yachtsmen still love to congregate, and are always sure of finding simple but excellent fare; while the town can also boast of various smaller inns, so that there is plenty of accommodation for the distinguished folk who find their way hither in the summer time. It was from Brightlingsea, by the way, that Lord and the late Lady Brassey started on their first voyage round the world, in the "Sunbeam," and hence sailed the "Kara," on her

Arctic Expedition. Nowhere else, of course, along the Eastern shore is there a yachting station which can compare for size with this enterprising little village, and at the rate at which its progressive inhabitants proceed with their improvements it should not be long before it develops into a flourishing town of maritime importance. Already, as a member of the Cinque Ports, being attached to the most ancient of them all, Sandwich, it has its Deputy-Mayor and Corporation of twelve; and just recently it has been presented with a public recreation ground by an enthusiastic yachtsman, who, sailing into the waters of Brightlingsea three or four years ago to have his yacht repaired, has ever since remained aboard it just without the harbour. To the little port he has found so attractive he has been a most generous benefactor; for, not only will it thus be made the possessor of fine lawn tennis-courts, a cricket ground, and, in fact, a miniature "Lord's," but its grand old church (whose lofty flint tower is one of the most beautiful in Essex) has been enriched by him with a peal of ten bells, which ring out to him across the water, as he sits hermit-like in his curious aquatic home. Up here the beloved shepherd of this flock of fishers has ofttimes kept lonely vigil on stormy winter nights when "Brickelsea" men have been away on the fierce North Sea, and their wives trembled for their safety as they shudderingly remembered the long list of victims claimed by the cruel, crawling sea, whose names the vicar has had inscribed on the interior walls. For far out at sea the tower can be seen, and he has hoped that the lamp he has kept alight through the dark watches might cheer and help any who were steering homewards. When he came here, a couple of decades since, he found this magnificent church in a deplorable condition; it is now thoroughly and carefully restored, and within and without has now few rivals in Essex. The church itself is singularly fine with its splendid Perpendicular tower, nave, aisles, Lady Chapel, and Baptistry. The fisher-folk are very proud of their church, its richly-appointed high altar, and their vicar, who is always the first on the "Hard" and the last to leave if the weather has been rough and there is any doubt about the safety of his men. And on Sundays it is a fine sight to see the bronze-faced lads and smart-looking yachtsmen streaming up the hill to the old church, whose bright and reverent services would not be unworthy of much more important and richer places of worship in East Anglia.

To the vicar's enterprise and thoughtfulness, too, Brightlingsea folk owe their excellent Reading Room, and many other features which amaze the visitors who come here anticipating none of the resources of civilization and go away marvelling at its public spirit, its bustle and ceaseless activity, and its unexpected interest. Nobody can ever complain of dulness in this offshoot of decayed Sandwich, that is, at least, if they are so happily constituted as to be able to seek out diversion for themselves. It is true that at present it boasts no pier and no town-band, but for those who find special delight in attractions of this kind there are amusements calculated to meet their requirements. "Jack" is not a dull dog. He likes music and dancing, and he is a patron of the drama, and consequently he is not unprovided at times and seasons with his needs in these directions. But those who come to Brightlingsea to see its wonderful array of resting yachts, to pursue the oyster to its native lair, and watch skeleton yawls and cutters, hard by at Wivenhoe, growing into smart crafts that shall perhaps become famous by-and-bye, will not find the time "hang heavy" on their hands, even though they are not perpetually sailing to Walton or Mersea, over the oyster grounds, or talking of boats and bivalves with the human natives. There is St. Osyth within a walk, and Colchester is close at hand to supply the antiquarian with plenty of interest; cricket, in due season, is always in progress, and the frequent water sports attract excursionists from all parts. But it is, after all, for the oysters and the shipping that we come to Brightlingsea. The rest can be had elsewhere along the Saxon shore, but otherwhere the sweet-flavoured "native" cannot be roused from his "bed" for luncheon, nor the fitting of yachts, their coming and going, and the simple, homely ways of the North Sea fishers be better studied. Moreover, when across the marshes the east winds blow keen and one may fancy that even the figure-heads of the harboured yachts look pinched and chill, sportsmen may go further and fare worse in pursuit of the wild-fowl, which here, at Mersea, and St. Osyth, make merry at the expense of the oysters, and with those excellent products of these shores are subsequently brought low by the hungry hunter.

CHAPTER XXVI.

A FLORAL SHRINE.

ACROSS the wild, lonely marshes the wind is blowing in from the sea. And as the breeze sweeps over the land and stirs the fine Lombardy poplars—the first planted in England—swaying high above the Abbot's Tower of the old Priory, the mingled perfumes of the flower-farm are borne to us. Each breath of wind is laden with fresh fragrance, and the whole village filled with the strong, sweet odours of the blossoms that make acres of land in the very centre of the hamlet to glow with dazzling brilliance. The windows, too, of the white cottages in the Street are all aglow with geraniums, the garden patches about them are a mass of bright blooms, there are flowers everywhere to greet the eye, and the air is heavy with their sweetness. Here, in this remote corner of Essex between the sea and the waving fields of rich corn, we seem to have discovered the land of flowers, the very bower of Flora herself; but apparently there are others, too, who have been attracted hither by the fame of the flower-farm and the ancient Priory, and the legend of the gentle saint whose name has been for ever perpetuated in the church and the village built in her memory. For in the windows of the few shops there is an announcement to the effect that "Tickets to view the Priory" may be had within, and the fact that "Refreshments" are obtainable is made manifest many times on the way to the farm. Yet, though the tourist has invaded it and the sight-seer is not unknown, the quietude and sleepiness of "Toozey," as it is locally called, remain undisturbed.

There is no one about, so far as can be seen, this afternoon. We stroll through the Street, past the village shops, till the little gate that leads to the flower-fields is reached, and St. Osyth

PHLOX.

herself is not apparently more dead than the inhabitants. Not a soul is to be seen. Not a sound breaks the silence: one wonders if everybody is drowsy with the heavy odour of the flowers, or if their patron, the headless Mercian damsel, who fell a victim to

SWEET PEAS.

the Danes in 870, holds them under a spell. In Nun's wood, within the Priory grounds, the scene of her martyrdom, an old fountain still flows that is said to have sprung from the ground as the saint's head fell beneath the Danish knife. Can it be that the waters of Lethe flow here, and that the dwellers in "Toozey" have drunk of them deeply and so forgotten to arise to their daily labour? No, there is life here after all. The flowers are not destined to blush unseen. For presently we come upon the labourers at work among the dazzling floral crops in the fields stretching before us. It is a glorious sight.

Like a gaudy carpet the farm is spread in the midst of the village. Instead of fields of stately wheat and whispering barley, metallic green mangolds and richly-coloured beets, this farm is made up of patches of gay and fragrant blossoms, flung together regardless of their colours, yet completely harmonious as a whole. Closer inspection, however, shows that the flowers are not in sole possession of the land, for here and there is a corner where monster "blue" peas hang in Brobdingnagian pods; where waxen turnips—outrivalling in size the models in the show-cases of the Crystal Palace— gigantic celery, and such marrows as an agriculturist in Giant-land might be proud to rear, hob-nob with the gladioli and sunflowers, the lilac and red and orange chrysanthemums, soon to reach the zenith of their glory. Presently, too, a miniature field of wheat is discerned among the acres of flowers, and even the humble broccoli and the pungent radish may be found for the seeking. But as the beautiful blossoms that scent the air and delight the eye are only born to die that their seeds may be spread far and near, so are these culinary specimens not directly destined to find their way into the cook's hands. It is when the seed-harvest is come that they shall one and all be gathered in, and in this form go forth to presently delight, when the time of their blossoming and maturity shall come

Threshing Seeds at St. Osyth.

again, the suburban horticulturist, the kitchen gardener, and the grower of grain.

Across the fields yonder, among the stacks of graceful and delicately perfumed sweet peas of a thousand hues, the rich but formal dahlias and the great purple patches of ageratum, the women and boys are busy reaping the harvest of flowers. They are well-nigh hidden as they stoop over the patches, for the sunflowers and nicotines that make the night air languid, and the heavy, bulging poppy heads tower above them. Some are weeding among the vegetables, but most of them are rapidly picking off the seedpods which will by-and-bye be carried into the barns close at hand, to undergo the various processes through

which they must pass before they are ready to send up to
the huge warehouse of Messrs. Carter and Co., in High
Holborn, whence they are dispatched all over the kingdom.
The autumn sun shines brightly upon the workers, albeit
the air blows keenly from the sea, and the bees are still
busily buzzing about their work, finding a very *embarras de
richesses* in the surrounding fields, while the rooks caw lazily
overhead. And like the bees, one scarce knows which way
to first turn that the sweetness of the flowers may be
gathered. Mignonette literally carpets the ground, its
fragrance struggling to overmaster the perfumes of the
gaudy petunias, the belated stocks, and the myriads of
pansies, white, purple, and yellow. Either way, before or
behind, colour and fragrance await one. When the eye is
weary of the huge yellow masses of sanvitalia and the
dazzling clumps of blue lobelia and less vivid ageratum,
there are the glowing pinks and deep rich reds of the
lordly gladioli to lend the charm of variety. Phlox, of
which there are no less than nineteen different kinds, is
made specially evident by the striking, poppy-red variety
which may be easily detected in this wilderness of perfume,
where surely the cravings of all noble souls, whom Ruskin
has declared to be lovers of bright colour, may be abundantly
satisfied.

It is almost with a sigh of relief, though, that we turn
from the dazzling scene without to the sombre picture
within. A miniature thresher is at work in the barns, and
as the rich, ripe grain falls into the huge troughs, the men
are shovelling it with milk-white wooden spades into the
clean dun-coloured sacks, of which there are piles of all
sizes, that will be filled in due time with seeds of every
possible kind. With such clean and pleasant work in
progress here, it is hardly surprising to find that the women
of "Toozey" have found an industry at their doors in

which they may easily engage. At this season there is
plenty for their hands to do. Some of them are sitting
round a huge sheet spread upon the barn-floor, stalking the
dried pods that are presently carried without and threshed
by the men and boys with flails; while others, when the
seeds are brought back again, pass them, according to their

Stripping Seed Pods at St. Osyth.

species, through various-sized sieves, till all the foreign
matter is separated from them, and they are then ready to
be finally winnowed in the huge wicker fans that clear them
of all dust. All the year round there is work of some kind
in hand here, and while the men of the village are tilling

the land for the corn and the root-crops, their women-kind can busy themselves among the flower-buds and the seeds in this nursery of mammoth blossoms, whence year after year some new "specimens" are sent forth to be the pride of flower-beds or the glory of kitchen gardens.

But though the attractions of this charming seed-farm are sufficient in themselves to lure all lovers of flowers to quiet St. Osyth, which is on the road to nowhere in particular, the pride of this little village is centred in its huge church and its Priory, now the property of Sir John Johnson, a City of London Alderman, whose father purchased it from the Nassaus, the sole representatives of the Earl of Rochford, in whose family it had been since the reign of Edward VI. Somewhere in the seventh century a nunnery existed at Chiche, as the village was then called, over which St. Osyth, a daughter of Penda, King of the Mercians, presided, and thence onward the Church seems to have regarded the Priory as a very

Church of St. Osyth.

desirable possession, if one may judge from the frequent disagreements and schemes which arose as to its occupation. When Henry VIII. was casting about for some suitable little reward for Cromwell's zeal, he threw in St. Osyth's Priory with some five-and-twenty other monastic buildings in this county and presented them to "my good Cromwell," who appears to have regarded it as a valuable acquisition, since he clung to it despite Lord Chancellor Audley's discouraging description of it as "onholsom for dwellyng, by cause yt ys nere the sea and mershes. This house," he repeats, "also stondith in the confyne of the realms nere the sea." Evidently Lord Chancellor Audley would have risked the marshy mists and "onholsomeness" himself if he had got the chance, but the astute Cromwell was not to be so easily "put off" this desirable seaside residence, though his possession of it was brief. It has been carefully restored by Sir John Johnson, and of its beautiful flint Norman gateway, overgrown with ivy, the "Toozey" villagers have good reason to be proud. Essex cannot boast of many interesting monastic remains, but all that there are at St. Osyth are of exceeding interest. Probably the excursionists who flock over here in the summer from noisy, "tripper"-ridden Clacton and waning Walton-on-the-Naze are not particularly interested in the beautiful sixteenth-century oriel window, the quadrangle with its Tudor remains, the Abbot's Tower and ancient chapel in the beautiful grounds; nor would they, were they offered for their inspection, think much of the old carvings and the ancient Scandinavian pottery within doors. They clamber up to the tower, it is true, to look across the marshes to the sea, and apparently derive much satisfaction from freely inscribing their names therein; and their sixpences, moreover, help to bring hither in the summer many parties of

Gateway to Existing Priory.

Interior of Quadrangle of Existing Priory.

pallid-faced little Londoners, for whom good Sir John provides a country holiday within the Priory from the funds thus collected. They neither know nor care, probably, that they are walking over the same ground that twelve centuries ago St. Osyth and her nuns trod. It is supposed that this was the oldest monastic establishment in Essex, and the present church of St. Peter and St. Paul can likewise trace its history back to the days when this famous East Anglian saint dwelt in this village of flowers. Many centuries later her arm was brought with great solemnity and deposited in the then existing church, and as each 7th of August—her festival—recurred, there were solemn services held in her honour within its walls. At this period—1120—St. Osyth village was apparently not quite as slow as it is now. The monks and priors had rather a pleasant time of it down here, for under a charter granted by Henry II., they not only instituted fox-hunting—a sport hitherto unknown—but they established a Sunday fair under the shadow of the Priory, and from time to time they further enlivened themselves, it would seem, by burning occasional "heretics." The Sunday fair and the "heretics" have had their day, but St. Osyth is still a famous hunting centre, and what

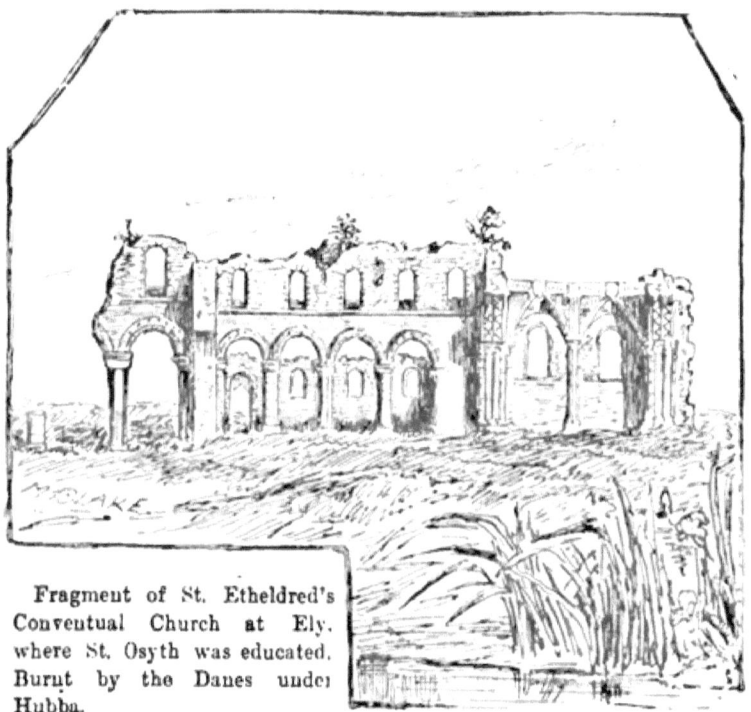

Fragment of St. Etheldred's Conventual Church at Ely, where St. Osyth was educated. Burnt by the Danes under Hubba.

sportsman in the county does not know its "Flag" and Green, the scene of many a well-remembered meet? Thanks to Sir John Johnson and a careful vicar, the interior of the present church is beginning to assume a reverent aspect. It was awhile ago in the most dilapidated condition, but its chancel has now been restored, the quaint old wooden "Fold" replaced by a stone one, a handsome reredos erected, and the altar—once wholly obscured by the "Fold," the fine Darcy monuments, and the Squire's pew—now made conspicuous, while stained glass has been placed in the east and other windows of the chancel. But there is still much to be done in the splendid old building. There are beautiful tombs that need care, the roof and walls of the nave and aisles are in a bad state, and the rest of the church needs to be fitly appointed and restored. If the work already taken in hand could be completed, this grand memorial of the county's most popular saint would undoubtedly be one of the finest of the churches in the county.

There is truly little temptation to hurry from this quaint East Anglian corner, where Elizabeth, who doubtless feasted right royally on the famous oysters to be found hard by, appears to have been sumptuously entertained by Lord Darcy, one of whose descendants married the Earl of Rochford, a name freely associated with the Junius Letters. This nobleman, evidently more cultivated than most of the companions of the Second George, who could not "see any use in bainting and boetry," subsequently became a personal friend of George III., and twice entertained that unhappy monarch at St. Osyth. From the tower one may look over the marshes to the lonely beach where, amid the scanty tufts of wild ranunculus and the coarse, reed-like grass, or sea-bent, that flourishes here as on the Dutch coast, wild duck, bar-geese, and widgeon have their haunts. Sometimes the shrill whistle of the curlew is heard when the mists are rising, and then, as the shadowy vessels are seen turning the "Point," and the sound of bells in Brightlingsea tower just across the creek rises and falls on the breeze, is the fitting opportunity to hear how, in the dark October nights when the wind moans through the now almost leafless trees in the park, St. Osyth, carrying her head in her hand, revisits the scene of her former labours, passing from the fountain in the wood to the church of St. Peter and St. Paul, against whose closed doors she may be heard to rap by any who have the temerity to wait for her coming.

CHAPTER XXVII.

'TWIXT THE COLNE AND THE NAZE.

ST. OSYTH, with its flower-farm and Priory, forms a common point of interest to the two holiday-haunts on the northern corner of the Essex shore. It is said that having visited the village of flowers and the headless saint, you are left stranded at Walton or Clacton with nothing whatever to do. True, the surrounding country is flat, as flat as any part of Essex, and there are no churches or ruins of interest or drives of particular beauty in the vicinity; yet there is something to be said in favour of these two resorts which have, at all events, attained popularity.

Of the two, Clacton is decidedly the more flourishing. It has indeed a big future before it, for it is one of those pushing places that are ever seeking how to improve themselves. From a mere village it has grown with surprising rapidity to a comparatively large and prosperous town; and there seems to be every chance of its further development into a kind of East Anglian Margate when a few more years have rolled, and time has been given for all the prospective "improvements" to be carried into effect. Even now it has fine houses, and their number annually increases at a rate which leaves no doubt as to the ever-growing popularity of the place. It has large hotels, yet their accommodation is always all too limited in the season; a pier already furnished with a pavilion always occupied by theatrical and operatic companies in the summer months, and of which great things are promised in the future, for this pier, like the rest of Clacton, has been growing fast. A decade or so since, it was an unpretentious small wooden jetty; then it was "done up" and enlivened after the fashion of piers, with a band and other accessories. Now the elaborate pavilion has been added, and when the band is playing and the London boat is alongside, and the sun streams down on the fine sea, Clacton pier is indeed a centre of gaiety, a Margate jetty in miniature.

At no time could Clacton ever be truly described as dull, though its gaiety is sometimes of a somewhat overpowering description, when the train pours thousands of jam-factory girls, playing-card makers, and envelope-folders into its midst. These maidens do their best to impart to Clacton all the "life" of the Commercial and Mile End Roads, as, linked arm-in-arm and five or six abreast, they rush down the broad avenues to the sea, warbling the latest popular melodies and stopping occasionally to execute *pas seuls*. Their costumes are always alike. Plush enters largely into their confection, and the much be-feathered hat of prismatic hues is, of course, indispensable on these festive occasions. The spirits of these damsels are unflagging, for when they are not dancing, they are singing or playfully placing sand down each others' backs. The sands are a great vantage-ground for their saltatory efforts, and music of all kinds is so liberally provided here that Terpsichore is given every chance.

Clacton, being wise in her generation, has in every way met the requirements of her patrons. With visitors of

Sea-Front, Clacton.

this type it has coped to their intense satisfaction and its own profit. At every turn you are implored to have "joint and two vegetables at a shilling a head," or to remember that "this is the shop for tea and shrimps." "Refreshments" stare you in the face here, there, and everywhere, testifying abundantly to the fact that if you come to Clacton it is a foregone conclusion that you will eat; and they will tell you in the hotels, in the lodging-houses, aye, even in the Charing Cross Hospital Convalescent Home itself, that a state of hunger is the normal condition of everybody after a week spent in the fine strong air that sweeps over both this little town and its neighbour, Walton-on-Naze. Some day, undoubtedly, there will be huge restaurants here along the sea-front, if the handsome great houses, that are so rapidly putting in an appearance north and south of the pleasant Royal Hotel, do not first occupy all the available space. "Estates" were long since laid out, and how great was the faith of the speculative builders in the evolution of Clacton is evidenced by the imposing mansions and handsome Queen Anne villas lining the prettily-planned roads. So fast have they found tenants that ready-built houses are now scarcely purchaseable; and it is only by buying land, that becomes more valuable each year, and building thereon for oneself, that a *pied à terre* is obtainable at all. The late Sir Andrew Clark long ago built himself a residence here, and, firmly believing in the beneficial effects of Clacton air, constantly urged upon his patients to try its restorative effects; and but recently the authorities of the Middlesex Hospital elected to build their Convalescent Home here on a plot of ground five acres in extent. Poor Fred Leslie, too, was an occasional resident, and his pretty villa has been the head-quarters from Saturday to Monday of numbers of popular players, many of whom have since found their way back to Clacton again and again. Perhaps the day is not so far distant when some of them, at all events, may return in a professional capacity, for the Public Hall and Assembly Rooms are none too large for the accommodation of visitors who like "somewhere to go of an evening." When the electric light illumines the town, Clacton will be well advised to consider a theatre; and as in all probability the former will be established by next year, the latter may not be an altogether nebulous project. There can be no doubt of the success of such a venture here. The young person of both sexes already finds Clacton an alluring holiday-resort; it would become ideal with a Hall-by-the-Sea or a Theatre Royal in its midst.

But it is not only with the young men and maidens, who flirt so continuously and so recklessly on the pier, that Clacton finds favour. Perhaps it is not too much to say that it owes a very large amount of its success as a watering-place to the fact that it just meets the requirements of the London as well as the local *paterfamilias*, who cannot take a holiday *en bloc*. If he is a Londoner, tied all the week to the busy mill-wheel of business, to what more convenient place could he possibly dispatch his wife and children when holiday-time comes round? He is sure that they will be getting full value for their money here. They will come home brown and full of strength, and they will not have spent half the holiday expenses on travelling; while he himself can, at a trifling outlay, and in an almost incredibly short space of time, run down from Saturday to Monday, from Friday to Tuesday, or even on Sunday, only just to see how they are, and have a romp with them on the sands. There never was, surely, a more accessible place. The railway authorities have reduced the fare to Clacton to its least common denominator, while they whirl you there and back in a couple of hours, from sunrise till long past sunset. And then, if time is no object, there is the water-way to Clacton, and only those who have tried it and who know, can realize how much enjoyment is to be had at the outlay of four or five shillings. It is one of the summer sights of Clacton to see the passengers land from the excellent boats that daily ply between London and Harwich—making Clacton one of the stopping-places—especially if the sea has been choppy and the journey unusually long. On a calm, fine day, a trip from London to Clacton on the well-appointed "Clacton Belle," for instance, is, as Mr. Pepys would have said, "vastly pleasant." The boat service is admirable, the passengers, as a rule, well-conducted, and the way hither, down the Thames and along the Essex shore, past Hadleigh and Southend, and thence into the open sea to Clacton, is mostly interesting. By way of diversion, it is good fun, when the boats come in, to run on to

Harwich or Felixstowe, if you are already "located" in Clacton, returning the same way when the boats start homeward again. By this means a good sea-blow is obtained, for the boats get well clear of the coast when they leave the pier-end; and at Harwich, as one knows, there is plenty of stir and life of a marine character. A trip of the kind disposes, moreover, of an occasional afternoon in an agreeable fashion; for truth to tell there is not much to be done by road when St. Osyth has been visited.

There is, however, a long and breezy walk over the cliffs to Frinton, by which means a grand appetite is established, and a particularly fine seascape opened to view. Towards this promising little village of bungalows, fast growing into a "resort," the cliffs gradually rise till they attain a fairly respectable height, and, compared with Walton on the left and Clacton on the right, Frinton stands on a dizzy eminence. What an ideal retreat this mushroom holiday-haunt would make for a novelist in search of perfect quiet and stimulating air! Nothing whatever occurs here. There is an absurdly small church with accommodation for about half a hundred people, a handful or two of pretty villas, a good hotel, and a shop or two, and nothing to do but to lie on the cliffs or firm white sands, eat, drink, play tennis, and sleep as one only can sleep in this splendid East coast air.

Down at Walton, a mile or so further on, they like to fancy they are "gay dogs;" but try as they will, they cannot shake off that air of depression that must necessarily hang over a townlet rapidly crumbling away into the sea, which has already swallowed up one Walton, church and all. At the cost of several thousands of pounds the Local Board recently built a sea-defence of concrete, which likewise forms an admirable esplanade; but already a part of it has been washed away, and the cost of repairing it constantly threatens to make a heavy drain upon the resources of the poor little place. Enterprise is hardly one of its characteristics; but it jogs along and has its admirers; and it is not pretentious. It has a small wooden pier, on which a local band plays very well on summer nights; its sailing yachts and rowing boats are the best of their kind; and the lodging-houses beyond reproach. Indeed, it produces the best specimens of

Walton.

seaside landladies to be met with round the coast, and this is "greatly to its credit." In the matter of hotels, too, it is reliable. The "Marine" is well situated and well appointed; the "Clifton" literally overhangs the sea, and is the chief centre of gaiety here. But Walton does not pretend to be smart or fashionable or high-class. The same lower-middle-class families come down year after year, expecting nothing more than Walton can give them, and they are perfectly satisfied with what it offers. It is neither picturesque nor lively nor noisy, nor is it a good head-quarters for interesting excursions; but it always sends its visitors home with a healthy glow on their cheeks, and fills their lungs with fine bracing air. The children make the most of the sands; the boys of the boating; the fathers and mothers of the restfulness; the young folks of the humble little pier and moonlight nights; and for those who cannot get far afield and have to consider that formidable item in holiday expenses, the railway fare, Walton is, after all, not such a bad place. The Great Eastern brings its passengers down for next to nothing, and the opportunities for spending much money when you get here are certainly not illimitable. It has no arcade of smart shops like Clacton, which, in this matter, can hold its own with most East coast watering-places; but there is plenty of everything to be had here, and very good dinners to boot, either at the "Marine," or the "Clifton," or the "Portobello" Hotels.

Walton speaks of Clacton as a place of wild dissipation and revelry; Clacton regards Walton as a dismal and decaying little village. Fortunately there are admirers for both, and those who delight in the one will surely not appreciate the other. It is very certain that poor little Walton stands no chance against its younger rival. All the money and enterprise and promise are at Clacton; and the sea has undoubtedly marked Walton for its own. As each winter comes round the waves make greater inroads. Until the sea-defence was built, the railway station itself was threatened with ultimate destruction; and the Honourable Artillery Company's lifeboat, which does such excellent service, has more often than not to face a sea which runs as high here as anywhere on the coast. There is brave work done on winter nights, and Waltonians are justly proud of their lifeboat's record. Candidly, they have not much else, save the air and the sea, of which to boast. Almost the whole of the tiny town might be included in one of Clacton's spacious streets. The church is modern and dull in every way, and the walks uninteresting, save when you stroll past the large foundry of Messrs. Warner and Co., the birthplace of bell-buoys, ships' engines, and lighthouse contrivances, to enjoy the view of Harwich and Felixstowe from the Naze, where plovers and oyster spat do grow, and the sea holds high revels, lashing and splashing in splendid fashion round the promontory.

CHAPTER XXVIII.

THE CAMP ON THE COLNE.

IF one were suddenly asked to name the products of this quiet yet most famous little town, the answer undoubtedly would be "soldiers, oysters, and antiquities." Geographical works and guides to Colchester will not be found to include these in their list; but they certainly seem, to the general observer, to be the chief features of this ancient city. Whether they are given in the right order of precedence is a matter of individual determination and taste. At all events, the soldiers are more invariably plentiful than the oysters, if less interesting, though, in favour of the antiquities taking a first place, it may be urged that they encompass the entire town. The oysters, unhappily, do not obtrude themselves quite so much upon the visitor as the red-coats, though, on the occasion of the annual Oyster Feast, it is said that they make their appearance, not in the ordinary dozens of commerce, but in millions; and having their shell upon their native heath, so to say, literally take possession of the ancient Camulodunum until the Mayor and Corporation and their guests take possession of them. Colchester has always done honour to the oyster. An ancient civic custom of opening the fishery is annually celebrated, the Mayor and Corporation inspecting the "grounds" in a kind of state barge, returning afterwards to "gin and gingerbread," and extras thereto. In the old Moot Hall—now unfortunately pulled down—long before it possessed the mace of which it is so proud, the Corporation kept oyster-knives and "oyster cloths," and oysters figure in almost all the old records of this famous town.

Returning to the soldiers, however, it must fain be admitted that as a general rule they are all-prominent. Their gay tunics enliven every corner and every thoroughfare. The North station literally glows with red-coats at all times of the day, and turn to right or to left, go eastwards or westwards from Lexden to Hythe, there is scarlet everywhere. The High Street, the only really important thoroughfare in the town, is ever ringing with the jingle of spurs; and from *reveille* to roll-call, up and down North Hill there always seem to be regiments coming in or regiments going from the camp, which has the largest cavalry barracks in the kingdom.

From time immemorial Colchester has been a city of soldiers. Eighteen hundred years ago in these same streets was heard the clatter of the mounted *miles* riding to and from the *castra* at Lexden, where the Roman fortifications, the cemetery, theatre, and other remains of the oppidum that undoubtedly existed here, are still to be seen. Cuirasses and helmets, shields and greaves glittered then in the sunlight as the legions and cohorts "gleaming with purple and gold" passed through the avenues of the city, just as in these days the cobbled streets of Colchester ring with the sound of mounted military, and are made gay with the colour and dazzling splendour of cavalry accoutrements. Thus, in an unbroken line, as it were, on from generation to generation, from A.D. 44, when "Camulodunum" was established, until this day, when

Colchester camp holds, as a rule, about two thousand troops at a time, soldiers have dwelt within its walls and constituted the greater portion of its inhabitants. And as "there were giants in those days," so have there been great battles in Colchester. It has stood a siege, memorable in history, and was likewise the scene of the great rising of the Iceni, when Boadicea led her troops in person, and the infuriated Britons, rolling southwards, fell upon the Romans and smote them hip and thigh. Of the famous siege of 1648 indelible marks remain upon the town, for Fairfax, who chose for his camp the

Colchester Castle.

identical ground where the Romans met and fought the Britons centuries before, made sad havoc with shot and shell of its churches and its buildings. Colchester's architectural ruin dates from this memorable siege; but it still remains one of the most interesting of all antiquarian haunts, since the traces of its Roman origin are so numerous and distinct.

A walk round Colchester, miniature though the town is, is not to be lightly and unadvisedly taken. For it is

perched on the top of a high hill, and go which way
you will, either you are climbing up or running down
an eminence, now looking upon roofs below or gazing
upwards at the houses and churches, which appear to
be slipping down the sides of the hilly streets. Betwixt
breakfast and luncheon the whole of the cheerful little
town may be seen, unless it be market day, when
soldiers and farmers, smart country carts, and droves of
cattle fill the streets to overflowing, and make locomotion
agreeably impossible to the crowds who delight in this
weekly glimpse of bustling activity.

The Colchester walls run the Colchester "natives" very
close as regards fame; in point of antiquity the bivalves
probably have the advantage, for the epicurean Roman
had a nice taste for the oyster, and not impossibly took
the ostreal advantages of the creeks round about into
consideration before settling down in the neighbourhood.
However, the walls date from the time of the Roman
occupation, and starting from the summit of the hill, from
the old postern in Balkerne Lane, close to the handsome
church of St. Mary on the Walls, one may trace their
whole circuit, and in so doing discover the most interesting
of the ancient buildings in the town. It was, by the way,
in the yard of the church that the Royalists had a battery
during the siege, and the tower then destroyed has only
been recently rebuilt. A little further along, one of
the principal bastions of the fortification, known as the
"Balcon," and a most picturesque corner of the town,
represents, so local tradition says, the castle of the original
old King Cole, whose claim to fame does not rest, according to the legend, solely upon the fact of his having
been "a merry old soul" of a convivial turn, and with
a taste for instrumental music. Up at Lexden may be
seen King Cole's kitchen, in which possibly the contents

of that "glass," for which he called in conjunction with his pipe, were brewed. Alas! the antiquarians and the Archæological Society have set their foot down very firmly in old King Cole's kitchen, and proved it without doubt to have been the theatre of the Roman settlers. There is no reason, however, why the legendary Duke of Kaercolin, to give the "merry old soul" his other title, should not be left in undisturbed possession of his castle on the walls. There is a certain picturesqueness in the association of Cole with Colchester, and the legends connected with the native monarch lend an interest to the town of which it is a thousand pities to rob it. It is very certain, for instance, that Constantine, the first Christian Emperor, did not visit Britain till he was a young man; but the romantic Colchestrians assert that he first saw the light in Colking's Castle, his mother having been Helena, daughter of Cole, and wife of the Roman senator who succeeded to the crown and presumably to "the fiddlers three" when the "merry" monarch died. And as the municipal arms would drop all to pieces without this story, it is perhaps as well to let Cole and his descendants severely alone. Whether or not King Cole inhabited the castle on the Balcon, there is "no possible doubt whatever" as to the reality and the antiquity of Colchester's real castle, hidden away behind the pleasant little High Street that a few years ago contained buildings dating back, so the story runs, to Saxon times, but now, unhappily, swept away by "improving" hands. It is eminently picturesque, this old castle, with its ivied walls and the fine old trees surrounding it, and the recently opened public park in its immediate vicinity has added in no small measure to its attractiveness from this point of view. Round it circle the usual antiquarian myths and mendacities; but as it is by far the largest Norman keep in England, and the whole structure, marvellously solid, is an excellent example of Norman architecture, it is not much good burrowing further back than the Conqueror for its foundation.

One Eudo, a "Dapifer," or "Lord High Executioner," or some other Court functionary to the first William, is credited with the erection of the castle by those who do not maintain it to be part of the Roman temple of Claudius, and if he performed his official duties as well as he built castles and churches, he must have been invaluable to his royal master. Doubtless he robbed and pillaged freely in the course of his building operations, but that is a mere detail. Those who suffered for his enterprise would probably have been swindled and

Ruins of Priory, Colchester.

tortured in any case, and it is philosophical, at all events, as one looks at Colchester Castle, to think that the net result was so eminently successful. The majority of folks who visit the Castle are much more interested in its Roman than its Norman aspect. They are prone to turn their backs on Eudo, so to say, and become absorbed in the wonderfully interesting collection of relics contained in the museum of the Essex Archæological Society, for which the Castle chapel has been utilised. In the course of building operations, in and around the town and in the neighbouring villages, some extraordinary discoveries have been made. Vases, glasses, pottery, statuary, implements of various kinds, and tiles have been unearthed and deposited here. At Lexden they are even unto this day continually finding coins, bronzes, and other Roman remains; and after the earthquake of 1884, urns and pots were freely disgorged round about.

Just without the castle walls, probably close to the garden of the old Crutched Friars, now converted into a botanical garden, Sir Charles Lucas and Sir George Lisle suffered death by order of the merciless Fairfax, though not improbably he was but a tool in the hands of the implacable Ireton, Cromwell's son-in-law, who is said to have witnessed the sight. Death filled these gallant soldiers with no dread. They had bravely borne a seventy-six days' siege of the town, during which time the starving garrison had lived on horses and dogs, no less than three hundred of the former being consumed; but Fairfax eventually forced them to surrender, and the generals were given but short shrift, for the same evening Lucas was first brought out into this little space behind the castle and there shot. Lisle shortly followed, kneeling to kiss his brave companion's body, before he, too, bared his breast to the rebels' muskets. The bodies of these faithful adherents of the king were afterwards secretly buried in St. Giles' Church, and after the Restoration a marble slab, still to be seen in the church, was laid above their remains. Close by this church is St. John's Abbey Gate, another relic of the architecturally-inclined Eudo, who evidently invested his savings—and the unconsidered trifles he picked up—in house property. The gateway, now restored, and once part of a huge Benedictine monastery, was ingeniously used as a gallows for the last abbot, who was one of the twenty-four mitred barons of England. This way the barracks are now reached; and in St. John's Abbey Gardens, where once the old Benedictines exercised themselves, and later on, the Lucases, who bought the place, took their pleasure, the children and nursemaids of the officers now promenade with the ubiquitous and fascinating "pretty soldier" in convenient proximity.

Round St. John's Green, whence one looks down on the factories and churches and crooked little streets of Colchester, the odour of gunpowder may be fairly said to cling about every stone, and if the soldiers of to-day have the martial spirit strong within them, they cannot tread its ground without some thought of the gallant fight of which this was the scene. Upon St. John's Gate the besiegers made their first attack, "undaunted Capel" shutting it in the face of the enemy; and it was on this same green that the most determined struggle between the Royalists and Fairfax's followers took place.

Hard by, the ruins of St. Botolph's Priory, founded in 1103, and once the leading Augustinian priory of England, to which Order the martyred Becket belonged, stand as a memorial of Fairfax's merciless attack upon the town. His heaviest cannon were levelled on this fine old building from the high ground at Wivenhoe—now famous for its yacht-yards—and there is very little left

St. John's Gateway.

save a few picturesque arches and the west front, which, curiously enough, bravely withstood the shock of earthquake in 1884, that brought down modern and some of the other old buildings in the town like packs of cards.

St. Botolph, whose name, bestowed upon the railway

station in the town under the shadow of the old Priory, is locally pronounced " Bottles," was a Saxon saint, much favoured by East Anglians ; but his memory is by no means honourably perpetuated in the ghastly modern church built close to the original St. Botolph's. Within and without it is ugly and bare, and altogether a poor substitute for the work of Ernulph and his followers.

Colchester's churches are anything but interesting, strange to say, though they are picturesquely situated, nor are its public buildings likely to add to its fame ; but it can hold its own in the matter of shops. The " gallant officers" and their wives, even if they have not much money to spend, like to believe they have, and they will not patronise the shops that cannot make a brave show. On Saturday, when the hilly High Street is crowded with carriers' carts, cheap-Jacks, agricultural implements, farmers' carts, and stalls devoted to the sale of every imaginable commodity, from sweet stuff and live animals to old books and pills, the "quality" are conspicuous by their absence from the town. Burly farmers, having transacted their business in the Corn Exchange and Cattle Market, and dined substantially at the old " Red Lion," whence Lucas and Lisle were summoned to execution, are sure of finding wives and daughters round the excellent shops that line either side of the High Street. Everything and everybody wakes up on Saturday. North Hill, veiled in clouds of dust, is alive with flocks of bleating "ship," obstreperous pigs, and sad-eyed cattle, driven by shouting hucksters, blue-bloused butchers, and shepherds, who utter weird but musical cries to their four-footed charges. The young farmers, emboldened by the fact that they are in the town, become quite jocular with the girls from neighbouring villages ; the elders potter round the famous fish-shop by the Exchange and devote their spare time to shopping. But on other days of the week, business Colchester is apparently almost as sound asleep as old King Cole himself. Then the officers and their womenkind have it all to themselves, and the fashionable side of the town is presented to view. From the leafy avenues of Lexden, from the Military Road and the out-lying halls come smart little Ralli-cars, dog-carts, and well-appointed broughams to rattle over the quiet cobbled roadway in place of the heavy wagons and traps that block it on Saturdays; the recruiting sergeant is not

A Bit in Colchester.

in evidence, and nothing whatever seems to be going on. Down at "Bottles," maybe, one meets a few golfers off to play on the beautiful village green at Great Bentley; occasionally there is a movement in the direction of the Castle if a bazaar is in progress. Life is not altogether "a round of petty pleasures" in Colchester. Being but an hour's journey from London, folks prefer to run up to town to do their "pleasuring" rather than take what they can get sent to them, although at the Theatre Royal and the

Corn Exchange some leading lights of the theatrical and musical professions are often to be seen and heard; and dances and tennis-parties are of course plentiful enough. Withal the enterprising Colchestrian has a variety of interests. There is a pleasing blend of the military, nautical, bucolic, and commercial elements; the first and last of which one need not leave the town to find, for, besides the soldiers, no inconsiderable proportion of the population is composed of factory operatives. And is not Brightlingsea close at hand, the land of fisher-folk and sailors, and the nursery of the "natives" for which the town is famous? Colchester may have its faults, but with these advantages it is not to be sneered at. After all, life in a town full of soldiers and oysters cannot be altogether dull, especially when a neighbouring yachting station and a couple of contiguous watering-places are thrown in.

Jarrold and Sons, Printers, Norwich, Yarmouth, and London.

INDEX TO ADVERTISERS.

Bristol—   PAGE
  J. S. Fry & Sons, Cocoa Manufacturers ... ix.

Cambridge—
  E. Bolton, Furniture Remover ... xxii.
  Leys School ... *Facing Front Cover*

Cromer—
  H. J. Limmer and Co., Auctioneers and House Agents ... xi.

Felixstowe—
  F. E. Brown, Chemist ... xvi.
  W. H. Cordy, Confectioner ... xiv.

Fordingbridge—
  J. R. Neave & Co., Patent Food Manufacturers *Second Page Cover*

Ipswich—
  C. B. Bartlett, Picture Frame Manufacturer ... xvii.

London—
  Great Eastern Railway Co. ... x.

Lowestoft—
  H. J. Limmer and Co., Auctioneers and House Agents ... xi.
  St. Margaret's College ... xii.
  Titcomb and Few, Auctioneers and House Agents ... vi.
  A. Wright, Chemist... ... xix.

Norwich—
  J. E. Barnes, Seedsman... ... xviii.
  S. J. Hook, High Class Tailor ... xx.

Nottingham—
  Coombs' Eureka Aerated Pastry Flour ... xxi.

Yarmouth—
  F. J. Lane, Chemist ... xiii.
  S. Randell, The Tailor King... ... xv.

"Strongest and Best."—*HEALTH.*

Purchasers should ask specially for FRY'S PURE CONCENTRATED COCOA, to distinguish it from other varieties manufactured by the Firm.

GREAT EASTERN RAILWAY.

SEA-SIDE, & BROADS & RIVERS OF NORFOLK & SUFFOLK.

Tourist, Fortnightly, and Friday to Tuesday Tickets
ARE ISSUED AS UNDER BY ALL TRAINS:—

LIVERPOOL STREET OR ST. PANCRAS TO	Tourist.		Fortnightly.		Friday to Tuesday.	
	1 Class.	3 Class.	1 Class.	3 Class.	1 Class.	3 Class.
Hunstanton	30/6	18/0	25/0	13/0	15/0	9/6
Lowestoft	33/0	19/9	27/6	15/0	20/0	10/0
Yarmouth	34/0	20/0	27/6	15/0	20/0	10/0
Cromer	34/0	20/0	27/6	15/0	20/0	10/0
Norwich	31/10	18/11	—	—	—	—
LIVERPOOL STREET TO						
Southend-on-Sea } Burnham-on-Crouch }	8/8	4/4	7/0	4/4	6/0	3/6
Walton-on-the-Naze, Clacton-on-Sea, Frinton-on-Sea, Harwich, or Dovercourt	20/0	12/0	17/6	10/0	12/6	7/6
Felixstowe	23/4	14/3	17/6	10/0	12/6	7/6
Aldeburgh	27/9	16/9	25/0	13/0	15/0	9/6
Southwold	31/3	18/5	27/6	15/0	20/0	10/0

TOURIST TICKETS are issued daily from 1st May to the 31st of October, and are available for return any day up to and including the 31st of December of the year of issue.

FORTNIGHTLY TICKETS are issued daily, and are available for return any day within 15 days, including days of issue and return.

FRIDAY TO TUESDAY TICKETS are issued every Friday and Saturday, and are available for return on the day of issue, or on any day up to and including the following Tuesday.

TOURIST, FORTNIGHTLY, AND FRIDAY TO TUESDAY TICKETS to the above Stations are also issued from Great Eastern Stations within 12 miles of London at the same fares as from Liverpool Street. Passengers are allowed to travel to and from Liverpool Street to join or leave the fast Sea-Side Trains; also to and from Stratford to join or leave the Trains booked to call at that Station. They are also issued from New Cross (L. B. & S. C.) and all Stations on the East London Railway, at the same fares as Liverpool Street.

The above Tickets are available to and from additional Stations as follows:— *Southend-on-Sea Tickets* at Prittlewell; *Burnham-on-Crouch Tickets* at Southminster, *Clacton-on-Sea Tickets* at Frinton, Walton, Harwich, Dovercourt; *Walton-on-the-Naze Tickets* at Frinton, Clacton, Harwich, Dovercourt; *Frinton-on-Sea Tickets* at Clacton, Walton, Harwich, Dovercourt; *Harwich Tickets* at Dovercourt, Parkeston, Frinton, Clacton, Walton; *Felixstowe Tickets* at Trimley, Harwich; *Aldeburgh Tickets* at Leiston; *Southwold Tickets* at Darsham; *Hunstanton Tickets* at Heacham; *Lowestoft Tickets* at Beccles, Reedham, Carlton Colville, Oulton Broad, Yarmouth, Cromer; *Yarmouth Tickets* at Beccles, Reedham, Acle, Lowestoft, Cromer; *Cromer Tickets* at Wroxham, North Walsham, Gunton, Yarmouth Lowestoft. Passengers must pay the ordinary local single fares when travelling from one Station to the other.

EXTRA JOURNEY RETURN TICKETS AT REDUCED FARES are issued at the above Stations, except Southend-on-Sea and Burnham-on-Crouch, to the Station from which the Tickets were issued, to holders of not less than two Tourist or Fortnightly Tickets.

EXTENSION OF TICKETS.—Passengers holding Friday to Tuesday Tickets and wishing to stay for a Fortnight or a shorter period, may do so by paying the difference between the Friday to Tuesday and Fortnightly Fares; and in the same manner Fortnightly Tickets may be extended to Tourist Tickets by paying the difference between those fares.

List of Farmhouse and County Lodgings in the Eastern Counties, and Pamphlets on the "Broads" District of Norfolk and Suffolk can be obtained (post free) on application to the Superintendent of the Line, Liverpool Street Station, London, E.C.

Liverpool Street Station, 1894.   WILLIAM BIRT, *General Manager.*

H. J. LIMMER & Co., A.A.I.,

AUCTIONEERS & VALUERS,

House, Yacht, Estate, & Business Agents.

A Large Selection of SEASIDE & COUNTRY

FURNISHED HOUSES,

Private Residences, Farmhouses, and

APARTMENTS,

In and around

LOWESTOFT & CROMER,

ALSO

YACHTS & PLEASURE WHERRIES

FOR THE

NORFOLK AND SUFFOLK BROADS.

Unfurnished Houses, Residences, Boarding and Lodging Houses, and Businesses in the Best Positions in various Towns on the East Coast

TO LET & FOR SALE.

Applicants when writing are respectfully requested to state their EXACT requirements, when

Full Particulars Free of Charge will be forwarded.

OFFICES:—

Next Railway Station, LOWESTOFT,

AND

Jetty Street, CROMER.

St. Margaret's College.

[LOWESTOFT PUBLIC SCHOOL.]

*****

Reasonable Terms for Boarders.

*****

Masters:—

High School: T. WILSON-WARD, F.S.Sc. (Lond.)

Lower School: A. M. HAWTHORNE, M.A.

French Master: F. H. ACQUIER, B. es L.

Art Master: E. MINNS, C.M.

Drill Inst.: SERGT.-MAJOR KEATES, Norf. Regt.

Advertisements.

For Summer or Winter Use.

GLYCERINE & CUCUMBER CREAM,

For rendering the Skin Soft and White.

Prevents Chapping and Roughness in Winter; Sunburn and Freckles in Summer. **In Bottles, 6d. & 1/-.**

LANE'S
Vitalizing Effervescent Saline.

This pleasant and refreshing Saline will be found exceedingly valuable in PURIFYING THE BLOOD and COOLING THE SYSTEM, and thus preventing those unpleasant eruptions and pimples so common to many at the change of the seasons.

For the relief of HEADACHE and all BILIOUS DISORDERS it will be found very beneficial, acting as a mild aperient and also on the liver and kidneys. **In Bottles, 1 6.**

DR. MONK'S
TIC & TOOTH-ACHE SPECIFIC.

A remedy first taken by himself with success for Tic-Doloreux or Face-Ache; and as a general Tonic in Debility and Loss of Appetite, cannot be too highly recommended. **In Bottles, 1/-.**

SWEET ZEPHYR.

A most fragrant and lasting perfume. **In Bottles, 1/-, 2/-, and 3 6.**

PHOTOGRAPHIC PLATES & SUNDRIES.

PREPARED BY

F. J. LANE,

FAMILY & DISPENSING CHEMIST,
19, MARKET PLACE, GT. YARMOUTH.

Purveyor to H.I.M. The Empress of Germany.

W. H. CORDY, Baker, Confectioner, & Dairyman,
9 & 13, PARADE, FELIXSTOWE.

Branch Establishment: HIGH ST., WALTON.

CORDY'S RESTAURANT: Bent Hill, Felixstowe.
(7 Minutes from Station.)

→ SCHOOLS AND CHOIRS CATERED FOR. ←

NORFOLK COAST.

Paying Guests taken for the Season.

LADIES AND GENTLEMEN who intend visiting the delightful neighbourhood of Holkham, Wells-next-the-Sea, and Walsingham, are invited to communicate with

Messrs. Jarrold & Sons,
The Library, Norwich,

as they have pleasure in confidently recommending a Lady, who has every facility for making them comfortable.

Over 5,000,000 of these Stories have already been sold in their various editions.

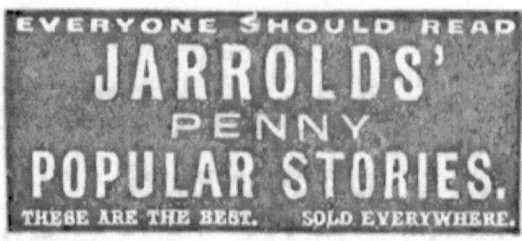

EVERYONE SHOULD READ JARROLDS' PENNY POPULAR STORIES. THESE ARE THE BEST. SOLD EVERYWHERE.

Issued Fortnightly on the 2nd and 4th Tuesdays in each month.

DO YOU WANT TO SAVE MONEY?

DO YOU WANT

CLOTHING for YOURSELF?

DO YOU WANT

SUITS for your BOYS?

DO YOU WANT

HATS or CAPS?

DO YOU WANT

A SUIT TO MEASURE?

IF YOU WANT TO SAVE MONEY

GO TO

RANDELL,

The Tailor King,

41, MARKET PLACE, GT. YARMOUTH;

31, LONDON ROAD, LOWESTOFT;

AND AT NORWICH.

DISPENSING CHEMIST.

F. E. BROWN,
(Late Tyler,)

From S. B. Maggs, St. Leonard's-on-Sea, Chemist to Her Majesty the Queen and the Royal Family,

8, PARADE, FELIXSTOWE.

PRESCRIPTIONS ACCURATELY DISPENSED.

Toilet Requisites.   Invalid Appliances.

GOLF CLUB BOUQUET, THE FASHIONABLE PERFUME.

SEASIDE LOTION FOR SUNBURN, &c.

Friedrichshall, Hunyadi Janos, Æsculap, Vichy, and other Natural Waters.

SCHWEPPES' SODA, POTASH, SELTZER,
And other Mineral Waters in Syphons, of guaranteed purity.

BATHING CAPS.   METHYLATED SPIRIT.

HOMOEOPATHIC MEDICINES.

Medalist in Practical Dispensing and Pharmacy.

Advertisements. xvii

C. B. BARTLETT,

46 & 48, Westgate St., IPSWICH.

AND

King's Quay Street, HARWICH,

IMPORTS

Mouldings from BERLIN, HAMBURG and COLOGNE; and has **STOCK** also of English and Room Bordering Mouldings. Prices now from 3d. per length of 9 ft.

PATTERNS FREE.

Also Glass in Cases or cut to measure. Screw Eyes, Rings, BACKBOARDS, MOUNTS CUT, &c., &c.

PICTURES, FRAMES, MOULDINGS.

IF YOU require **PICTURE FRAMES,** Call or send for Prices. A GOOD STAFF of WORKMEN KEPT, and satisfaction guaranteed at REASONABLE CHARGES.

RESTORING

AND

RE-GILDING.

OLD ENGRAVINGS, PRINTS, OLD SPORTING SUBJECTS, &c., carefully treated by very Experienced Men.

𝔈stimates for 𝔖how 𝔊ards.

THE GREAT EASTERN SEED STORES

TRY
Barnes' Reliable & Popular Seeds.

Everything for the Garden, the Greenhouse, the Allotment, and the Farm.

ECONOMY IN THE GARDEN.

PRIZE SEEDS A SPECIALITY.

Prize Seeds A SPECIALITY.

Purchase your supplies of HIGH-CLASS RELIABLE SEEDS at Store Prices, and effect a Saving of 20 to 25 per cent. on your outlay.

CATALOGUES GRATIS.

J. E. BARNES,
SEEDSMAN, SEEDGROWER, & MERCHANT,
Horticultural Sundriesman,
NURSERYMAN & FLORIST,
THE GREAT EASTERN SEED STORES,
9, Exchange Street, Norwich.

Seed Trial Grounds, Newmarket Road.   Telegraphic Address "Reliable," Norwich.

A Fact That None Can Dispute.

S. J. HOOK,

FAMILY TAILOR,
6, Goat Lane, Norwich,

Has by maintaining great excellence in his work given satisfaction to his patrons for the last 25 years.

YOU may find it difficult to get a nice suit, and above all, good fit.

TRY HIM, His Style will Suit You.

YOU may be wanting a genteel and yet smart Overcoat.

Patronize Him, & You will Receive Satisfaction.

ONCE YOU TRY HIM, YOU WILL ALWAYS BUY OF HIM.
A TRIAL ORDER IS THEREFORE RESPECTFULLY SOLICITED.

The Address is GOAT LANE, NORWICH.

An Admitted Antidote for Indigestion.

COOMBS'
EUREKA
ÆRATED PASTRY FLOUR!

16 Good Reasons why everybody should use Coombs' Flour.

BECAUSE it is an Admitted Antidote for Indigestion.
BECAUSE it is recommended by the highest Medical Authorities.
BECAUSE it is suitable for the most delicate constitutions.
BECAUSE it pleases the most fastidious.
BECAUSE it makes Delicious Cakes and Pastry of every description.
BECAUSE thousands eat and enjoy it.
BECAUSE it is within the reach of the Poor as well as the Rich.
BECAUSE the Quality and Price are always Uniform.
BECAUSE of the smallness of the quantity needed for Pastry.
BECAUSE it has gained the highest awards at important Exhibitions.
BECAUSE of the immense saving in shortening properties.
BECAUSE of the saving of Barm and Baking Powder.
BECAUSE of the time saved in Preparation.
BECAUSE English, French, and German Chefs speak highly of it.
BECAUSE it is used by the leading Lecturers on Cookery.
LAST BUT NOT LEAST—
    BECAUSE OF ITS SUPERIORITY AND GENERAL EXCELLENCE.

Annual Sales 3,000,000 lbs.

AWARDS: FIVE GOLD MEDALS.

SOLD in 3d., 6d., 1s., and 2s. 6d. BAGS.

ESTABLISHED 1869.

THE
Cambridge Pantechnicon Warehouse,
FOR THE SAFE STORAGE OF VALUABLE FURNITURE.
ESTIMATES OF ALL KINDS FREE.

EDWARD BOLTON
22, Hills Road, & 76, Newmarket Road,
CAMBRIDGE,
Contractor for Household Removals,
TO OR FROM ANY DISTANCE,
WITHOUT PACKING, RISK, OR EXPOSURE TO WEATHER.

Household Removals throughout the entire system of Railways in the United Kingdom and Continent. By this system the cost of packing is entirely avoided, and the Furniture, &c., remain in the same lock-up Van throughout the whole journey, irrespective of distance.

ALL ORDERS PUNCTUALLY ATTENDED TO.
Brick, Tile, Lime, Cement, Gravel, Sand, and Drain Pipe Merchant.

E. B. begs to inform the public that he purchased the business of his late Father, Thomas Bolton, of 26 Union Road. Terms are most reasonable, and will compare favourably with any other house in the Kingdom.

A TRIAL SOLICITED.
All communications should be addressed to 22, Hills Road.

Novels for Holiday Reading.

POPULAR 3/6 NOVELS,
BY
MRS. LEITH ADAMS, HON. IZA DUFFUS HARDY,
AND OTHER WELL-KNOWN AUTHORS.

1. **LOUIS DRAYCOTT.** By Mrs. Leith Adams (Mrs. De Courcy Laffan). 2nd Edition.

   "The whole tone of the book, in common with all Mrs. Laffan's works, is ennobling."—*Birmingham Gazette.*

2. **GEOFFREY STIRLING.** By Mrs. Leith Adams (Mrs. De Courcy Laffan). 5th Edition.

   "It may be assumed how highly we think of this novel, when, in summing up its imperfections, we can only find one very venial fault."—*Standard.*

   "The portraiture of Hester Devenant is a really fine and powerful dramatic study, even better fitted for the actual stage than for a novel."—*Globe.*

3. **BONNIE KATE.** By Mrs. Leith Adams (Mrs. De Courcy Laffan). 2nd Edition.

   "Melissa is fresh and natural, and has a charm of her own, and the twin-sisters are genuine and pleasing."—*Saturday Review.*

4. **A NEW OTHELLO.** By Hon. Iza Duffus Hardy. 2nd Edition.

   "One of the most powerfully-written books this talented author has yet produced, engrossing throughout, enthralling in interest."—*Vanity Fair.*

   "The closing chapters are tremendous in their intensity."—*Athenæum.*

   "The reader will at once perceive that 'A New Othello' is constructed with real skill, and told with vigour and directness."—*Spectator.*

5. **THE MAID OF LONDON BRIDGE.** A Story of the Time of Kett's Rebellion. By Somerville Gibney, Author of "The Hovellers of Deal," "John o' London," &c.

   "An historical story. . . . The author shows a praiseworthy intimacy both with the geography of Old London and with the particulars of Kett's Rebellion and subsequent disturbances."—*Athenæum.*

6. **EVELINE WELLWOOD.** A Tale of Modern Irish Life. By Major Norris Paul.

   "A rattling good story, as many, both young and old, will heartily pronounce it."—*Sunday Times.*

7. **OLD LATTIMER'S LEGACY.** By J. S. Fletcher, Author of "The Winding Way," "Andrewlina," "Mr. Spivey's Clerk," "Frank Carisbroke's Stratagem," &c.

   "'Old Lattimer's Legacy' is cleverly written and interesting."—*Vanity Fair.*

London: Jarrold & Sons, 10 & 11, Warwick Lane.
And of all Booksellers.

Novels for Holiday Reading.

POPULAR 3/6 NOVELS,

By CURTIS YORKE,

8. **THAT LITTLE GIRL.** By CURTIS YORKE. 4th Edition.
   "A very charming and well-written story."—*Queen.*

9. **DUDLEY.** By CURTIS YORKE. 3rd Edition.
   "It is some time since such a fresh, pleasant book has come under our notice as 'Dudley.'"—*Whitehall Review.*

10. **THE WILD RUTHVENS.** By CURTIS YORKE. 3rd Edition.
    "An enchanting work—the story runs on with happy blithesome tread to the end, which is reached all too soon."—*St. Stephen's Review.*

11. **THE BROWN PORTMANTEAU, and other Stories.** By CURTIS YORKE. 2nd Edition.
    "The stories are all interesting and the volume is sure of a welcome."—*Literary World.*

12. **HUSH!** By CURTIS YORKE. 3rd Edition.
    "Is in many ways a remarkable novel, and from every point of view superior to the current fiction of the day."—*Morning Post.*

13. **ONCE!** By CURTIS YORKE. An entirely New Work. 2nd Edition.
    "A story showing all Curtis Yorke's capacity for vigorous and vivid writing, and for skilful construction of plot."—*Scottish Leader.*

14. **A ROMANCE OF MODERN LONDON.** By CURTIS YORKE. 2nd Edition.
    "May be classed among the best modern works of fiction."—*Cambridge Chronicle.*

15. **HIS HEART TO WIN.** By CURTIS YORKE. An entirely New Work.
    "The pleasantest and brightest of Curtis Yorke's stories."—*Newcastle Daily Leader.*

16. **DARRELL CHEVASNEY.** By CURTIS YORKE.

17. **BETWEEN THE SILENCES.** By CURTIS YORKE.

18. **THE PEYTON ROMANCE.** By MRS. LEITH ADAMS. 2nd Edition. [*Ready Shortly.*]

Others in preparation for issue at short intervals.

London: Jarrold & Sons, 10 & 11, Warwick Lane.
And of all Booksellers.

POPPYLAND.

Papers Descriptive of Scenery on the East Coast.

By CLEMENT SCOTT.

4th EDITION.

26 ILLUSTRATIONS BY F. H. TOWNSEND.

Crown 8vo, 172 Pages, Illustrated Paper Cover, 1/-.
Superior Edition, Cloth, 2/6.

LONDON: JARROLD & SONS, 10 & 11, WARWICK LANE.

Selections from Jarrolds' New Books.

Dr. Gordon-Stables' 'Health Series.'

Crown 8vo, cloth, 2/6 each. (Postage 4½d.)

SICKNESS OR HEALTH? or, The Danger of Trifling Ailments. 2nd Edition.

"The work is practical, and written in a readable style. It merits a place in every public and private library in the land. The publishers are to be warmly congratulated on the publication of this excellent volume." — *Hull Examiner*.

"'Sickness or Health?' is an excellent book in every way, and we trust its success will be equal to its merits."— *Literary World*.

THE GIRL'S OWN BOOK OF HEALTH AND BEAUTY. 2nd Edition.

"Teems with useful hints and good suggestions. Ought to be in the hands of every young woman."— *The Leicester Chronicle*.

"The reader who follows Dr. Gordon-Stables' instructions may hope for a long respite from the ills that flesh is heir to."— *Woman's Gazette*.

BOYS' BOOK OF HEALTH AND STRENGTH. 2nd Edition. With portraits of Dr. GORDON-STABLES, C.M., R.N.; R. G. GORDON-CUMMING (the Lion Hunter); W. McCOMBIE SMITH (Champion Scottish Athlete); J. D. MACPHERSON (Champion Putter); G. H. JOHNSTONE (Champion Hammer Thrower of Scotland); and **Special Letter to Boys** by W. McCOMBIE SMITH, the Champion Scottish Athlete.

"Such a common sense *vade mecum* to health and strength, should find a place on every boy's bookshelf."— *Star*.

"Straightforward manly talks, pregnant with wise counsel. Our advice is let every boy get the book."— *Christian Age*.

THE WIFE'S GUIDE TO HEALTH AND HAPPINESS.

"This book reads like a novel, and is just as interesting as a novel, and far more instructive. The advice given is sensible, and up to date. Dr. Stables handles difficult and delicate subjects with great skill. A great deal of misery would be prevented if the young wife would adhere to the advice given in this book."— *The Medical Monthly*.

"Every mother ought to possess one of Dr. Gordon-Stables' 'Wife's Guide to Health and Happiness.'"— *The Princess*.

London: Jarrold & Sons, 10 & 11, Warwick Lane.

And of all Booksellers.

Selections from Jarrolds' New Books.

SUN PICTURES
OF THE
NORFOLK BROADS.
BY PAYNE JENNINGS.

With Descriptive Letterpress by E. R. SUFFLING.   Price 8/6 nett.

Post free, 4½d. extra.

"Payne Jennings, the celebrated photographer, who has brought an artistic feeling to bear on the taking of 'Sun Pictures,' has found in the Norfolk and Suffolk Rivers and Broads plenty of scenes eminently suitable for reproduction in pictorial form. Everyone who loves the Broads and has spent days upon them will be sure to have a copy on the drawing-room table, as each half page of it is filled with a picture which gives a more graphic idea of a bit of Broad country than would a chapter of prose by the most eloquent writer.'"—*Eastern Daily Press.*

"We fancy that many will be tempted by the pictures in this book to join the yearly increasing number of those who visit the charming spots here depicted."—*John Bull.*

"A handsome volume of views of the far-famed Broads of Norfolk, exquisitely printed from photographs."—*West Herts Post.*

"One hundred of Payne Jennings' well-known studies of the Broads reproduced in calotype and handsomely bound. In commending such an album to photographers, it is only necessary to say that its style of production is quite worthy of Mr. Payne Jennings, and the price is only 8/6."—*The Practical Photographer.*

"The far-famed Norfolk Broads are worthy of being illustrated in the highly artistic fashion that is here presented. The Sun pictures that lie before us do full justice to the romantic spots which they illustrate. They have been taken by hands that know how to use a camera and are produced in faultless style by the printer."—*Kensington Express.*

"Mr. Jennings' photographs (100 in number) are splendid. No one can look at them without wishing himself on the spot."—*Weekly Despatch.*

London: Jarrold & Sons, 10 & 11, Warwick Lane.
And of all Booksellers.

www.ingramcontent.com/pod-product-compliance
Lightning Source LLC
Chambersburg PA
CBHW020234240426
43672CB00006B/528